Also by America's Test Kitchen

The Complete Modern Pantry

Everyday Bread

The Healthy Back Kitchen

The Complete Small Plates Cookbook

Fresh Pasta at Home

Desserts Illustrated

Vegan Cooking for Two

The Complete Guide to Healthy Drinks

Modern Bistro

More Mediterranean

The Complete Plant-Based Cookbook

Cooking with Plant-Based Meat

Boards

The Savory Baker

The New Cooking School Cookbook:
Advanced Fundamentals

The New Cooking School Cookbook:
Fundamentals

The Complete Autumn and
Winter Cookbook

One-Hour Comfort

The Everyday Athlete Cookbook

Cook for Your Gut Health

Foolproof Fish

Five-Ingredient Dinners

The Ultimate Meal-Prep Cookbook

The Complete Salad Cookbook

The Chicken Bible

The Side Dish Bible

Meat Illustrated

Vegetables Illustrated

Bread Illustrated

Cooking for One

The Complete One Pot

How Can It Be Gluten-Free
Cookbook Collection

The Complete Summer Cookbook

Bowls

100 Techniques

Easy Everyday Keto

Everything Chocolate

The Perfect Cookie

The Perfect Pie

The Perfect Cake

How to Cocktail

Spiced

The Ultimate Burger

The New Essentials Cookbook

Dinner Illustrated

America's Test Kitchen Menu Cookbook

Cook's Illustrated Revolutionary Recipes

Tasting Italy: A Culinary Journey

Cooking at Home with Bridget and Julia

The Complete Mediterranean Cookbook

The Complete Vegetarian Cookbook

The Complete Cooking for Two Cookbook

The Complete Diabetes Cookbook

The Complete Slow Cooker

The Complete Make-Ahead Cookbook

Just Add Sauce

How to Braise Everything

How to Roast Everything

Nutritious Delicious

What Good Cooks Know

Cook's Science

The Science of Good Cooking

Master of the Grill

Kitchen Smarts

Kitchen Hacks

100 Recipes

The New Family Cookbook

The Cook's Illustrated Baking Book

The Cook's Illustrated Cookbook

The America's Test Kitchen
Family Baking Book

America's Test Kitchen Twentieth
Anniversary TV Show Cookbook

The Complete America's Test Kitchen
TV Show Cookbook 2001–2024

Healthy Air Fryer

Healthy and Delicious Instant Pot

Mediterranean Instant Pot

Cook It in Your Dutch Oven

Vegan for Everybody

Sous Vide for Everybody

Air Fryer Perfection

Toaster Oven Perfection

Multicooker Perfection

Food Processor Perfection

Pressure Cooker Perfection

Instant Pot Ace Blender Cookbook

Naturally Sweet

Foolproof Preserving

Paleo Perfected

The Best Mexican Recipes

Slow Cooker Revolution
Volume 2: The Easy-Prep Edition

Slow Cooker Revolution

The America's Test Kitchen
D.I.Y. Cookbook

Cook's Country Titles

Big Flavors from Italian America

One-Pan Wonders

Cook It in Cast Iron

Cook's Country Eats Local

The Complete Cook's Country
TV Show Cookbook

For a Full Listing
of All Our Books

CooksIllustrated.com

AmericasTestKitchen.com

Praise for America's Test Kitchen Titles

Selected as the Cookbook Award Winner of 2021 in the Health and Nutrition category

INTERNATIONAL ASSOCIATION OF CULINARY PROFESSIONALS (IACP) ON *THE COMPLETE PLANT-BASED COOKBOOK*

"An exhaustive but approachable primer for those looking for a 'flexible' diet. Chock-full of tips, you can dive into the science of plant-based cooking or just sit back and enjoy the 500 recipes."

MINNEAPOLIS STAR TRIBUNE ON *THE COMPLETE PLANT-BASED COOKBOOK*

"In this latest offering from the fertile minds at America's Test Kitchen the recipes focus on savory baked goods. Pizzas, flatbreads, crackers, and stuffed breads all shine here . . . Introductory essays for each recipe give background information and tips for making things come out perfectly."

BOOKLIST (STARRED REVIEW) ON *THE SAVORY BAKER*

"A mood board for one's food board is served up in this excellent guide . . . This has instant classic written all over it."

PUBLISHERS WEEKLY (STARRED REVIEW) ON *BOARDS: STYLISH SPREADS FOR CASUAL GATHERINGS*

"Reassuringly hefty and comprehensive, The Complete Autumn and Winter Cookbook by America's Test Kitchen has you covered with a seemingly endless array of seasonal fare . . . This overstuffed compendium is guaranteed to warm you from the inside out."

NPR ON *THE COMPLETE AUTUMN AND WINTER COOKBOOK*

"Here are the words just about any vegan would be happy to read: 'Why This Recipe Works.' Fans of America's Test Kitchen are used to seeing the phrase, and now it applies to the growing collection of plant-based creations in Vegan for Everybody."

THE WASHINGTON POST ON *VEGAN FOR EVERYBODY*

Selected as the Cookbook Award Winner of 2021 in the General category

INTERNATIONAL ASSOCIATION OF CULINARY PROFESSIONALS (IACP) ON *MEAT ILLUSTRATED*

"Another flawless entry in the America's Test Kitchen canon, Bowls guides readers of all culinary skill levels in composing one-bowl meals from a variety of cuisines."

BUZZFEED BOOKS ON *BOWLS*

Selected as the Cookbook Award Winner of 2021 in the Single Subject Category

INTERNATIONAL ASSOCIATION OF CULINARY PROFESSIONALS (IACP) ON *FOOLPROOF FISH*

"The book's depth, breadth, and practicality makes it a must-have for seafood lovers."

PUBLISHERS WEEKLY (STARRED REVIEW) ON *FOOLPROOF FISH*

"The Perfect Cookie . . . is, in a word, perfect. This is an important and substantial cookbook . . . If you love cookies, but have been a tad shy to bake on your own, all your fears will be dissipated. This is one book you can use for years with magnificently happy results."

HUFFPOST ON *THE PERFECT COOKIE*

"The book offers an impressive education for curious cake makers, new and experienced alike. A summation of 25 years of cake making at ATK, there are cakes for every taste."

THE WALL STREET JOURNAL ON *THE PERFECT CAKE*

"The go-to gift book for newlyweds, small families, or empty nesters."

ORLANDO SENTINEL ON *THE COMPLETE COOKING FOR TWO COOKBOOK*

"If you're one of the 30 million Americans with diabetes, The Complete Diabetes Cookbook by America's Test Kitchen belongs on your kitchen shelf."

PARADE.COM ON *THE COMPLETE DIABETES COOKBOOK*

"True to its name, this smart and endlessly enlightening cookbook is about as definitive as it's possible to get in the modern vegetarian realm."

MEN'S JOURNAL ON *THE COMPLETE VEGETARIAN COOKBOOK*

THE OUTDOOR COOK

USING YOUR GRILL, FIRE PIT, FLAT-TOP GRILL, AND MORE

HOW TO COOK ANYTHING OUTSIDE

AMERICA'S TEST KITCHEN

Library of Congress Cataloging-in-Publication Data has
been applied for.

ISBN 978-1-954210-41-7

America's Test Kitchen
21 Drydock Avenue, Boston, MA 02210

Printed in Canada
10 9 8 7 6 5 4 3 2 1

Distributed by Penguin Random House Publisher Services
Tel: 800.733.3000

Pictured on Front Cover Paella for a Crowd (page 262)

Pictured on Back Cover Fireside Chili (page 254),
Grilled Strip Steak and Potatoes with Blue Cheese Butter
(page 142), Glazed Rotisserie Pineapple with Salted Rum
Butterscotch Sauce (page 304), Smoked Turkey (page 206)

Editorial Director, Books Adam Kowit

Executive Food Editor Dan Zuccarello

Deputy Food Editors Leah Colins and Stephanie Pixley

Executive Managing Editor Debra Hudak

Senior Editors Valerie Cimino, Joseph Gitter, and Sara Mayer

Project Editor Cheryl Redmond

Additional Editorial Support Amelia Freidline, Katrina Munichiello,
and April Poole

Test Cooks Olivia Counter, Carmen Dongo, Hisham Hassam,
José Maldonado, Patricia Suarez, and David Yu

Additional Recipe Development Garth Clingingsmith and Eva Katz

Kitchen Intern Olivia Goldstein

Design Director Lindsey Timko Chandler

Deputy Art Director Janet Smith Taylor

Photography Director Julie Bozzo Cote

Senior Photography Producer Meredith Mulcahy

Senior Staff Photographers Steve Klise and Daniel J. van Ackere

Staff Photographer Kevin White

Additional Photography Joseph Keller and Carl Tremblay

Food Styling Joy Howard, Sheila Jarnes, Catrine Kelty, Chantal Lambeth,
Gina McCreadie, Kendra McNight, Ashley Moore, Christie Morrison,
Elle Simone Scott, and Kendra Smith

Project Manager, Publishing Operations Katie Kimmerer

Senior Print Production Specialist Lauren Robbins

Production and Imaging Coordinator Amanda Yong

Production and Imaging Specialists Tricia Neumyer and Dennis Noble

Copy Editor Elizabeth Wray Emery

Proofreader Karen Wise

Indexer Elizabeth Parson

Chief Creative Officer Jack Bishop

Executive Editorial Directors Julia Collin Davison and Bridget Lancaster

Contents

Welcome to America's Test Kitchen

This book has been tested, written, and edited by the folks at America's Test Kitchen, where curious cooks become confident cooks. Located in Boston's Seaport District in the historic Innovation and Design Building, it features 15,000 square feet of kitchen space including multiple photography and video studios. It is the home of *Cook's Illustrated* magazine and *Cook's Country* magazine and is the workday destination for more than 60 test cooks, editors, and cookware specialists. Our mission is to empower and inspire confidence, community, and creativity in the kitchen.

We start the process of testing a recipe with a complete lack of preconceptions, which means that we accept no claim, no technique, and no recipe at face value. We simply assemble as many variations as possible, test a half-dozen of the most promising, and taste the results blind. We then construct our own recipe and continue to test it, varying ingredients, techniques, and cooking times until we reach a consensus. As we like to say in the test kitchen, "We make the mistakes so you don't have to." The result, we hope, is the best version of a particular recipe, but we realize that only you can be the final judge of our success (or failure). We use the same rigorous approach when we test equipment and taste ingredients.

All of this would not be possible without a belief that good cooking, much like good music, is based on a foundation of objective technique. Some people like spicy foods and others don't, but there is a right way to sauté, there is a best way to cook a pot roast, and there are measurable scientific principles involved in producing perfectly beaten, stable egg whites. Our ultimate goal is to investigate the fundamental principles of cooking to give you the techniques, tools, and ingredients you need to become a better cook. It is as simple as that.

To see what goes on behind the scenes at America's Test Kitchen, check out our social media channels for kitchen snapshots, exclusive content, video tips, and much more. You can watch us work (in our actual test kitchen) by tuning in to *America's Test Kitchen* or *Cook's Country* on public television or on our websites. Listen to *Proof*, *Mystery Recipe*, and *The Walk-In* (AmericasTestKitchen.com/podcasts) to hear engaging, complex stories about people and food. Want to hone your cooking skills or finally learn how to bake—with an America's Test Kitchen test cook? Enroll in one of our online cooking classes. And you can engage the next generation of home cooks with kid-tested recipes from America's Test Kitchen Kids.

However you choose to visit us, we welcome you into our kitchen, where you can stand by our side as we test our way to the best recipes in America.

 Join Our Community of Recipe Testers Our recipe testers provide valuable feedback on recipes under development by ensuring that they are foolproof in home kitchens. Help the America's Test Kitchen book team investigate the how and why behind successful recipes from your home kitchen.

- f facebook.com/AmericasTestKitchen
- ⊙ instagram.com/TestKitchen
- ▶ youtube.com/AmericasTestKitchen
- ♪ tiktok.com/@TestKitchen
- ⌄ twitter.com/TestKitchen
- ⓟ pinterest.com/TestKitchen

AmericasTestKitchen.com
CooksIllustrated.com
CooksCountry.com
OnlineCookingSchool.com
AmericasTestKitchen.com/kids

Let's Go Outside

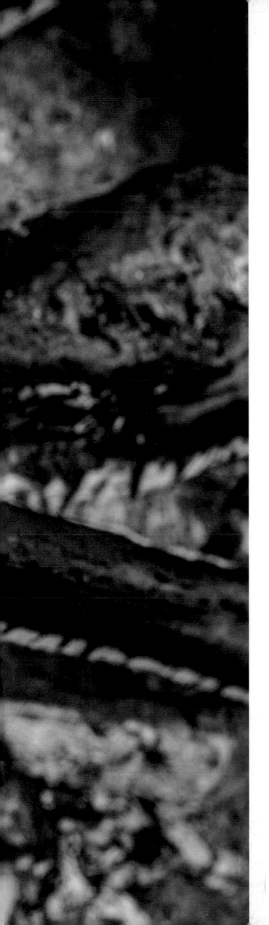

START THE FIRE

There's a primal pull toward cooking food over flames. Enticing wisps of smoke beckon you to the heat; the sizzling sound of fat dripping onto hot coals gets your juices flowing; the dark stripes of char against a bright green pepper, rosy pork tenderloin, or tawny pizza crust signal that you're about to enjoy something special. The intense heat and kiss of smoke make for outsize texture and flavor contrasts as well; think of crackling-crisp mahogany chicken skin giving way to moist, perfectly seasoned meat. Cooking outdoors transforms an ordinary meal into an all-senses-engaging feast.

The Outdoor Cook shows you how to cook outside with panache, whether your fuel of choice is charcoal, gas, or wood and whether your equipment is a grill, a fire pit, a flat-top grill, or a smoker. We tested these recipes extensively using all kinds of grilling and smoking gear so that whatever your setup, you'll find recipes that work for you. What's more, many of them can be easily converted between different pieces of equipment.

To help you make the most of your outdoor cooking experience, we show you how to set up an outdoor prep station so that you can minimize trips back and forth to the kitchen—meaning you can turn out everything from speedy dinners such as Grilled Steak Fajitas or Grilled Chicken Thighs with Butternut Squash and Cilantro Vinaigrette to entertaining-worthy showstoppers like Rotisserie Leg of Lamb with Cauliflower, Grape, and Arugula Salad without leaving your family and friends on the patio. There's also plenty of information on how to maintain your equipment and build your fires for peak performance.

We've also expanded the notion of what's possible to achieve outdoors by developing methods for adapting traditionally "indoor" dishes, from Grilled French Toast (cooked right on the grate) to Smoked Nachos to Fried Rice with Ham, Gai Lan, and Mushrooms. Maybe you've never considered firing up a grill to make dinner rolls, quesadillas, or Philly cheesesteaks, but we've got the recipes to convince you it's well worth it.

There are practical reasons for cooking outdoors—it lets you avoid heating up the house, it cuts down on pots and pans to wash, it opens up more breathing room for entertaining friends and family—but those pieces don't tell the whole story. There's just something about the magic of fire that attracts us and draws us together. Outdoor cooking is more exciting than cooking indoors. At the same time, it's relaxing: Even when you make the most of the latest gear, you can still unplug, enjoy being outside, and focus on the here and now. So let these recipes spark your desire to keep the fire, and the fun, going.

GRILLING 101

Gas Grills

Gas grills give you an outdoor cooking experience with a generous side of convenience: Just turn a couple of knobs and you're good to go. Gas grills heat up quickly and, as long as you have enough propane, they maintain a consistent temperature whether you're cooking for 20 minutes or 2-plus hours. A large gas grill with multiple burners provides plenty of space to cook for a crowd. For quickly grilled foods, such as boneless chicken breasts, there's little to no difference in flavor between gas and charcoal. Finally, they're easy to clean—no ashes to dispose of.

Gas grills can be pricey, but you don't have to spend a fortune to get a sturdy, reliable model. You want a solidly built grill with powerful burners—three are better than two—and a generously sized cooking grate. Also important: a cast-iron grate, metal heat diffusers ("flavorizer bars" in manufacturers' lingo), a tight-fitting lid, and sturdy wheels. We like the **Weber Spirit II E-310**, which has a heavy-duty cookbox of thick cast aluminum and enameled steel with just one narrow vent across the back, helping to maintain steady heat and distribute smoke.

Best-Practice Tips for Gas Grills

Check Your Fuel

Check your propane level before you start cooking by pouring hot water down the side of the tank. Propane is both a liquid and a gas; the liquid sits at the bottom of the tank, and the gas portion is at the top. Because gas doesn't conduct heat well, the part of the tank holding gas will feel warm when hot water is poured over it. The liquid in the bottom will make the tank feel cool to the touch. The more of the tank that feels cool, the more grilling time you have.

Don't Skip Preheating

Gas flames don't produce much radiant heat, so metal bars, ceramic rods, or lava rocks are positioned between the flames and cooking grate. It takes about 15 minutes for these items to convert the heat of the flames into radiant heat to get the grate searing hot.

Keep It Clean

Always scrape down the preheated grill grate and oil it to prevent sticking (see page 9). Many gas grills have grease traps underneath, which should be thoroughly cleaned a couple of times a year.

Keep It Covered

Directions for grilling foods with gas often call for closing the grill lid. Gas grills don't burn as hot as charcoal grills, and an uncovered gas grill loses a lot of heat; only the side of the food facing the flames gets hot. This is OK for faster-cooking foods such as burgers, but for many dishes, trapping heat by keeping the lid down makes for more efficient cooking.

Charcoal Grills

Admittedly, there's more of an art to cooking with charcoal than with gas, but once you get the hang of it, you'll appreciate its versatility. Charcoal grills can achieve much hotter temperatures than most gas grills, leading to enhanced color and char. The smoke from the charcoal and from the sizzling drippings of the food on the grates adds flavor and aroma to whatever you cook.

Charcoal grills are basic in design, but details make a difference. An ample cooking surface is important, not just for food capacity but also so that you can create different heat zones. The lid should fit well and be domed enough to accommodate a large roast. Top and bottom vents should effectively draw smoke over cooking food and be easily adjustable.

We love the classic **Weber Original Kettle Premium Charcoal Grill**. With a 22-inch diameter, it's an expert griller and maintains heat well, and its well-positioned vents allow for excellent air control. It has a sturdy ash catcher and a secure leg attachment system, and it's fast and easy to assemble and move.

If you want the convenience of gas plus the flavor of charcoal, the **Weber Performer Deluxe Charcoal Grill** is a worthwhile (albeit pricey) upgrade. Built around a 22.5-inch kettle is a roomy, easy-to-roll cart with a pullout charcoal storage bin; a lid holder; and, most significant, a gas ignition system that lights coals with the push of a button.

Best-Practice Tips for Charcoal Grills

Fire It Up

A chimney starter heats coals evenly and efficiently. Fill the bottom of the chimney starter with two sheets of crumpled newspaper, set it on the lower charcoal grate (make sure the bottom vent is open), and fill the top with charcoal. Allow the charcoal to burn until the top briquettes are partially covered with a thin layer of gray ash. The ash is a sign that the coals are fully lit and ready to be turned out into the grill. Don't pour out the coals prematurely; you'll be left with unlit coals at the bottom of the pile that may never ignite, as well as a cooler fire.

Keep It Clean

To ensure that food will release with ease, scrape the heated grate clean and then oil it (see page 9). Clean the inside of the grill lid regularly by scrubbing it with steel wool and water to prevent the carbon buildup from flaking off onto your food.

Dispose of Spent Coals

After grilling, cover the grill and close both the bottom and top vents; let the coals and ash cool for at least 48 hours. For quicker disposal, pour them into a metal bucket with 2 inches of water in it (be careful of steam); add more water to cover the coals and ashes and stir until cool. Dump into a doubled trash bag.

Gas and Charcoal Fire Setups

Single-Level Fire

Heat level Low, medium, or high for gas; medium (½ chimney) to high (full chimney) for charcoal

Purpose Delivers a uniform level of heat across the entire cooking surface

Good for Small, quick-cooking pieces of food such as sausages, burgers, fish fillets, and some vegetables. Try Blistered Shishito Peppers (page 40), Grilled Turkey Burgers with Spinach and Feta (page 88), or Grilled Shrimp, Corn, and Avocado Salad (page 162).

Gas Method
After preheating grill, turn all burners to desired heat setting (low, medium, or high).

Charcoal Method
Distribute lit coals in even layer across bottom of grill.

Two-Level Fire

Heat level High / medium

Purpose Creates two cooking zones: a hotter area for searing and a slightly cooler area for gentler cooking

Good for Thick chops, bone-in poultry pieces, and recipes with multiple foods that require different heat levels. Try Lamb and Summer Vegetable Kebabs with Grilled Focaccia (page 158), Grilled Caesar Salad with Salmon (page 170), or Paprika and Lime-Rubbed Chicken with Grilled Vegetable Succotash (page 130).

Gas Method
After preheating grill, leave primary burner on high and turn other burner(s) to medium.

Charcoal Method
Evenly distribute two-thirds of lit coals over half of grill, then distribute remainder of coals in even layer over other half.

Half-Grill Fire

Heat level High / low

Purpose Creates two cooking zones with a greater difference between heat levels than the two-level fire, with one side intensely hot and the other side comparatively cool.

Good for Large cuts of meat such as porterhouse steaks and pork tenderloin, bone-in poultry pieces, and foods that need both searing and gentle cooking. Try Tacos al Pastor (page 110), Sweet and Tangy Barbecue Chicken Thighs with Sweet Potatoes and Scallions (page 128), or Grilled Stone Fruit (page 302).

Gas Method
After preheating grill, adjust primary burner as directed in recipe and turn off other burner(s).

Charcoal Method
Distribute lit coals over half of grill, piling them in even layer. Leave other half of grill free of coals.

Banked Fire

Heat level Low

Purpose Similar to a half-grill fire, except the heat is concentrated in an even smaller area. The large flame-free or coal-free area can accommodate a pan of water to prevent food from drying out.

Good for Large foods such as brisket, pulled pork, or whole poultry, as well as foods that need both browning and gentle cooking. Try Smoked Bourbon Chicken (page 198) or Rustic Summer Fruit Tart (page 308).

Gas Method
After preheating grill, adjust primary burner as directed in recipe and turn off other burner(s).

Charcoal Method
Bank all lit coals steeply against 1 side of grill, leaving rest of grill free of coals.

Gas and Charcoal Fire Setups

Double–Banked Fire

Heat level   High / Low

Purpose   Sets up a cooler area between two heat sources so that food cooks evenly without having to rotate it; it's also the ideal setup when using a rotisserie.

Good for   Whole poultry and small roasts. Try Pollo a la Brasa (page 202), Rotisserie Leg of Lamb with Cauliflower, Grape, and Arugula Salad (page 226), or Glazed Rotisserie Pineapple with Salted Rum Butterscotch Sauce (page 304).

Gas Method
Requires at least three burners, preferably running front to back. After pre-heating grill, turn primary burner and burner at opposite end of grill to desired heat level and turn off center burner(s).

Charcoal Method
Divide lit coals into 2 steeply banked piles on opposite sides of grill, leaving center empty. (Disposable pan is sometimes placed in center to catch drips and keep coals banked.)

Concentrated Fire

Heat level   Very high

Purpose   Creates a contained area of intense heat to sear quick-cooking foods

Good for   Stir-fries, burgers, and scallops. Try Grind-Your-Own Sirloin Burgers (page 96) or Stir-Fried Cumin Beef (page 132).

Gas Method
After preheating grill, leave all burners on high.

Charcoal Method
Poke holes in bottom of disposable aluminum roasting pan and set in center of charcoal grate. Pour lit coals into disposable pan.

How to Clean and Oil a Grill Grate

1. Preheat grate thoroughly and scrub it with grill brush until bars have been stripped of any old food residue.

2. Using grill tongs, dip wad of paper towels in vegetable oil and rub it along bars of grate.

Make It Nonstick

For delicate foods that are prone to sticking, such as fish, create a nonstick surface by repeating step 2 with well-oiled paper towels until the grate is black and glossy, 5 to 10 times.

How to Measure Charcoal

We find that a large, 6-quart chimney starter is the best way to get a charcoal fire going. But if you don't have a chimney starter, you can measure the amount of briquettes or hardwood charcoal you need by volume. A quick way to do this is to use a clean, empty half-gallon milk or juice carton, which holds about 2 quarts.

Mounded chimney starter	7 quarts, or 115 briquettes
Full chimney starter	6 quarts, or 100 briquettes
Three-quarters full chimney starter	4½ quarts, or 75 briquettes
Two-thirds full chimney starter	4 quarts, or 65 briquettes
Half-full chimney starter	3 quarts, or 50 briquettes

Flat-Top Grills

Cooking on a flat-top grill is the closest thing to bringing your stovetop outdoors, but with more surface area and more firepower. The intense heat on the carbon steel surface gives foods a great sear, and the griddle becomes seasoned and more nonstick over time. And because of its large size, you can double or even triple recipes, making this a primo way to cook for a crowd. The multiple burners of flat-top grills mean multiple heat zones, so you can cook foods at different temperatures at once. However, because of their flat surface, these grills cannot be used for barbecuing or smoking foods, nor for items where you'd want grill marks, such as grilled pizza.

Our favorite flat-top grill, the **Nexgrill 4-Burner Propane Gas Grill** in Black with Griddle Top, is easy to use, simple to clean, and produces great results. It easily accommodates enough food to feed a crowd and has distinct hotter and cooler zones, making it possible to successfully sear burgers and gently toast burger buns at the same time. Side and back walls make it easy to flip and contain food.

Best-Practice Tips for Flat-Top Grills

Fire It Up

Heat all the burners on medium-high heat for 10 minutes; this helps minimize any hot spots and creates an even initial heat. (User manuals for many flat-top grills warn to never preheat over high, as it might warp the surface.) After the initial preheat, you can adjust to the specified cooking level; the heat will adapt quickly.

Keep It Clean and Seasoned

The best time to clean and season your flattop is right after cooking, letting the griddle cool for 5 to 10 minutes first. We find the best cleaning tool to be a bench scraper (or a metal fish spatula). Be careful not to pour too much water onto the griddle, as a sudden temperature drop can actually crack the nonstick patina finish that you're trying to build up. Besides rubbing it with oil after cleaning, one of the best forms of seasoning is simply cooking on your flattop. The more you use it and build up the patina, the fewer hot spots and the better heat conduction you'll get.

If you want to enjoy some of the advantages of a flat-top grill without investing in one, try a cast-iron plancha (see page 20), a portable griddle that lets you sear foods such as Blistered Shishito Peppers (page 40) or Gambas a la Plancha (page 64) on your grill or over an open fire. While it doesn't offer the surface area of a flattop, a plancha is a great way to expand your grilling repertoire.

How to Clean and Season a Flat-Top Grill

1. Squirt small amount of water onto any built-up residue on hot griddle; it will steam and bubble.

2. Gently scrape water and residue into dripwell or remove it using scraper.

3. With cooking surface still hot, turn heat to medium and lightly coat cooking surface with vegetable oil.

4. Wipe griddle clean with paper towels and tongs. Once finished, turn off grill and let it cool down.

OPEN-FIRE COOKING 101

Fire Pits

Using a fire pit is a full-on embrace of the outdoor cooking experience that engages all your senses; plus, it's a lot of fun. Open-fire cooking is less predictable and more improvisational than other methods. Approach it with a sense of adventure and you'll be rewarded with unique flavors and justifiable pride in your accomplishment.

Freestanding fire pits have made this style of outdoor cooking much more accessible. They come in several shapes; one of our favorites, the **Solo Stove Bonfire 2.0**, resembles a sleek, stainless-steel washing machine drum. About 20 inches in diameter and 18 inches tall, the Bonfire is big enough to gather around but small enough (25 pounds) to still be portable. To cook using the Bonfire, you'll need to buy a two-part attachment: a "hub" or metal crown that goes atop the fire pit and a cast-iron grill grate that rests on the crown, about 8 inches above the fire. (Solo also sells a griddle and a wok, which both fit on the crown.)

Another fire pit we like, the **Kudu Open Fire Grill**, consists of a 2-foot-diameter ceramic-coated heavy-gauge steel fire pit base on legs that hold it about 32 inches off the ground. Two vertical bars attach to the base; one holds a stainless-steel grill grate and the other a cast-iron pan. Both can be adjusted to different heights and can swing out of the way of the flames. The Kudu is sturdy, spacious, and versatile. The long legs are removable, leaving 4-inch legs that bring the pit closer to the ground. The Kudu weighs about 75 pounds, but handles on both sides make moving it manageable for two people.

Establishing proper airflow to maintain a hot fire in the Kudu can be more challenging than it is for a Solo stove, since the former doesn't have a perforated bottom. The Solo stove's fixed grate sits farther from the coals than the Kudu's grate, but the Solo's chamber insulates the heat and funnels it to the grate. The shallow sides of the Kudu allow heat to dissipate, but its cooking grate can be set quite close to the coals. So despite their differences, you can get great results cooking with both fire pits.

Best-Practice Tips for Fire Pits

Fire It Up

Get your fire going early. The wood needs to cook down to mostly coals before you can put the food on, and this takes 30 minutes to 1 hour. (For more about firewood, see page 18.)

Keep It Clean and Seasoned

While the stove and grate are heating, use a pair of tongs to dip a wad of paper towels in vegetable oil and brush the grate (or pan). After cooking, clean the hot grate while it's still on the fire pit, using a grill brush. Then oil the grate again, leaving it to heat on the fire pit to let the oil create a seal. This seasons the grate, making it more nonstick over time and discouraging rust. If rust does occur, do this the next time you use the stove: While it's preheating, brush the surface with a grill brush to remove debris and then rub it well with paper towels soaked in vegetable oil. The grate will look glossy and black again in no time.

Check the Temperature

Place your hand 2 inches above the grate and count until it feels too hot to keep your hand there.

Hot fire	2 seconds
Medium-hot fire	4 seconds
Medium fire	6 seconds
Medium-cool fire	8 seconds
Cool fire	10 seconds

How to Set Up a Fire Pit

Building a 3-Layer Log Cabin Fire

1. Arrange small bundle of tinder in center of grill. Lean thinnest pieces of kindling against each other over tinder to form cone shape. Continue leaning larger pieces of kindling on top, making sure to leave gaps for air to circulate. Arrange 2 largest pieces of fuel wood on either side of cone, parallel to each other.

2. Stack next 2 largest pieces on top of and perpendicular to the first two. Repeat once more with next 2 largest pieces to create log cabin shape. Ignite tinder and let kindling and logs catch fire.

3. As fire burns, use fire tongs or poker to concentrate burnt logs that begin to break down into center. Allow to burn until most logs have carbonized and broken down into large coals.

4a. Single-Level Hot Fire
Spread coals evenly into 1-inch-thick layer over grill. Arrange any logs that have not broken down on perimeter of fire.

4b. Half-Grill Hot Fire
Spread coals evenly into 2-inch-thick layer over half of grill. Arrange any logs that have not broken down on perimeter of fire, away from cool side.

To maintain fire, use fire tongs to pull fresh coals created by burning logs onto spent coals and feed in fresh logs through space between pit and cooking grate. Flames should be no more than 3 inches below cooking grate.

COOKING WITH SMOKE 101

Smokers

Smoke when you're cooking outdoors is not only OK, it's sometimes the main goal. Barbecued foods are beloved for their smoky goodness—the mark of a good batch of Texas-Style Smoked Beef Ribs (page 224) is that pink smoke ring you find when you take a bite.

A charcoal or gas grill can certainly get the job done (and we'll show you how), but if you love barbecue and make it often, you could invest in a dedicated smoker. In contrast to grills, which smoke foods at 275 to 325 degrees, most good smokers can maintain a significantly lower temperature range: from 225 to 250 degrees. (You don't necessarily need to go that low, though; see our

Best-Practice Tips on page 15.) In addition, most smokers allow you to maintain temperatures more consistently and precisely than you can on a grill. Many also have larger fuel capacities (and some models are electric or propane-fueled), so you won't have to worry much about running out of heat during long cooking times.

While there are many types available—including vertical smokers, horizontal smokers, and pellet smokers—broadly speaking, they all work similarly. The fuel provides the smoker with heat, turning it into a vented oven. You add wood chunks or chips directly on top of that fuel or contain them in metal pans suspended over the heat. The wood heats up, producing that signature smoke that is essential to barbecue flavor.

We like the **Weber Smokey Mountain Cooker Smoker**, a charcoal-fueled vertical smoker that's easy to assemble. It has a large charcoal basket that lets you cook for many hours, and it's simple to add more briquettes or wood as needed to maintain the cooking temperature. The largest model is 22 inches and has two grates arranged one over the other, so you can smoke multiple racks of ribs, many pork butts, and at least two spatchcocked turkeys at a time.

Whichever variety of dedicated smoker you have, always follow the manufacturer's instructions to maintain the temperature given in our recipes; that way, the cooking times we provide will line up across different models.

Best-Practice Tips for Vertical Charcoal Smokers

How Low Should You Go?

While barbecue experts say 225 to 250 degrees is the optimal smoking temperature range for turning large, tough cuts of meat tender without drying them out, there is a tradeoff: very long cooking times. We found that briskets cooked for 8 hours at 290 degrees turned out just as good as those cooked for 14 hours at 230 degrees. Our recipes are designed so that you don't need to wake up at 3 a.m. to start your smoking project.

Make It a Charcoal Copycat

You can modify a low-and-slow charcoal grill recipe for your dedicated smoker. For grill recipes that use a charcoal "C" (see page 17), add an extra single row of briquettes on top of your two double rows. This gives you a more hands-off setup so that you need to tend your smoker only once or twice during a long smoking project. Be sure to use a disposable aluminum roasting pan rather than the smoker's water pan. For grill recipes that use a half-grill or banked fire, use the same coal and wood setup, but add an extra 1 quart coals and extend the cooking time to the suggested range in the recipe's smoker conversion.

It's Good to Vent

The smoker's vents give you an easy way to modify the heat level: More open means more air flow, leading to a faster burn and a higher temperature. More closed means less air flow and a lower temperature. If you notice a fluctuation in temperature while smoking, try simply adjusting the air vents on the smoker to regulate the heat before adding more coals or removing the lid.

Check It Out

Keep tabs on the temperature inside the smoker by using a probe thermometer set at the cooking grate level. (The temperature gauge in the lid can be inaccurate.) And if you've got our winning smoker, you can use the side door to check the coal and wood situation and quickly add more fuel if needed, without moving the food or grate.

Keep It Clean

It's a good idea to scrape and wipe down the cooking grates after use while they're still warm. If you're using the water pan, clean it out to get rid of any rendered fat. Unlike a charcoal grill, a vertical smoker doesn't have an ash collector; instead, you lift the upper section off the bottom to empty the ashes.

How to Use Your Grill for Smoking

Use Wood Chip Packets

Wood chips (see page 19) deliver deep, smoky flavor to ribs, brisket, salmon, and more. Charcoal grills can use wood chips or chunks, but if you grill with gas, a foil packet of chips is the way to go.

- For 45 minutes to 1 hour of smoke, you'll need about 2 cups of chips. If you prefer to weigh your chips, 2 cups equals about 4.75 ounces.

- We don't usually soak wood chips when smoking food; soaking delays the onset of smoke, since the wood can't smolder until the water is driven off.

- A foil packet measuring 8 by 4½ inches is just the right size to fit under the grates of most gas grills and won't risk blocking too much heat from the burner. Make sure you don't use so much foil that you need to fold it in more than two layers. Multiple layers, with air trapped between them, end up insulating the chips from the heat so they don't get hot enough to smoke.

- Cutting slits in the packet is the key to wood chips that smolder but don't ignite. Two 2-inch-long slits should let in just enough oxygen for a steady smolder but not enough for the chips to burn. If the chips aren't smoking, insert the tip of a paring knife to gently widen the openings just a little at a time. (And make sure that the slits aren't blocked by the grate's bars when the packet is on the burner.)

Make a Charcoal "C"

You can make truly magnificent barbecue on a kettle grill, including Texas-Style Barbecue Brisket (page 222), with the help of a charcoal snake, a formation in the shape of the letter C.

1. Open bottom vent completely. (This maximizes airflow so that the charcoal and wood chunks burn cleaner, producing better smoke flavor.)

2. Arrange 2 rows of briquettes around perimeter of bottom grate, overlapping slightly, to form "C" shape. Leave at least 8-inch gap between ends. Top each row with second layer of briquettes. (The completed "C" will be 2 briquettes wide by 2 briquettes high.)

3. Place wood chunks at even intervals on top of charcoal. (These will smolder to infuse your food with smoke flavor.) Place disposable aluminum roasting pan in center, running lengthwise into gap of C. Pour 6 cups of water into pan. (This will keep the temperature more consistent.)

4. Light chimney starter filled with 15 briquettes. When top coals are partially covered with ash, pour them over 1 end of charcoal C. (Use tongs as needed to arrange the coals so they touch only 1 end.) Set cooking grate in place. Cook food covered, leaving lid vent completely open.

FUEL FOR THE FIRE

Charcoal

Charcoal is an extremely efficient fuel source for outdoor cooking: It's lighter and more portable and burns more evenly than firewood. Charcoal produces a lot of radiant heat (produced by the frenetic motion of charged particles in the air around the food), which enables superior browning.

There are two types: lump (aka hardwood) and briquettes, both of which produce great-tasting food. Lump resembles the wood it comes from. Briquettes, the most common form, are compact pucks made from sawdust and other materials. Both briquettes and lump charcoal are great for direct, fast grilling (think steaks, chops, burgers, and hot dogs). If you're grilling something that takes more than 40 minutes to cook or you're planning to grill several items over a period of time, go for briquettes, since they stay hot longer. In our testing, a chimney full of briquettes kept grill temperatures above 300 degrees for 2½ to 3½ hours, whereas a chimney full of lump charcoal lasted 40 minutes to 2 hours before temperatures dipped below the 300-degree mark.

If you're cooking multiple foods and need to extend your grill time, you can light another chimney of charcoal (make sure you do this on a safe surface, such as concrete) and add it to your grill when the top coals are partially covered with ash. Remove any food on the grate and then carefully remove the grate and add the lit coals in your desired configuration. This method allows for more consistent heat than adding unlit coals.

There are many excellent products on the market, including **Kingsford Original Briquets**, **B&B Competition Oak Briquets**, and **FOGO Premium All-Natural Lump Charcoal**.

Wood for Open-Fire Cooking

Open-fire cooking requires a hot, clean-burning fire, achieved with dry, seasoned wood. Green wood will burn poorly, creating excess smoke and unnecessary pollution. The ideal wood for a cooking fire is hardwood such as oak, ash, birch, or maple. All of our open-fire recipes use split logs about 12 inches long. We prefer to split all fuel wood into smaller 2-inch-thick pieces in order to quickly create usable coals. If you don't have your own source of dry hardwood, you can often buy precut fuel wood bundles from the grocery store or loose logs from your local landscaping store.

In addition to fuel wood, you need tinder and kindling to build a fire. Tinder is what you'll light first to get your fire started, so it can be anything that catches fire and burns quickly and easily. A small bundle of crumpled newspaper works well, as do combustible items such as wood shavings, dryer lint, or torn-up cardboard egg cartons. Kindling helps bridge the gap between the burning tinder and the larger logs. Kindling needs to be able to catch fire easily and keep burning for a while. Small sticks between ½ and 1 inch thick work best.

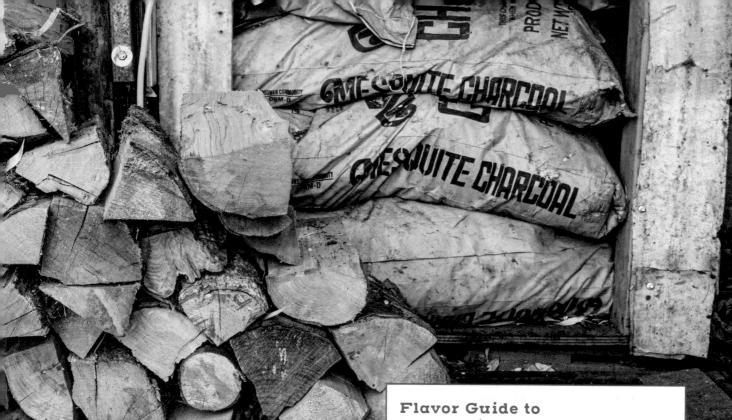

Wood Chips and Chunks

We use wood in two different forms on the grill: chips and chunks. Wood chips can be used on gas grills and charcoal grills, while wood chunks are used only on charcoal grills. Chips are smaller and burn faster than chunks and thus are better for giving flavor to foods that cook more quickly. It's typically not necessary to soak them in water before use: Just place them inside a foil packet with slits cut into it for ventilation (see page 16). Since wood chunks are bigger (most are roughly the size of a tennis ball), they work well for long-cooked foods. Wood chunks are placed directly on the coals for long, slow-smoking Southern-style recipes such as brisket or ribs. We don't typically soak wood chunks when using them on a charcoal grill or in a dedicated smoker.

Flavor Guide to Wood Chips and Chunks

There are many varieties of wood chips and chunks out there for cooking, and each type provides a uniquely flavored smoke to flavor your food. Here are our tasting notes on some of the most common types.

Fruit (Apple, Cherry, Peach)
Produces lightly sweet, mild smoke. Great for seafood and poultry.

Hickory
A balanced though intense smoke that works with almost any food.

Maple
Relatively mild and tasty smoke good for pork and poultry; some tasters found it "resiny" on salmon.

Mesquite
A potent smoke that works best with stronger-tasting cuts of beef, pork, lamb, and game.

Oak
A nutty and well-balanced smoke. The traditional choice for many pitmasters.

FAN THE FLAMES: EQUIPMENT

Your outdoor cooking space doesn't have to be fancy, but a choice selection of efficient cookware, tools, and gear will give you better end results and make getting there a lot more fun.

Chimney starter

Charcoal chimney starters light charcoal in a controlled manner and are our top choice for charcoal grilling. The **Weber Rapidfire Chimney Starter** features a roomy charcoal chamber, an insulated handle, and a helper handle to make it easier to precisely distribute the lit coals.

Plancha

Popular in Spanish cooking, a plancha is a flat griddle that fits on top of a gas or charcoal grill grate. Its flat surface puts a good sear on meat, chicken, or fish and also prevents smaller foods from falling through the grate. We use the **Lodge Pro-Grid Reversible Grill/Griddle**, which is 20 by 10½ inches and made of seasoned cast iron.

Dutch oven

For outdoor cooking, we like to use non-enameled cookware. **Lodge seasoned cast-iron Dutch ovens** come in a range of sizes. You can successfully use enameled Dutch ovens on the grill, though outdoor cooking may be a bit rougher on them than indoor cooking.

Cast-iron skillet

Our choice for outdoor cooking is the **Lodge 12 Inch Cast Iron Skillet**. You may already have this in your kitchen, but if not, you'll need to follow the seasoning instructions before using it on the grill.

Wok

Relatively lightweight woks with stay-cool wooden handles and a generous flat cooking surface work the best for stir-frying on the grill. We favor carbon-steel woks for their efficient heat transfer, which sears foods more effectively than woks made of stainless steel or clad materials or nonstick woks. Carbon steel gradually acquires nonstick seasoning through regular use. **Taylor and Ng Natural Nonstick Wok Set**; **Joyce Chen Classic Series 14-Inch Carbon Steel Wok with Birch Handles**; and **IMUSA 14" Non-Coated Wok with Wood Handle, Silver** are all good choices.

Grill rotisserie

We fell head over heels for rotisserie grilling after discovering how easy it was to produce extra-juicy, crispy-skinned chicken and beautifully roasted, juicy lamb with the **Weber 2290 22-inch Charcoal Kettle Rotisserie**. It has a powerful motor and well-designed food-securing forks so it rotates smoothly and holds food in place.

Grill brush

With short metal bristles and a tri-angular head, the **Weber 12" Three-Sided Grill Brush** makes it easy to clean grill grates by sweeping the top of the grill or by holding the brush at an angle and wedging it between the bars. And for the occasional deep cleaning, the tough-scrubbing pumice block on the **GrillStone Value Pack Cleaning Kit** by Earthstone International works well.

Sheet pans

Rimmed baking sheets have a host of uses for outdoor cooking prep. Use them as a tray to carry ingredients out to the grill or dirty utensils back indoors, as well as to hold cooked ribs or roasts. Our winning sheets, **Nordic Ware Naturals Baker's Half Sheet** and **Nordic Ware Naturals Quarter Sheet**, are sturdy and warp resistant.

Disposable aluminum roasting pans

Positioned beneath the grill grate on a charcoal grill, a pan acts as a drip tray, cutting down on flare-ups; it holds water to add humidity; or it corrals a pile of lit briquettes for a concentrated fire. You can use them to braise food on the grill, such as Grilled Beer Brats and Onions (page 78). On a flat-top grill, they serve as easy-to-maneuver lids for melting cheese on top of Philly-Style Cheesesteaks (page 76) or cooking the eggs-in-a-hole in the Diner-Style Breakfast (page 186). We like 13 by 9-inch moderately deep pans.

Skewers

For most jobs, we prefer metal skewers, which are flameproof and reusable. Thin, flat **Norpro 12-Inch Stainless Steel Skewers** support thick kebabs, can be threaded through delicate foods without tearing them, and turn easily. Plus, their looped handles cool quickly. For certain tasks, such as holding butterflied chicken flat on the grill, slender, disposable wooden or bamboo skewers work better; 12 inches is a good, versatile length.

Tongs

You'll need long tongs to safely move food around the grill. We like the **OXO Good Grips Grilling Tongs**, which have just the right combination of light but tough construction, precise pincers that can grip asparagus spears or racks of ribs, and an easy locking tab.

Spatulas

You'll want more than one of these in your outdoor kitchen; using two spatulas helps a lot with controlling and moving/flipping food, including delicate fish fillets. We love the **Char-Broil Comfort-Grip Spatula** for its flared shape that fits into tight spaces and its comfortable, rounded handle that lends the griller agility, a sense of control, and confidence. Particularly when the grill is really packed, this is your spatula.

FAN THE FLAMES: EQUIPMENT

Bench scraper

A bench scraper can help you transfer food to and from a flat-top griddle (think piles of chopped peppers and onions for fajitas) and scrape down a flattop to clean it. The textured polypropylene handle of the **Dexter-Russell Sani-Safe 6" x 3" Dough Cutter/Scraper** is thick enough to provide a sturdy grip and is easy to grab onto even when slick.

Plastic squeeze bottles

Beyond their uses storing barbecue sauce and burger condiments, squeeze bottles allow you to easily dispense controlled amounts of oil or water onto a flattop for seasoning and cleaning. **TableCraft Widemouth Squeeze Bottles** are made of flexible plastic that's very easy to squeeze and won't deform.

Instant-read thermometer

The **ThermoWorks Thermapen ONE** has a large, grippy handle; a rotating screen with large, highly legible numbers; and a backlight that goes on when viewing conditions are dim. As its name indicates, it takes just 1 second to measure a temperature.

Probe thermometer

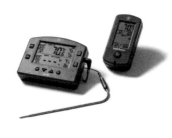

A probe thermometer tells you when your food is ready without having to lift the grill lid and thus slow down the cooking process. It consists of a probe that's inserted into the food you're cooking and connects by a thin wire to a base that sits outside the grill. The base displays the readout so you can monitor the food's temperature. Clip-on probe thermometers are useful only as long as you're standing next to the grill, while remote-probe thermometers also transmit temperature data to portable receivers. We prefer this style, especially for longer-cooking foods such as barbecue or roasts, because you can walk away from the grill or smoker; the receiver lets you know when your food has reached its target temperature. The **ThermoWorks Smoke 2-Channel Alarm** is ready to use right out of the box. The base and receiver have clear displays that can be read in any light conditions, and the unit maintains a connection for up to 300 feet.

Smoker box

If you want to avoid fussing with foil packets, a smoker box is a worthy, reusable investment. We like using the **GrillPro Cast Iron Smoker Box** made by Onward Manufacturing Company. It's easy to fill, empty, and clean and, at just slightly over an inch tall, it will fit in almost any grill.

Pizza peel

Essentially a large, very thin metal spatula, the **American Metalcraft Pizza Peel 2814** does an excellent job of sliding under pizzas or breads to rotate or remove them.

Grill gloves

When you're working over a scorching-hot grill, oven mitts won't cut it. **Steven Raichlen Best of Barbecue Extra Long Suede Grilling Gloves** give great control when manipulating tongs and grabbing hot grill grates. They're made of pliant leather and have long, wide cuffs that protect your forearms and let air circulate to keep you relatively cool.

Basting brush

Long-handled barbecue basting brushes allow you to safely apply oil or sauce to food on the grill without burning your fingers. The silicone bristles of the **OXO Good Grips Grilling Basting Brush** pick up an impressive volume of sauce. Although the bristles are heat resistant to a high temperature, the handle is not, so be careful not to set it on the grill.

Fireplace tools

Why are these here, you ask? Well, we found in recipe development that a decent set of fireplace tools is the best equipment to turn to when cooking over an open fire. The tongs and poker let you safely move and adjust burning logs, and the small shovel is helpful for removing ashes from the pit.

Cooler

A cooler is indispensable outdoor "pantry" gear whether you're planning on cooking at a campground, a beach, or just your backyard. Generally speaking, the more insulating power a cooler has, the heavier it is and the smaller the capacity for its size. The **Yeti Tundra 45 and 65** fall into this category. They're durable and easy to open and close, and ice lasts a whole week in them. The budget-friendly **Coleman 50 QT XTreme Wheeled Cooler** does a decent job of cooling, keeping ice for six days. Its wheels make it more portable, and it has a roomy interior.

Pizza oven

While you can make excellent pizza on your grill (see page 276), dedicated outdoor portable pizza ovens are an intriguing and increasingly popular option. They're fueled by propane gas and/or wood or charcoal; we prefer gas-fueled ovens for their ease of use and their ability to maintain the necessary high temperatures for producing the professional results they promise. The best-performing ovens are well insulated and easily portable, and have burners placed at the back (rather than under the cooking surface), which allows them to produce great results in a variety of pizza styles. The compact, reliable **Ooni Koda 12 Gas Powered Pizza Oven** is our recommendation for most home cooks who want to cook amazing pizzas outdoors quickly and easily. A gas flame located at the rear of the oven heats up the baking stone relatively evenly while also heating the inside of the oven. An angled heat deflector on the roof of the oven helps direct heat to the tops of the pizzas as they bake. If you want the ability to make 16-inch pizzas, the **Ooni Koda 16** does a great job, although it's heavier and bulkier. See our recipes developed especially for an outdoor pizza oven, along with tips for baking fantastic pizza in it, on pages 280–282.

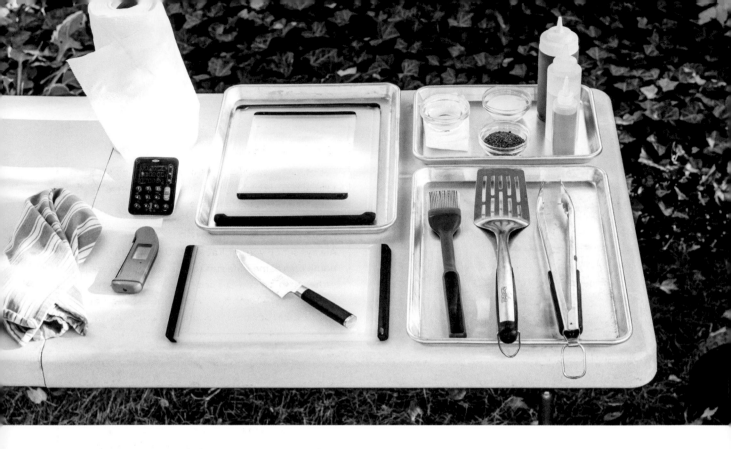

KEEP YOUR COOL: SETUP AND SAFETY

Outdoor Kitchen Setup

Minimize the need to keep running indoors by organizing an outdoor prep station near your grill.

Your Prep Table

A sturdy, portable table gives you a dedicated place to prep food that's separate from where you'll be eating. Make sure it's big enough to allow you prep space as well as storage space. Plan for the following equipment:

- A sheet pan holding plastic squeeze bottles of oil, water, and any condiments you need, along with mise bowls holding spices.

- Another sheet pan holding cutting boards and serving platters. Having a stack of lightweight cutting boards or mats on hand makes it easy to avoid cross-contamination; use separate boards to hold raw meat and vegetables.

- A third sheet pan or a tray holding any cooking utensils that you need: spatulas, knives, scissors, metal skewers, and so on.

Alongside Your Prep Table

Here are some other handy items for your outdoor kitchen:

- A dish tub filled with warm soapy water is a great place to stash grilling utensils when you're done with them. Soaking the used tools gives you a head start on cleanup—no dried-on food to contend with.

- A cooler keeps raw meat and other foods safe until you use them and also holds cold drinks for the cooking crew.

- A plastic storage tub is handy for storing grill gear that can live outside for the season, such as grill gloves, grill brush, long tongs, grill lighter, stash of disposable aluminum roasting pans, and more.

- A wide-mouthed trash barrel makes an easy target for discards; a tight-fitting lid discourages flying pests and other critters.

- A fire extinguisher is a safety feature that every kitchen, outdoors or indoors, should have.

Safety First!

Let's face it, part of the fun of outdoor cooking is the primal thrill of playing with fire. Here are four tips to keep that thrill accident-free.

Location Is Everything

Always set up your grill at least 10 feet from your home on a flame-safe surface—a driveway or patio rather than grass or a wooden deck—and away from where children and pets might wander. Pay special attention when cooking with charcoal or wood in windy weather, as sparks can fly out of the grill or fire pit.

Cleanliness Counts

It's important that the interior basin of your gas or charcoal grill, or your smoker, be cleaned a few times each season to wash away built-up food matter that can ignite (or lend off-flavors) to whatever you're cooking. Empty drip pans and ash-catchers frequently to reduce mess and minimize risk.

Prep Food Carefully

Flare-ups are often caused by fat or by excess oily marinade dripping off the meat and catching fire. Trim meat carefully and pat dry any oil-marinated foods with paper towels before grilling. In case a flare-up still happens, keep long tongs and grill gloves handy so that you can quickly and safely move the food to an area of the grill not directly over the fire. Briefly covering the grill can also help squelch flare-ups.

Food Safety Matters

It's easy to skip basic rules when cooking outside. Don't forget to always use separate platters for raw and cooked foods to avoid cross-contamination, and always dispose of excess marinade for raw proteins. Also be mindful of basting brushes: If you brush something onto a protein early in cooking, use a clean brush and separate bowl of sauce for any finishing swipes of sauce.

FIRE UP THE MEAL: MENUS

Once you've got the fire going, take advantage of the heat to cook your entire meal outdoors with smart timing. Our Weeknight Dinners chapter (page 119) gives you more than 30 complete meals, but you can branch out and create your own menus. Get started by working your way through these examples.

Gas Grill Glory

Grilled Vegetable and Halloumi Salad (page 180)

Mana'eesh Za'atar (page 272)

This summery meal comes together with less than an hour of grilling time. While you're waiting for the vegetables to cool so that you can chop them, toss the flatbreads on the grate; they'll cook within minutes, so you can serve them warm with the salad.

Grilled Potato Wedges with Lemon-Dill Mayo (page 42)

Grill-Roasted Butterflied Chicken (page 200)

Skillet Brownie (page 300)

Grill-bake the brownie in advance and then gently warm it on the grill right before serving. Grill the potato wedges on the hotter side of the grill while the chicken cooks on the cooler side.

Charred Pineapple Margaritas (page 67)

Charred Guacamole (page 32)

Grilled Chicken and Vegetable Quesadillas (page 56)

Watermelon with Grilled Queso de Freir, Serrano, and Pepitas (page 44)

Start with the guacamole, charred pineapple, and queso, grilling them on the grate before cooking the quesadillas on the plancha.

Charcoal Cred

Grilled Vegetable Platter (page 234)

Grilled Turkey Burgers with Spinach and Feta (page 88)

For a quick, efficient meal, grill all the vegetables at once over a single-level hot fire, followed by the turkey burgers over the slightly cooled, now medium-hot fire.

Bruschetta with Marinated Grilled Tomatoes and Fresh Mozzarella (page 46)

Grilled Pork Loin with Apple-Cranberry Filling (page 208)

Cherry Spoon Cake (page 314)

Grill-bake the cake on the cooler side of the grill while charring the tomatoes for the bruschetta ahead of time; they'll develop flavor as they marinate. At mealtime, start the pork on the cooler side of the grill and toast the bread for the bruschetta on the hotter side. Serve the bruschetta while the pork continues to cook. Warm the spoon cake over the dwindling heat of the charcoal while you enjoy your dinner.

Mini Lamb Kofte (page 60)

Grilled Cod and Summer Squash Packets (page 172)

After grilling the kofte, use the concentrated hot fire to cook the cod and squash packets.

Open-Fire Improv

Grilled Polenta Wedges with Grilled Scallions and Gorgonzola (page 48)

Grilled Halibut Steak with Spicy Orange and Fennel Salad (page 258)

Maintaining a hot single-level fire is all you need to do to grill all the elements in these two recipes.

Grilled Clams, Mussels, or Oysters with Soy-Citrus Sauce (page 62)

Thick-Cut Rib Steaks with Ember-Baked Potatoes (page 250)

Ultimate S'mores (page 296)

While the potatoes and garlic roast in the embers and the steaks cook on the cooler side of the grill, quickly cook the shellfish on the hotter side to enjoy while the steaks finish. Keep the fire lit while enjoying dinner so you can toast marshmallows for dessert.

Baba Ghanoush (page 34)

Grilled Flatbreads (page 270)

Grilled Harissa-Rubbed Rack of Lamb with Ember-Baked Carrots (page 256)

Grill the eggplant and prepare the baba ghanoush. Grill the flatbreads directly over the flames to serve with the dip while the carrots and lamb roast over the fire.

Flattop Flair

Blistered Shishito Peppers (page 40)

Japanese Steak House Steak and Vegetables (page 140)

The large surface area of the flattop gives you the option to cook both recipes at the same time or to quickly sear the shishitos before cooking the steaks and assorted vegetables.

Gambas a la Plancha (page 64)

Grilled Chicken Thighs with Butternut Squash and Cilantro Vinaigrette (page 126)

Grilled Stone Fruit (page 302)

These recipes all cook relatively fast, making this an elegant but manageable menu to serve to company outdoors.

GRILL IT,
YOU'LL LIKE IT!

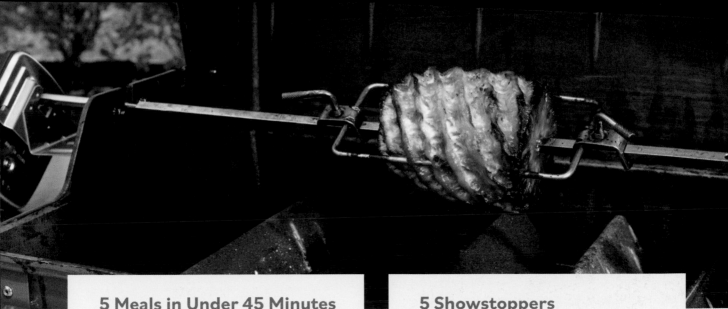

5 Meals in Under 45 Minutes

Grilled Red Curry Chicken Sandwiches with Spicy Slaw (page 74)

Grilled Strip Steak and Potatoes with Blue Cheese Butter (page 142)

Grilled Sausages and Polenta with Arugula Salad (page 146)

Grilled Pork Chops with Plums (page 150)

Grilled Swordfish with Potatoes and Salsa Verde (page 168)

5 Showstoppers

Grilled Clams, Mussels, or Oysters with Soy-Citrus Sauce (page 62)

Smoked Bourbon Chicken (page 198)

Rotisserie Leg of Lamb with Cauliflower, Grape, and Arugula Salad (page 226)

Grill-Roasted Whole Cauliflower with Tahini-Yogurt Sauce (page 232)

Glazed Rotisserie Pineapple with Salted Rum Butterscotch Sauce (page 304)

5 Superfun Recipes to Make on a Flattop or Plancha

Blistered Shishito Peppers (page 40)

Grilled Chicken and Vegetable Quesadillas (page 56)

Smashed Burgers (page 90)

Japanese Steak House Steak and Vegetables (page 140)

Diner-Style Breakfast (page 186)

5 Must-Cook Open-Fire Dishes

Fireside Chili (page 254)

Ember-Roasted Beet Salad (page 264)

Grilled Whole Trout with Wilted Swiss Chard and Apple-Cherry Relish (page 260)

Mana'eesh Za'atar (page 272)

Ultimate S'mores (page 296)

1 Snacks and Small Plates

Charred Guacamole

SERVES 6 to 8   **TOTAL TIME** 40 minutes

1   jalapeño chile

¼   small red onion

2   garlic cloves, unpeeled

3   ripe but firm avocados,
     halved and pitted

2   tablespoons chopped
     fresh cilantro

¼   teaspoon grated lime zest
     plus 2 tablespoons juice,
     plus extra juice for seasoning

½   teaspoon table salt

Why This Recipe Works Putting a little char on guac ingredients adds intensity to this perennial party favorite. This recipe employs heat strategically by grilling the aromatics until well charred, grilling the avocados lightly, and leaving the lime off the grill entirely so that its fresh juice brightens the smoky flavors. Threading the jalapeño, onion, and garlic onto a skewer makes them easier to manage over the flames. Since over-heating avocados can bring out bitterness, grill them just long enough for the hot grate to leave its marks. The rustic flavor of this guacamole calls for a chunky texture, so you'll mash one avocado into the aromatics and then coarsely chop the other two before folding everything together. You can make this dip ahead and chill it for up to a day, but it also tastes great still slightly warm from the grill; you might find yourself spooning it over grilled chicken, steak, or shrimp, as well as scooping it up with chips (or a spoon!). For a spicier guac, include a portion of the chopped jalapeño's seeds. You will need one 12-inch metal skewer.

1A   For a charcoal grill Open bottom vent completely. Light large chimney starter filled with charcoal briquettes (6 quarts). When top coals are partially covered with ash, pour evenly over grill. Set cooking grate in place, cover, and open lid vent completely. Heat grill until hot, about 5 minutes.

1B   For a gas grill Turn all burners to high; cover; and heat grill until hot, about 15 minutes. Leave all burners on high.

2   Clean and oil cooking grate. Thread jalapeño, onion, and garlic onto 12-inch metal skewer. Grill skewer (covered if using gas), turning occasionally, until vegetables are well charred, 4 to 6 minutes; transfer to cutting board. Grill avocados (covered if using gas), cut side down, until lightly charred, about 3 minutes; transfer to cutting board with vegetables and let cool slightly, about 5 minutes.

3   Using paper towel, peel away skin from jalapeño, then remove stem and seeds and chop fine. Peel and mince garlic and chop onion fine. Combine vegetables with cilantro, lime zest and juice, and salt in large bowl.

Flare Trade

Open Fire Prepare hot single-level fire in open-fire grill. Set cooking grate at least 6 inches from coals and flames and heat grill until hot, about 5 minutes. Proceed with step 2.

4 Scoop flesh from 2 avocado halves directly into bowl with vegetable mixture. Using tines of fork, mash avocado until just combined. Scoop flesh from remaining 4 avocado halves onto cutting board and chop coarse. Gently fold chopped avocado into mashed avocado mixture until it has broken down just enough to coat other ingredients but is still chunky. Season with extra lime juice and salt to taste. Serve. (Guacamole can be covered with plastic wrap, pressed directly onto surface of mixture, and refrigerated for up to 24 hours. Bring guacamole to room temperature still covered, removing plastic wrap at last moment before serving.)

Baba Ghanoush

SERVES 4 to 6   **TOTAL TIME** 1¼ hours

2 (12-ounce) eggplants

1 tablespoon lemon juice,
  plus extra for seasoning

1 garlic clove, minced to paste

1 teaspoon table salt

¼ cup tahini

¼ cup extra-virgin olive oil,
  divided

1 tablespoon chopped
  fresh parsley

Why This Recipe Works Cooking eggplants over flames gives you baba ghanoush as it's meant to be: beguilingly smoky and ultrasilky. To help evaporate moisture, which would dilute the flavor, and to keep them from bursting, pierce the skins of the eggplants. You'll grill the eggplants for a good half-hour, until they're completely soft. Plenty of tahini underlines the dip's toasty flavor, and olive oil enhances the creaminess. Letting the minced garlic soak in lemon juice before combining it with the eggplants tempers its pungency. The finished product should be assertive but not overpowering. Baba ghanoush is best served the day you make it. Serve with pita bread, tomato wedges, and/or cucumber slices.

1A   For a charcoal grill Open bottom vent completely. Light large chimney starter filled with charcoal briquettes (6 quarts). When top coals are partially covered with ash, pour evenly over grill. Set cooking grate in place, cover, and open lid vent completely. Heat grill until hot, about 5 minutes.

1B   For a gas grill Turn all burners to high; cover; and heat grill until hot, about 15 minutes. Turn all burners to medium-high.

2 Clean and oil cooking grate. Poke each eggplant about 6 times with paring knife. Grill eggplants, covered, for 20 minutes. Flip eggplants and continue to grill, covered, for 10 minutes. (Skin should be charred and have aroma of burning leaves, and eggplants should be uniformly soft when pressed with tongs.) Transfer eggplants to plate and let cool completely, about 30 minutes.

3 Meanwhile, combine lemon juice, garlic, and salt in medium bowl; set aside.

4 Working with 1 eggplant at a time, split lengthwise on 1 side through skin and peel back skin to expose flesh. Using spoon, scoop out eggplant flesh; discard eggplant skin. Chop eggplant flesh fine with chef's knife and transfer to bowl with lemon juice mixture.

5 Add tahini and 2 tablespoons oil to eggplant mixture and whisk to combine. Let baba ghanoush sit for 20 minutes to allow flavors to blend, stirring occasionally. Season with extra lemon juice and salt to taste. Spread baba ghanoush in shallow bowl and drizzle with remaining 2 tablespoons oil. Sprinkle with parsley and serve.

Flare Trade

Open Fire Prepare hot single-level fire in open-fire grill. Set cooking grate at least 6 inches from coals and flames and heat grill until hot, about 5 minutes. Proceed with step 2, turning eggplants occasionally, until skins are charred and eggplants are uniformly soft when pressed with tongs, 30 to 40 minutes.

Grilled Buffalo Chicken Dip with Spicy Monkey Bread

SERVES 8 to 10   **TOTAL TIME** 1½ hours

6 tablespoons hot sauce, divided

2 tablespoons unsalted butter, melted

1 pound pizza dough, room temperature

8 ounces cream cheese, softened

2 ounces blue cheese, crumbled (½ cup), divided

⅓ cup ranch dressing

1 teaspoon Worcestershire sauce

1 (6- to 8- ounce) boneless, skinless chicken breast, trimmed

2 scallions

Why This Recipe Works This cast-iron skillet creation is so messily fun to eat, you'll be extra-glad you're outside. The whole shebang "bakes" to golden, lightly smoky perfection on the grill. Rolling the dough balls in hot sauce and butter before tucking them around the perimeter of the skillet reinforces the buffalo flavor. Grilled and shredded chicken breast, charred scallions, cream cheese, both crumbled blue cheese and ranch dressing (to please everybody), and more hot sauce all go into the dip. The bread gets a head start on the grill before the dip goes into the skillet. Then it all cooks over the fire until it's browned and bubbling. Ready-made pizza dough from the local pizzeria or supermarket works great here, but if you'd like to make your own, see page 276. A vinegar-forward Louisiana-style hot sauce tastes best here. You will need a 10-inch cast-iron skillet.

1   Combine 2 tablespoons hot sauce and melted butter in large bowl; set aside. Place dough on lightly floured counter and pat into rough 8-inch square. Cut dough square into 32 pieces (½ ounce each) and loosely cover with greased plastic wrap. Working with one at a time (keep remaining pieces covered), roll dough pieces into tight balls, then coat with butter mixture. Reserve remaining butter mixture. Evenly space 16 balls around edge of 10-inch cast iron skillet, keeping center of skillet clear. Place remaining 16 balls on top, staggering them between seams of balls underneath. Cover loosely with greased plastic and let sit until slightly puffed, about 20 minutes.

2   Whisk cream cheese and remaining ¼ cup hot sauce in bowl until smooth and no lumps of cream cheese remain. Stir in ¼ cup blue cheese, ranch dressing, and Worcestershire until combined (bits of blue cheese will remain); set aside.

3A   For a charcoal grill Open bottom vent completely. Light large chimney starter mounded with charcoal briquettes (7 quarts). When top coals are partially covered with ash, pour into steeply banked pile against side of grill. Set cooking grate in place, cover, and open lid vent completely. Heat grill until hot, about 5 minutes.

3B For a gas grill Turn all burners to high; cover; and heat grill until hot, about 15 minutes. Leave primary burner on high and turn off other burner(s). (Adjust primary burner as needed to maintain grill temperature between 450 and 500 degrees; if using 3-burner grill, adjust primary burner and second burner.)

4 Clean and oil cooking grate. Grill chicken and scallions on hotter side of grill until scallions are lightly charred, 2 to 4 minutes, and chicken is lightly browned and registers 160 degrees, 8 to 10 minutes, turning as needed. Transfer scallions and chicken to cutting board as they finish cooking.

5 Remove plastic from dough balls. Transfer skillet to cooler side of grill, cover, and cook until rolls are just beginning to brown, about 20 minutes, rotating skillet halfway through baking.

6 Shred chicken into bite-size pieces and thinly slice scallions. Stir chicken and scallions into cream cheese mixture. Off heat, spoon chicken mixture into center of skillet and sprinkle with remaining ¼ cup blue cheese. Return skillet to cooler side of grill, cover, and bake until dip is heated through and rolls are golden brown, 10 to 15 minutes. Brush bread with reserved butter mixture before serving.

Smoked Nachos

SERVES 6 to 8   **TOTAL TIME** 50 minutes

2 cups wood chips

2 ears corn, husks and silk removed

2 teaspoons vegetable oil

2 poblano chiles, stemmed, halved, and seeded

4 Fresno or jalapeño chiles, stemmed, halved, and seeded

1 (15-ounce) can black beans, rinsed

8 ounces Monterey Jack cheese, shredded (2 cups)

8 ounces sharp cheddar cheese, shredded (2 cups)

12 ounces tortilla chips

2 scallions, sliced thin

Lime wedges

Why This Recipe Works Take your next backyard get-together to the next level and wow everyone with these grilled skillet nachos. Using a foil packet of wood chips gives great smoky flavor that an oven broiler could never deliver. You'll char savory poblano and fruity Fresno chiles until their skins blister and ears of corn until their kernels turn chewy and sweet. To these you'll add black beans and two kinds of cheese for irresistible gooey-ness. The key to creating evenly coated, evenly delicious nachos is layering. When the nachos come off the fire, a squeeze of lime and a scattering of scallions brighten the cheesy, smoky goodness. If you'd like to use wood chunks instead of wood chips when using a charcoal grill, substitute two medium wood chunks for the wood chip packet. You will need a 12-inch cast-iron skillet for this recipe. Serve with sour cream, salsa, and/or Charred Guacamole (page 32).

1   Using large piece of heavy-duty aluminum foil, wrap wood chips in 8 by 4½-inch foil packet. (Make sure chips do not poke holes in sides or bottom of packet. If using gas, make sure there are no more than 2 layers of foil on bottom of packet.) Cut 2 evenly spaced 2-inch slits in top of packet.

2A   For a charcoal grill Open bottom vent halfway. Light large chimney starter mounded with charcoal briquettes (7 quarts). When top coals are partially covered with ash, pour two-thirds evenly over half of grill, then pour remaining coals over other half of grill. Place wood chip packet along 1 side of grill near border between hotter and cooler coals. Set cooking grate in place, cover, and open lid vent halfway. Heat grill until hot and wood chips are smoking, about 5 minutes.

2B   For a gas grill Remove cooking grate and place wood chip packet directly on primary burner. Set cooking grate in place, turn primary burner to medium, and turn other burner(s) to high. Cover and heat grill until hot and wood chips are smoking, 15 to 25 minutes. Leave primary burner on medium and other burner(s) on high.

3   Clean and oil cooking grate. Brush corn with oil. Grill corn, poblanos, and Fresnos on hotter side of grill (covered if using gas) until corn is charred on all sides and poblanos and Fresnos are well blistered, 5 to 10 minutes. As poblanos and Fresnos finish cooking, transfer to bowl, cover tightly with aluminum foil, and let sit until skins soften, about 5 minutes. Transfer corn to cutting board. Turn all burners to medium (if using gas).

4 Cut kernels from corn. Using paper towels, peel away skin from poblanos and Fresnos. Slice poblanos into ¼-inch-thick strips and thinly slice Fresnos. Combine corn, poblanos, Fresnos, black beans, Monterey Jack, and cheddar in bowl.

5 Spread one-quarter of tortilla chips evenly in 12-inch cast iron skillet. Sprinkle with one-quarter of vegetable-cheese mixture. Repeat layering of chips and vegetable-cheese mixture 3 more times. Place skillet on cooler side of grill (if using charcoal), cover, and cook until cheese is melted, 15 to 30 minutes. Sprinkle with scallions and serve with lime wedges.

Blistered Shishito Peppers

SERVES 4 to 6   **TOTAL TIME** 25 minutes

1 tablespoon vegetable oil

8 ounces shishito peppers

Why This Recipe Works Japanese shishito peppers boast thin skins; delicate flesh; and a fruity, grassy flavor reminiscent of jalapeño or serrano chiles, minus the heat. A cast-iron plancha gets ripping-hot on the grill and blisters these beauties in a matter of minutes, for a super-simple one-bite snack or appetizer to fortify everyone while the rest of the meal cooks. Once they're done, just toss them with flake sea salt or other seasonings and then pick them up by the stem and devour them whole. You will need a cast-iron plancha measuring at least 20 by 10 inches.

1A For a charcoal grill Open bottom vent completely. Light large chimney starter filled with charcoal briquettes (6 quarts). When top coals are partially covered with ash, pour evenly over grill. Set cooking grate in place, center plancha on cooking grate, cover, and open lid vent completely. Heat grill with plancha until hot, about 5 minutes.

1B For a gas grill Turn all burners to high; cover; and heat grill until hot, about 15 minutes. Center plancha on grill, cover, and heat for 5 more minutes. Leave all burners on high.

2 Toss peppers with oil in bowl. Arrange peppers in even layer on plancha and cook, without moving, until skins are blistered on first side, 1 to 3 minutes. Flip peppers and continue to cook until blistered on second side, 1 to 2 minutes. Transfer to serving bowl and season with flake sea salt to taste. Serve immediately.

Variations

Smoky Shishito Peppers with Espelette and Lime
Combine 1 teaspoon ground dried Espelette pepper, 1 teaspoon smoked paprika, ½ teaspoon flake sea salt or kosher salt, and ¼ teaspoon grated lime zest in small bowl. Sprinkle over cooked peppers in serving bowl. Serve with lime wedges.

Shishito Peppers with Mint, Poppy Seeds, and Orange
Combine 1 teaspoon dried mint, 1 teaspoon poppy seeds, ½ teaspoon flake sea salt or kosher salt, and ¼ teaspoon grated orange zest in small bowl. Sprinkle over peppers in serving bowl. Serve with orange wedges.

Flare Trade

Flat-Top Grill Turn all burners to medium-high and heat griddle until hot, about 10 minutes. Turn all burners to high. Clean griddle and proceed with step 2.

Open Fire Prepare hot single-level fire in open-fire grill. Set cooking grate at least 6 inches from coals and flames, place plancha on cooking grate, and heat plancha until hot, about 5 minutes. Proceed with step 2.

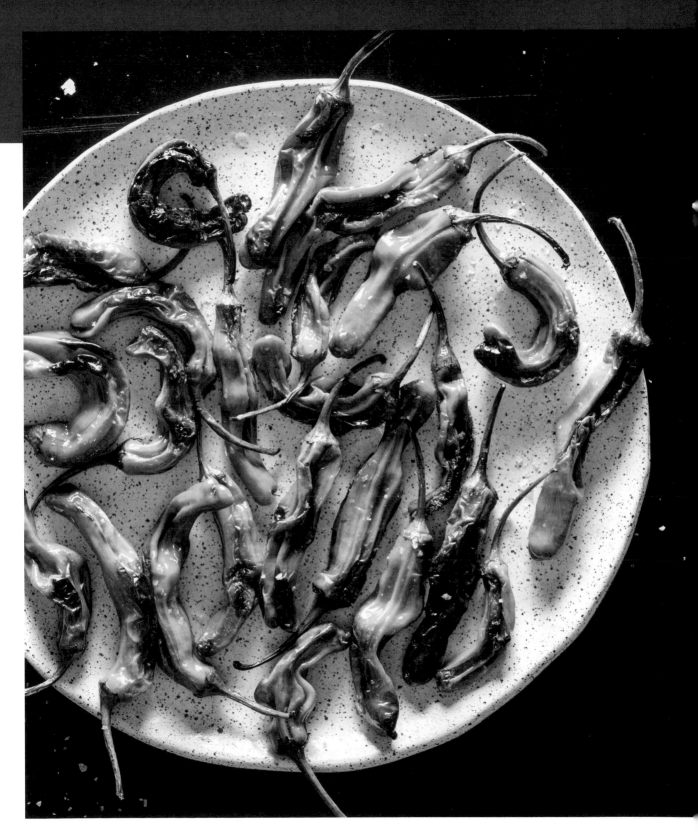

Grilled Potato Wedges with Lemon–Dill Mayo

SERVES 4   TOTAL TIME 50 minutes

Potatoes

- 2 pounds large Yukon Gold potatoes, unpeeled
- 2 tablespoons extra-virgin olive oil
- 1½ teaspoons granulated garlic
- ¾ teaspoon table salt
- ½ teaspoon pepper

Lemon–Dill Mayo

- ½ cup mayonnaise
- ¼ cup chopped fresh dill
- 2 tablespoons extra-virgin olive oil
- 1 teaspoon grated lemon zest plus 1 tablespoon juice
- 1 garlic clove, minced
- ¼ teaspoon pepper
- ⅛ teaspoon table salt

Flare Trade

Open Fire Prepare hot single-level fire in open-fire grill. Set cooking grate at least 6 inches from coals and flames and heat grill until hot, about 5 minutes. Proceed with step 4.

Why This Recipe Works Done right, grilled potatoes are creamy and soft inside and crisp and charry outside. Their density makes cooking them completely outdoors a challenge, but the microwave jump-starts the process nicely. Leave the skins on, cut the spuds into generous wedges, and toss them with oil and seasonings before microwaving until almost tender. Outdoors on the grill, they need just a few minutes on each side to achieve crispy-brown perfection. Mayo anchors a quick dip punctuated with garlic, lemon, and a big handful of fresh dill; you can stir it up while the potatoes are in the microwave. Look for large Yukon Gold potatoes that are at least 3 inches in diameter and weigh 8 to 12 ounces each.

1 **For the potatoes** Cut each potato lengthwise into 8 wedges, about ¾ inch thick. Toss potatoes with oil, granulated garlic, salt, and pepper in large bowl. Microwave, covered, until potatoes are nearly tender, 9 to 12 minutes, stirring every 3 minutes. (Potatoes should range in doneness from nearly completely tender to raw in spots.) Uncover and set aside while heating grill.

2 **For the lemon-dill mayo** While potatoes cook, combine all ingredients in bowl; set aside.

3A **For a charcoal grill** Open bottom vent completely. Light large chimney starter filled with charcoal briquettes (6 quarts). When top coals are partially covered with ash, pour evenly over grill. Set cooking grate in place, cover, and open lid vent completely. Heat grill until hot, about 5 minutes.

3B **For a gas grill** Turn all burners to high; cover; and heat grill until hot, about 15 minutes. Leave all burners on high.

4 Clean and oil cooking grate. Place potatoes on grill, cut side down and perpendicular to grate bars. Grill until well browned on all sides and lightly charred, 9 to 12 minutes (3 to 4 minutes on each cut side and on skin side). Transfer potatoes to serving platter and season with salt to taste. Serve with lemon-dill mayo.

Watermelon with Grilled Queso de Freir, Serrano, and Pepitas

SERVES 6   **TOTAL TIME** 35 minutes

3 tablespoons extra-virgin olive oil, divided

2 tablespoons chopped fresh cilantro

1 serrano or jalapeño chile, stemmed, seeded, and minced

1 teaspoon grated lime zest plus 1 tablespoon juice

1 teaspoon honey

¼ teaspoon table salt

16 pieces watermelon (either 1-inch cubes or 1½ by ½-inch triangles)

10 ounces queso de freir, sliced into ½-inch-thick slabs

2 tablespoons chopped roasted, salted pepitas

Why This Recipe Works The mild, fresh-yet-firm Mexican cheese queso de freir has a very high melting point, so grilling it turns the exterior golden and lightly crisp while the interior softens. The dynamic pairing of hot, creamy cheese with cool, crisp, juicy watermelon makes for al fresco magic. A lip-smacking honey-lime dressing unites both elements. To maximize the hot-cold contrast, you'll toss the watermelon with some of the dressing before the quick-cooking cheese hits the grill. After pairing the grilled cheese and watermelon pieces, drizzle the rest of the dressing over everything, scatter crunchy pepitas on top, and serve right away. Creating nonstick conditions for the grill grate is key here (see page 9). If queso de freir is unavailable, you can substitute halloumi.

1   Whisk 2 tablespoons oil, cilantro, serrano, lime zest and juice, honey, and salt together in small bowl; set aside.

2A For a charcoal grill Open bottom vent completely. Light large chimney starter filled with charcoal briquettes (6 quarts). When top coals are partially covered with ash, pour evenly over half of grill. Set cooking grate in place, cover, and open lid vent completely. Heat grill until hot, about 5 minutes.

2B For a gas grill Turn all burners to high; cover; and heat grill until hot, about 15 minutes. Leave primary burner on high and turn off other burner(s).

3   Clean and oil cooking grate. Just before grilling cheese, toss watermelon with 2 teaspoons dressing in large bowl. Pat queso de freir dry with paper towels and brush with remaining 1 tablespoon oil. Grill queso de freir on hotter side of grill (covered if using gas) until lightly charred and beginning to soften on first side, 30 to 60 seconds. Using thin metal spatula, gently flip cheese and cook until lightly charred on second side, 45 to 90 seconds. Transfer to cutting board and cut each slab in half crosswise.

4   Top queso de freir with watermelon and arrange on serving platter. Drizzle with remaining dressing and sprinkle with pepitas. Serve.

Flare Trade

Open Fire Prepare hot single-level fire in open-fire grill. Set cooking grate at least 6 inches from coals and flames and heat grill until hot, about 5 minutes. Proceed with step 3.

Bruschetta with Marinated Grilled Tomatoes and Fresh Mozzarella

SERVES 8   TOTAL TIME 1 hour

2 pounds ripe tomatoes, cored and halved along equator

6 tablespoons extra-virgin olive oil, divided, plus extra for serving

¾ teaspoon table salt, divided

½ teaspoon pepper, divided

8 ounces fresh mozzarella cheese, torn into bite-size pieces and patted dry

¼ cup chopped fresh basil

2 tablespoons red wine vinegar

Pinch red pepper flakes

1 (10 by 5-inch) loaf country bread with thick crust, ends discarded, sliced crosswise into ¾-inch-thick pieces

1 garlic clove, peeled

Why This Recipe Works Bruschetta features grilled bread, but why not grill the topping too? A delicious use for an abundance of summer tomatoes is to halve them and put them over a hot fire to quickly develop char and smoky depth. Milky fresh mozzarella balances the tomatoes' acidity. Cloaking them both in a blend of red wine vinegar and olive oil lets their flavors meld to create a topping bursting with flavor. For the best results, use in-season, round tomatoes that are ripe yet a bit firm so they will hold their shape on the grill. Plum tomatoes may be used, but they will have a drier texture. If using plum tomatoes, halve them lengthwise. Supermarket vine-ripened tomatoes will work but won't be as flavorful.

1   Toss tomatoes with 1 tablespoon oil, ½ teaspoon salt, and ¼ teaspoon pepper in large bowl. Let stand for at least 15 minutes or up to 1 hour.

2A   For a charcoal grill Open bottom vent completely. Light large chimney starter filled with charcoal briquettes (6 quarts). When top coals are partially covered with ash, pour evenly over grill. Set cooking grate in place, cover, and open lid vent completely. Heat grill until hot, about 5 minutes.

2B   For a gas grill Turn all burners to high; cover; and heat grill until hot, about 15 minutes. Leave all burners on high.

3   Clean and oil cooking grate. Grill tomatoes, cut side down (covered if using gas), until tomatoes are charred and beginning to soften, 4 to 6 minutes. Using tongs or thin metal spatula, carefully flip tomatoes and continue to cook (covered if using gas) until skin sides are charred and juice bubbles, 4 to 6 minutes. Transfer tomatoes to cutting board and let cool slightly, then chop coarse. Combine tomatoes, mozzarella, basil, vinegar, pepper flakes, ¼ cup oil, remaining ¼ teaspoon salt, and remaining ¼ teaspoon pepper in bowl.

4   Brush bread with remaining 1 tablespoon oil and grill until lightly charred, about 1½ minutes per side. Transfer bread to platter and rub each slice with garlic clove. Spread tomato mixture evenly over toast. Drizzle with extra oil and serve. (Tomato mixture can be refrigerated for up to 24 hours; bring to room temperature before serving.)

Flare Trade

Open Fire Prepare hot single-level fire in open-fire grill. Set cooking grate at least 6 inches from coals and flames and heat grill until hot, about 5 minutes. Proceed with step 3.

Grilled Polenta Wedges with Grilled Scallions and Gorgonzola

SERVES 6 to 8   **TOTAL TIME** 1¼ hours, plus 2½ hours cooling and refrigerating

2   cups water

1   tablespoon chopped fresh rosemary

½   teaspoon table salt

1   cup coarse-ground cornmeal

3   tablespoons plus 1 teaspoon extra-virgin olive oil, divided

4   scallions

4   ounces Gorgonzola cheese, softened

1   tablespoon heavy cream

1   tablespoon honey

Why This Recipe Works Grilled polenta triangles with a decadent sweet and smoky topping make a delicious alternative to crostini. Using a low liquid-to-cornmeal ratio when simmering the polenta ensures that the wedges will be sturdy enough to hold together during grilling. Fresh rosemary bolsters the outdoor flavors with its piney notes. After chilling in an 8-inch square baking pan, the cooked polenta is firm enough to slice into portions. Five minutes over a hot fire crisps and lightly chars the outside while the inside stays nice and soft. These versatile wedges lend themselves to plenty of other toppings, as well as to being served topping-free alongside grilled meat and vegetables. Be sure that the Gorgonzola is at room temperature so that it blends smoothly.

1   Grease 8-inch square baking pan, line with parchment paper, and grease parchment. Bring water to boil in medium saucepan over medium-high heat. Stir in rosemary and salt. Slowly pour cornmeal into water in steady stream while whisking constantly and return to boil. Reduce heat to medium-low and continue cooking until grains of cornmeal are tender, about 30 minutes, stirring every few minutes. (Polenta should be very thick.) Off heat, stir in 3 tablespoons oil. Transfer polenta to prepared pan, smooth top using rubber spatula, and let cool completely, about 30 minutes. Wrap tightly in plastic wrap and refrigerate until polenta is very firm, at least 2 hours or up to 3 days.

2   Remove polenta from pan and flip onto cutting board; discard parchment. Slice into 4 equal squares, then cut each square into 4 triangles; refrigerate until ready to grill. Toss scallions with remaining 1 teaspoon oil.

3A   For a charcoal grill Open bottom vent completely. Light large chimney starter filled with charcoal briquettes (6 quarts). When top coals are partially covered with ash, pour evenly over grill. Set cooking grate in place, cover, and open lid vent completely. Heat grill until hot, about 5 minutes.

3B   For a gas grill Turn all burners to high; cover; and heat grill until hot, about 15 minutes. Leave all burners on high.

Flare Trade

Open Fire Prepare hot single-level fire in open-fire grill. Set cooking grate at least 6 inches from coals and flames and heat grill until hot, about 5 minutes. Proceed with step 4.

4 Clean and oil cooking grate. Grill polenta triangles and scallions (covered if using gas) until polenta and scallions are lightly charred on both sides, 5 to 7 minutes, turning as needed. As polenta and scallions finish cooking, transfer polenta to serving platter and scallions to cutting board.

5 Chop scallions. Stir scallions, Gorgonzola, and cream in bowl until thoroughly combined. Season with salt and pepper to taste. Top polenta wedges with heaping teaspoon of Gorgonzola mixture and drizzle with honey. Serve.

Variation

Grilled Polenta Wedges with Grilled Oranges and Ricotta

Omit scallions and Gorgonzola. Cut peel and pith from 1 orange. Slice orange crosswise into ¼-inch-thick rounds. Brush rounds with 1 teaspoon extra-virgin olive oil and grill until lightly charred on both sides, 5 to 7 minutes, flipping as needed. Halve orange slices to make half-moons. Stir 4 ounces (½ cup) whole-milk ricotta cheese, 1 tablespoon cream, and 1 teaspoon minced fresh thyme together in bowl. Season with salt and pepper to taste. Top polenta wedges with heaping 1 teaspoon ricotta mixture and orange slices; drizzle with honey.

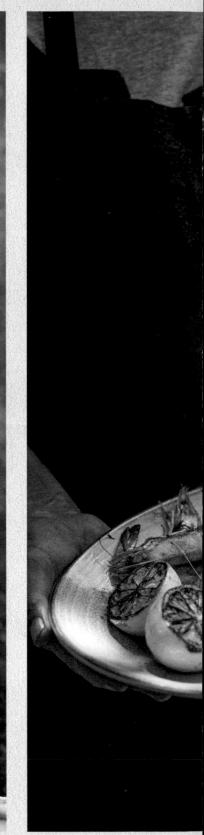

Grilled Onion, Pear, and Prosciutto Flatbread

SERVES 6 to 8   **TOTAL TIME** 1 hour

1 pound pizza dough, room temperature, split into 2 equal pieces

1 red onion, sliced into ½-inch-thick rounds

2 ripe but firm Bartlett or Bosc pears, peeled, halved, and cored

5 tablespoons extra-virgin olive oil, divided

½ teaspoon table salt

¼ teaspoon pepper

6 ounces firm Brie cheese, sliced thin

4 ounces thinly sliced prosciutto

2 teaspoons minced fresh thyme

Honey

Why This Recipe Works For this savory-sweet-salty flatbread, the pear and onion toppings go directly on the grate first to soften, sweeten, and pick up char. The dough is then grilled on one side, flipped, and topped with the grilled goodies, along with some Brie. Once the cheese is melty, the flatbreads are ready to serve, draped with ribbons of pink prosciutto and drizzled with honey. Using pizza dough from the local pizzeria or supermarket makes this recipe superconvenient, but if you'd like to make your own, see page 276. Make sure to flour the counter so the dough doesn't stick as you work with it. For the best flavor and texture, serve the grilled flatbread as soon as possible.

1   Cover dough pieces loosely with plastic wrap and set aside. Push toothpick horizontally through each onion round to keep rings intact while grilling. Brush onion and pear halves with 1 tablespoon oil and sprinkle with salt and pepper; set aside.

2   Line rimmed baking sheet with parchment paper and dust liberally with flour. Working with 1 piece of dough at a time, press and roll to form 12 by 8-inch rectangle on lightly floured counter. Transfer dough to prepared sheet, reshaping as needed, sprinkle with flour, and top with second sheet of parchment. Dust second sheet of parchment liberally with flour and repeat with remaining dough, stacking dough rectangle on floured parchment.

3A   For a charcoal grill Open bottom vent completely. Light large chimney starter filled with charcoal briquettes (6 quarts). When top coals are partially covered with ash, pour evenly over grill. Set cooking grate in place, cover, and open lid vent completely. Heat grill until hot, about 5 minutes.

3B   For a gas grill Turn all burners to high; cover; and heat grill until hot, about 15 minutes. Leave all burners on high.

4   Clean and oil cooking grate. Grill pear halves, cut side down, and onion (covered if using gas) until tender and charred, 8 minutes for pears and 18 to 22 minutes for onion, turning as needed. Transfer onion and pears to cutting board as they finish cooking. Remove toothpicks from onion rounds and discard any charred outer rings. Chop onion and slice pears thin.

Flare Trade

Open Fire Prepare hot single-level fire in open-fire grill. Set cooking grate at least 6 inches from coals and flames and heat grill until hot, about 5 minutes. Proceed with step 4.

5 Brush top of each dough rectangle with 1 tablespoon oil. Grill dough rectangles, oiled side down, until undersides are spotty brown and top is covered with bubbles, 2 to 3 minutes (pop any large bubbles that form). Brush top of each rectangle with 1 tablespoon oil, then flip. Layer flatbreads with Brie, pear, and onion. Cover and grill until second side of flatbreads is spotty brown and cheese is melted, 3 to 5 minutes. Transfer to cutting board.

6 Top flatbreads with prosciutto and thyme and drizzle with honey. Cut into wedges and serve.

Variation
Grilled Butternut Squash, Apple, and Goat Cheese Flatbread

Omit prosciutto and thyme. Substitute 1 pound butternut squash, peeled, halved lengthwise, seeded, and sliced crosswise ½ inch thick, for onion; do not thread on toothpicks. Substitute 1 Granny Smith apple, peeled, halved, and cored, for pears. Substitute crumbled goat cheese for Brie and maple syrup for honey. Sprinkle flatbreads with ground sumac before serving.

Malaysian Chicken Satay with Peanut Sauce

SERVES 4 to 6   **TOTAL TIME** 1¼ hours

Aromatic Paste

- 2 lemongrass stalks, trimmed to bottom 6 inches
- 3 shallots, chopped (⅔ cup)
- 3 tablespoons water
- 1 tablespoon vegetable oil
- 1 tablespoon packed brown sugar
- 3 garlic cloves, chopped
- 1 (1-inch) piece galangal, peeled and minced
- 1 (1-inch) piece ginger, peeled and sliced into ⅛-inch-thick coins
- 2 teaspoons table salt
- 1 teaspoon ground turmeric
- ½–¾ teaspoon red pepper flakes
- ½ teaspoon ground coriander
- ½ teaspoon ground cumin

Peanut Sauce

- ⅓ cup dry-roasted peanuts
- 2 tablespoons vegetable oil
- ¾ cup water, plus extra as needed
- 1 tablespoon tamarind paste
- 1 tablespoon packed brown sugar

Chicken

- 2 pounds boneless, skinless chicken thighs, trimmed and cut crosswise into 1- to 1½-inch-wide strips
- 2 tablespoons vegetable oil

Why This Recipe Works Malaysian chicken satay features tender pieces of chicken coated in a fragrant paste, skewered, and charred on the grill. Dark chicken meat is the way to go, as the collagen-rich thighs cook up juicy and can pick up deep char without drying out. Cutting the chicken into wide strips and stretching them between two skewers creates more surface area for coating with the paste and for charring. Loads of lemongrass, ginger, and galangal, plus garlic, shallots, spices, and a touch of sugar make for a complex, aromatic paste that develops savory character over the fire. A portion of the paste also serves as the base for a sweet and tangy peanut dipping sauce. If galangal is unavailable, increase the ginger to one 1½-inch piece. The aromatic paste can also be prepared using a mortar and pestle. For a spicier dish, use the larger amount of pepper flakes. Lime juice can be substituted for the tamarind paste. You will need eight 12-inch metal skewers.

1 For the aromatic paste Halve lemongrass lengthwise and, using meat pounder, lightly crush on cutting board to soften. Mince lemongrass and transfer to food processor. Add shallots, water, oil, sugar, garlic, galangal, ginger, salt, turmeric, and pepper flakes and process until uniform paste forms, about 2 minutes, scraping down sides of bowl as necessary. Measure out ⅓ cup paste and set aside. Transfer remaining paste to bowl and stir in coriander and cumin. Cover bowl and microwave paste for 1½ minutes, stirring halfway through microwaving. Transfer bowl to refrigerator and let paste cool while preparing sauce.

2 For the peanut sauce Place peanuts in now-empty processor and process until coarsely ground, about 15 seconds. Heat oil and reserved ⅓ cup paste in medium saucepan over medium-low heat until fond begins to form on bottom of saucepan and paste starts to darken, about 5 minutes. Stir in water, tamarind, sugar, and peanuts and bring to boil, scraping up any browned bits. Reduce heat to maintain gentle simmer and cook, stirring occasionally, until sauce is reduced to about 1 cup, 8 to 10 minutes. Season with salt to taste, cover, and set aside.

3 For the chicken Add chicken to cooled paste and toss to combine. Thread chicken onto 4 sets of two 12-inch metal skewers. (Hold 2 skewers 1 inch apart and thread chicken onto both skewers at once so strips of chicken are perpendicular to skewers.) Do not crowd skewers; each set

of skewers should hold 7 to 8 pieces of chicken. Transfer kebabs to large plate and refrigerate while preparing grill. (Kebabs can be refrigerated for up to 4 hours.)

4A   For a charcoal grill Open bottom vent completely. Light large chimney starter mounded with charcoal briquettes (7 quarts). When top coals are partially covered with ash, pour evenly over grill. Set cooking grate in place, cover, and open lid vent completely. Heat grill until hot, about 5 minutes.

4B   For a gas grill Turn all burners to high; cover; and heat grill until hot, about 15 minutes. Turn all burners to medium.

5   Clean and oil cooking grate. Brush both sides of kebabs with oil. Grill kebabs (covered if using gas) until browned and char marks appear on first side, about 5 minutes. Using large metal spatula, gently release

chicken from grill, flip, and continue to cook until chicken registers 175 degrees, 3 to 5 minutes longer. Transfer to large platter. Gently reheat peanut sauce, thinning with extra water, 1 tablespoon at a time, to desired consistency. Serve chicken, passing peanut sauce separately.

Flare Trade

Flat-Top Grill Turn all burners to medium-high and heat griddle until hot, about 10 minutes. Turn all burners to high. Clean griddle and proceed with step 5.

Open Fire Prepare hot single-level fire in open-fire grill. Set cooking grate at least 6 inches from coals and flames and heat grill until hot, about 5 minutes. Proceed with step 5.

Vegetable Quesadillas

SERVES 6 to 8   **TOTAL TIME** 45 minutes

5 tablespoons extra-virgin
   olive oil, divided

3 garlic cloves, minced

1 onion, sliced into
   ½-inch-thick rounds

1 red bell pepper, stemmed,
   seeded, and cut into quarters

1 small zucchini, sliced
   lengthwise into 4 planks

1½ pounds boneless, skinless
   chicken breasts, trimmed

¾ teaspoon table salt

½ teaspoon pepper

4 (12-inch) flour tortillas

8 ounces Monterey Jack cheese,
   shredded (2 cups), divided

   Lime wedges

Why This Recipe Works With the help of a plancha, you can take on the role of short-order cook, turning out quesadillas from start to finish on the grill as fast as your guests can devour them. Onion, bell pepper, zucchini, and chicken breasts all get a boost of grill flavor from being cooked right on the grate; then, the plancha is heated up and the assembled tortillas are pressed and griddled until they're evenly brown—and no melted cheese or bits of vegetable fall through the bars. For spicier quesadillas, use pepper Jack cheese in place of Monterey Jack. Serve with Charred Guacamole (page 32), sour cream, and/or salsa. You will need a cast-iron plancha measuring at least 20 by 10 inches.

1   Combine ¼ cup oil and garlic in bowl and microwave until bubbling, about 30 seconds. Push toothpick horizontally through each onion round to keep rings intact while grilling. Brush onion rounds, bell pepper, zucchini, and chicken with oil mixture and sprinkle with salt and pepper.

2A   **For a charcoal grill** Open bottom vent completely. Light large chimney starter filled with charcoal briquettes (6 quarts). When top coals are partially covered with ash, pour evenly over grill. Set cooking grate in place, cover, and open lid vent completely. Heat grill with plancha until hot, about 5 minutes.

2B   **For a gas grill** Turn all burners to high; cover; and heat grill until hot, about 15 minutes. Leave all burners on high.

3   Clean and oil cooking grate. Grill vegetables and chicken until vegetables are lightly charred and tender, and chicken is well browned and registers 160 degrees, 6 to 10 minutes, turning vegetables and chicken as needed. Transfer vegetables and chicken to cutting board as they finish cooking.

4   Clean cooking grate, then center plancha on now-empty grill. Turn all burners to medium-low (if using gas). Cover and heat plancha while assembling quesadillas.

5   Slice bell pepper, zucchini, and chicken thin. Remove toothpicks from onion rounds and separate into rings. Place tortillas on counter and brush tops of tortillas with remaining 1 tablespoon oil. Flip tortillas, oiled side down, and divide 1 cup Monterey Jack evenly among tortillas, sprinkling

cheese over half of each tortilla and leaving ½-inch border. Layer vegetables and chicken over cheese and sprinkle with remaining 1 cup Monterey Jack. Fold tortillas over filling and press gently to seal.

6   Transfer 2 prepared quesadillas to plancha and press firmly to reseal. Cook, covered, until quesadillas are crisp and golden brown on first side, 2 to 4 minutes. Using 2 spatulas, flip quesadillas and gently press down with spatula. Cook until second side is browned and crisp and cheese is melted, 2 to 4 minutes; transfer to cutting board. Repeat with remaining quesadillas. Cut each quesadilla into wedges and serve with lime wedges.

Flare Trade

Flat-Top Grill   Turn all burners to medium-high and heat griddle until hot, 10 minutes. Clean griddle. Halve and thinly slice onion, bell pepper, and zucchini and toss with half of prepared garlic oil. Toss chicken with remaining garlic oil. Arrange vegetables in even layer over half of griddle and cook, tossing frequently, until well browned and tender, 7 to 10 minutes. Cook chicken on open side of griddle until well browned and registers 160 degrees, about 3 minutes per side. Turn all burners to medium. Assemble quesadillas and cook in 1 batch in step 6.

Negimaki

SERVES 8 to 10   **TOTAL TIME** 1 hour, plus 30 minutes freezing

1 (2-pound) flank steak, trimmed

½ cup soy sauce

¼ cup sugar

3 tablespoons mirin

3 tablespoons sake

16 scallions, trimmed and halved crosswise

1 tablespoon sesame seeds, toasted

Why This Recipe Works Negimaki combines bold beef teriyaki flavor with the elegant presentation of sushi rolls. Flank steak is an afford-able, flavorful choice, and freezing the meat briefly makes it easy to slice thin so that you can form "wrappers" for the scallion bundles. A hot fire and a salty-sweet teriyaki-like glaze burnish the rolls to perfection. Since the meat slices are too thin to probe for doneness, temp the scallion core instead: When it registers between 150 and 155 degrees, the meat is cooked just right. A final sprinkling of toasted sesame seeds ensures every bite pops with a nutty, delicate crunch. Look for a flank steak that is as rectangular as possible, as this will yield the most uniform slices. You may end up with extra slices of steak; you can grill these alongside the rolls or make several smaller rolls.

1   Place steak on large plate and freeze until firm, about 30 minutes.

2   Bring soy sauce, sugar, mirin, and sake to simmer in small saucepan over high heat, stirring to dissolve sugar. Reduce heat to medium and cook until slightly syrupy and reduced to ½ cup, 3 to 5 minutes. Divide evenly between 2 bowls and let cool. Cover 1 bowl with plastic wrap and set aside for serving.

3   Place steak on cutting board. Starting at narrow, tapered end, slice steak against grain on bias ⅜ inch thick until width of steak is 7 inches (depending on size of steak, you will need to remove 2 to 3 slices until steak measures 7 inches across). Cut steak in half lengthwise. Continue to slice each half against grain on bias. You should have at least 24 slices. Pound each slice to ¼-inch thickness between 2 sheets of plastic.

4   Arrange 3 slices on cutting board with short side of slices facing you, overlapping slices by ¼ inch and alternating tapered ends as needed, to form rough rectangle that measures 4 to 6 inches wide and at least 4 inches long. Place 4 scallion halves along edge of rectangle nearest to edge of counter, with white tips slightly hanging over edges of steak on either side. Starting from bottom edge and rolling away from you, roll into tight cylinder. Insert 3 equally spaced toothpicks into end flaps and through center of roll. Transfer roll to platter and repeat with remaining steak and scallions. (Assembled rolls can be refrigerated for up to 24 hours.)

Flare Trade

Open Fire Prepare hot single-level fire in open-fire grill. Set cooking grate at least 6 inches from coals and flames and heat grill until hot, about 5 minutes. Proceed with step 6.

5A **For a charcoal grill** Open bottom vent completely. Light large chimney starter three-quarters filled with charcoal briquettes (4½ quarts). When top coals are partially covered with ash, pour evenly over half of grill. Set cooking grate in place, cover, and open lid vent completely. Heat grill until hot, about 5 minutes.

5B **For a gas grill** Turn all burners to high; cover; and heat grill until hot, about 15 minutes. Leave all burners on high.

6 Clean and oil cooking grate. Place rolls on grill (on hotter side if using charcoal) and cook until first side is beginning to char, 4 to 6 minutes. Flip rolls, brush

cooked side with glaze, and cook until second side is beginning to char, 4 to 6 minutes. Cook remaining 2 sides, glazing after each turn, until all 4 sides of rolls are evenly charred and thermometer inserted from end of roll into scallions at core registers 150 to 155 degrees, 16 to 24 minutes total. Transfer rolls to cutting board, tent with aluminum foil, and let rest for 5 minutes. Discard remaining glaze.

7 Remove toothpicks from rolls and cut rolls crosswise into ¾-inch-long pieces. Arrange rolls cut side down on clean platter, drizzle with 2 tablespoons reserved glaze, sprinkle with sesame seeds, and serve, passing remaining reserved glaze separately.

Grilled Lamb Kofte

SERVES 4 to 6   **TOTAL TIME** 1 hour, plus 1 hour chilling

Yogurt–Garlic Sauce

- 1 cup plain whole-milk yogurt
- 2 tablespoons lemon juice
- 2 tablespoons tahini
- 1 garlic clove, minced

Kofte

- ½ cup pine nuts
- 4 garlic cloves, peeled
- 1½ teaspoons smoked hot paprika
- 1 teaspoon table salt
- 1 teaspoon ground cumin
- ½ teaspoon pepper
- ¼ teaspoon ground coriander
- ¼ teaspoon ground cloves
- ⅛ teaspoon ground nutmeg
- ⅛ teaspoon ground cinnamon
- 1½ pounds ground lamb
- ½ cup grated onion, drained
- ⅓ cup minced fresh parsley
- ⅓ cup minced fresh mint
- 1½ teaspoons unflavored gelatin

Why This Recipe Works A traditional favorite in Turkey and found all over the Middle East, kofte are a highly seasoned type of meatball that are often cooked over live fire. They can be stuffed into pita bread, served with rice pilaf, or presented on a platter, as we do here. Corralling the coals into the center of the grill using a disposable pan concentrates the fire to create a smoky, crunchy coating of char. Kneading the ingredients together creates an almost sausage-like springiness, while gelatin helps the meat mixture retain juiciness without muting the flavors. Ground pine nuts add richness and keep the texture from being too bouncy. For the cooling yogurt sauce, a small amount of tahini, along with the traditional additions of garlic and lemon juice, gives the yogurt a depth to match that of the kofte itself. You will need eight 12-inch metal skewers and a 13 by 9-inch disposable aluminum roasting pan.

1   **For the yogurt-garlic sauce** Whisk all ingredients together in bowl. Cover and refrigerate until ready to serve.

2   **For the kofte** Process pine nuts, garlic, paprika, salt, cumin, pepper, coriander, cloves, nutmeg, and cinnamon in food processor until coarse paste forms, 30 to 45 seconds. Transfer mixture to large bowl. Add lamb, onion, parsley, mint, and gelatin and knead with your hands until thoroughly combined and mixture feels slightly sticky, about 2 minutes. Divide mixture into 24 equal portions (1¼ ounces each). Shape each portion into 2-inch-long cylinder about 1 inch in diameter. Using eight 12-inch metal skewers, thread 3 cylinders onto each skewer, pressing gently to adhere. Transfer kebabs to lightly greased baking sheet, cover with plastic wrap, and refrigerate for at least 1 hour or up to 24 hours.

3A   **For a charcoal grill** Using skewer, poke 12 holes in bottom of disposable pan. Open bottom vent completely and place pan in center of grill. Light large chimney starter two-thirds filled with charcoal briquettes (4 quarts). When top coals are partially covered with ash, pour into disposable pan. Set cooking grate in place, cover, and open lid vent completely. Heat grill until hot, about 5 minutes.

3B   **For a gas grill** Turn all burners to high; cover; and heat grill until hot, about 15 minutes. Leave all burners on high.

4 Clean and oil cooking grate. Place kebabs on grill (directly over coals if using charcoal) at 45-degree angle to bars. Cook (covered if using gas) until browned and meat easily releases from grill, 4 to 7 minutes. Flip kebabs and continue to cook until meat is browned on second side and registers 160 degrees, about 6 minutes. Transfer kebabs to serving platter and serve, passing yogurt sauce separately.

Flare Trade

Open Fire Prepare hot single-level fire in open-fire grill. Set cooking grate at least 6 inches from coals and flames and heat grill until hot, about 5 minutes. Proceed with step 4.

Grilled Clams, Mussels, or Oysters with Soy-Citrus Sauce

SERVES 4 to 6   **TOTAL TIME** 25 minutes

½ cup soy sauce

1 tablespoon lemon juice

1 tablespoon lime juice

1 scallion, sliced thin

1 teaspoon grated fresh ginger

30-35 mussels (about 2 pounds), scrubbed and debearded, or 24 clams or oysters

Lemon wedges

Why This Recipe Works Choose one, or grill a duo or trio of smoky, briny-sweet mollusks to elicit plenty of oohs and aahs at your outdoor gatherings. They look splashy, but they're incredibly simple. There's no shucking necessary—when they're open, they're done. While the grill heats, you'll want to scrub the shells carefully to rid them of any grit, and you can also stir together the drizzling sauce. Once the shellfish are on the grill, the keys to success are to not move them around too much and to handle them carefully once they open: As you transfer the open bivalves with tongs to a platter, hold them steady so as not to spill any of their flavorful juices. Always look for tightly closed clams, mussels, and oysters (avoid any that are gaping; they may be dying or dead).

1   Combine soy sauce, lemon juice, lime juice, scallion, and ginger in small bowl. Set sauce aside for serving.

2A   For a charcoal grill Open bottom vent completely. Light large chimney starter filled with charcoal briquettes (6 quarts). When top coals are partially covered with ash, pour evenly over grill. Set cooking grate in place, cover, and open lid vent completely. Heat grill until hot, about 5 min utes.

2B   For a gas grill Turn all burners to high; cover; and heat grill until hot, about 15 minutes. Leave all burners on high.

3   Clean and oil cooking grate. Place shellfish directly on cooking grate, cupped side down if grilling oysters. Grill (covered if using gas), without turning, until shellfish open, 3 to 6 minutes for mussels and oysters or 6 to 12 minutes for clams.

4   With tongs, carefully transfer opened shellfish to flat serving platter, trying to preserve juices. Discard top shells and loosen meat in bottom shells before serving, if desired. Serve with soy-citrus sauce and lemon wedges.

Flare Trade

Open Fire Prepare hot single-level fire in open-fire grill. Set cooking grate at least 6 inches from coals and flames and heat grill until hot, about 5 minutes. Proceed with step 3.

Variations

**Grilled Clams, Mussels, or Oysters
with Spicy Lemon Butter**
Omit soy-citrus sauce. Melt 4 tablespoons unsalted
butter in small saucepan over medium-low heat. Off heat,
add 1 tablespoon hot sauce, 1 teaspoon lemon juice, and
¼ teaspoon table salt. Serve sauce warm with grilled
clams, mussels, or oysters.

**Grilled Clams, Mussels, or Oysters
with Mignonette Sauce**
Omit soy-citrus sauce. Combine ½ cup red wine vinegar,
2 finely chopped shallots or ¼ cup minced red onion,
2 tablespoons lemon juice, and 1½ tablespoons minced
fresh parsley in small bowl. Serve with grilled clams,
mussels, or oysters.

Gambas a la Plancha

SERVES 4 to 6   **TOTAL TIME** 45 minutes

¼ cup table salt for brining

¼ cup sugar for brining

2 pounds shell-on, head-on extra-large shrimp (10 to 15 per pound)

2 tablespoons extra-virgin olive oil

2 large garlic cloves, minced to paste

2 teaspoons lemon juice, plus 1 lemon, halved

1 teaspoon smoked paprika

¼ teaspoon cayenne pepper

Why This Recipe Works This iconic tapas dish is supremely satisfying and elemental—a simple food that you eat with your hands, straight off the grill if you're impatient. The shrimp are traditionally served with their heads on so that after gently twisting apart the head and body, you can suck the flavorful juices out of the head. Brining the shrimp before grilling keeps them especially plump and juicy. Employing a plancha gives the shrimp the flavor of the grill while allowing them to retain those juices that would otherwise be lost between the bars of the grate. A lemony garlic paste adheres perfectly and then coats your fingers as you peel and eat the shrimp. If head-on shrimp are unavailable, you can substitute extra-large, unpeeled, head-off shrimp. You will need a cast-iron plancha measuring at least 20 by 10 inches.

1   Dissolve salt and sugar in 2 quarts cold water in large container. Submerge shrimp in brine, cover, and refrigerate for 15 minutes. Drain shrimp.

2   Combine oil, garlic, lemon juice, paprika, and cayenne in large bowl. Add shrimp and toss to coat. (Shrimp can be refrigerated for up to 1 hour.)

3A   **For a charcoal grill** Open bottom vent completely. Light large chimney starter filled with charcoal briquettes (6 quarts). When top coals are partially covered with ash, pour evenly over grill. Set cooking grate in place, center plancha on grill, cover, and open lid vent completely. Heat grill with plancha until hot, about 5 minutes.

3B   **For a gas grill** Turn all burners to high; cover; and heat grill until hot, about 15 minutes. Center plancha on grill, cover, and heat for 5 more minutes. Leave all burners on high.

4   Arrange half of shrimp on plancha in even layer and cook until shells are bright pink and just beginning to char and shrimp are opaque throughout, 2 to 6 minutes, turning halfway through cooking. Transfer shrimp to platter and repeat with remaining shrimp. Meanwhile, cook lemon halves, cut side down, on open space of plancha until well charred, 2 to 4 minutes; set aside for serving. Serve shrimp warm or at room temperature with lemon.

Flare Trade

Flat-Top Grill Turn all burners to medium-high and heat griddle until hot, about 10 minutes. Leave all burners on medium-high. Clean griddle and proceed with step 4.

Open Fire Prepare hot single-level fire in open-fire grill. Set cooking grate at least 6 inches from coals and flames, place plancha on cooking grate, and heat plancha until hot, about 5 minutes. Proceed with step 4.

COCKTAILS ON THE GRILL

Burnt Whiskey Sours

SERVES 2   **TOTAL TIME** 30 minutes

Why This Recipe Works This isn't your parents' whiskey sour. Grilling lemons caramelizes their sugars while softening their acidity. Squeezing the juice from grilled halves and muddling grilled slices builds complex citrus flavor. Charred rosemary sprigs add woodsy notes and make a rustic garnish. Tennessee whiskey or bourbon also works well here (decrease the simple syrup to ½ ounce). To make the simple syrup, whisk ¼ cup water and 6 tablespoons sugar in a bowl until the sugar is dissolved. Leftover syrup can be refrigerated for up to one month.

> 2 lemons (1 halved, 1 sliced thin)
>
> 6 rosemary sprigs
>
> 1 ounce simple syrup
>
> 4 ounces rye whiskey

1A For a charcoal grill Open bottom vent completely. Light large chimney starter filled with charcoal briquettes (6 quarts). When top coals are partially covered with ash, pour evenly over half of grill. Set cooking grate in place, cover, and open lid vent completely. Heat grill until hot, about 5 minutes.

1B For a gas grill Turn all burners to high; cover; and heat grill until hot, about 15 minutes. Leave primary burn on high and turn off other burner(s).

2 Clean and oil cooking grate. Grill lemon halves cut sides down, lemon slices, and rosemary (covered if using gas), turning as needed, until well charred, 3 to 6 minutes. Transfer lemon and rosemary to plate as they finish cooking. Squeeze 1 ounce (2 tablespoons) juice from lemon halves. Add 2 lemon slices, 4 rosemary springs, and simple syrup to base of cocktail shaker and muddle until broken down and all juice has been expressed, about 30 seconds.

3 Add rye and lemon juice to shaker, then fill with ice. Shake mixture until fully combined and well chilled, about 15 seconds. Strain cocktail into chilled cocktail glasses. Garnish with remaining 2 rosemary sprigs and lemon slices. Serve.

Flare Trade

Open Fire Prepare hot single-level fire in open-fire grill. Set cooking grate at least 6 inches from coals and flames and heat grill until hot, about 5 minutes. Proceed with step 2.

Charred Pineapple Margaritas

SERVES 4 to 6
TOTAL TIME 45 minutes, plus 1 hour chilling

Why This Recipe Works This is an absolute must to go along with any of the taco recipes in chapter 2, or any other recipe that strikes your fancy. Grilling imparts delicious char to fresh pineapple, no coring needed: The grilled rings are blended along with sugar, lime zest, and the juice from charred limes. After adding tequila and triple sec, you'll want to chill the mixture to let the flavors blend. A smoked salt rim reinforces the outdoor vibe (regular flake sea salt is great too).

  6 limes

  ½ pineapple, peeled and sliced crosswise into 1-inch-thick rings

  ¼ cup sugar

      Pinch smoked sea salt, plus ½ cup smoked sea salt for garnish (optional)

  8 ounces blanco or reposado tequila

  8 ounces triple sec

1A **For a charcoal grill** Open bottom vent completely. Light large chimney starter filled with charcoal briquettes (6 quarts). When top coals are partially covered with ash, pour evenly over grill. Set cooking grate in place, cover, and open lid vent completely. Heat grill until hot, about 5 minutes.

1B **For a gas grill** Turn all burners to high; cover; and heat grill until hot, about 15 minutes. Leave all burners on high.

2 Grate limes to yield 4 teaspoons zest; set zest aside and halve limes. Clean and oil cooking grate. Grill pineapple and lime halves, cut side down, (covered if using gas), turning pineapple as needed, until charred and tender, about 15 minutes. Transfer pineapple and limes to plate as they finish cooking and let cool slightly, about 5 minutes.

3 If salting glass rims, cut wedge from 1 lime half and reserve. Squeeze 4 ounces (½ cup) juice from lime halves. Transfer 2 pineapple slices to cutting board and cut into 6 wedges; set aside for garnish. Transfer remaining pineapple, lime zest and juice, sugar, and salt to blender and process on low speed until mixture is combined but still coarse in texture, about 10 seconds, scraping down sides of blender jar as needed. Gradually increase speed to high and process until completely smooth, about 1 minute. Transfer mixture to large bowl and stir in tequila and triple sec. (Mixture can be covered and refrigerated for up to 24 hours.)

4 Strain mixture through fine-mesh strainer set over serving pitcher or large container, pressing on solids to extract as much liquid as possible; discard solids. Keep margarita chilled in refrigerator until ready to serve.

5 Spread ½ cup smoked salt, if using, into even layer in shallow bowl. Moisten about ½ inch of chilled old-fashioned glass or margarita glass rims by running reserved lime wedge around outer edge; dry any excess juice with paper towel. Roll moistened rims in salt to coat. Remove any excess salt that falls into glass. Serve margaritas in prepared glasses filled with ice, garnishing individual portions with pineapple wedge.

BLOODY MARYS FOR A CROWD

SMOKY PEACH SANGRIA

COCKTAILS ON THE GRILL

Bloody Marys for a Crowd

SERVES 12

TOTAL TIME 15 minutes, plus 2 hours chilling

Why This Recipe Works This fuss-free big-batch cocktail must be made at least 2 hours ahead—which means you can serve your guests from the chilled pitcher the moment they arrive. We prefer Tabasco here, but you can use whatever hot sauce you like, adjusting the amount according to your taste. For tomato juice, Campbell's is classic, but feel free to use V8 if that's your thing. Be sure to buy refrigerated prepared horseradish, not the shelf-stable kind, which contains additives; don't use horseradish cream. Part of the fun with Bloody Marys is the anything-goes mindset of garnishing. Great options include grilled lemon slices, charred tomato or avocado wedges, grilled rosemary sprigs (see page 66), Blistered Shishito Peppers (page 40), grilled shrimp (see page 162), or griddled crispy bacon (see page 72).

48 ounces tomato juice

16 ounces vodka

4 ounces lemon juice (3 lemons)

1 ounce Worcestershire sauce

4 teaspoons prepared horseradish

2 teaspoons pepper

½–1 teaspoon hot sauce

1 Whisk all ingredients together in serving pitcher or large container. Cover and refrigerate until flavors meld and mixture is well chilled, at least 2 hours or up to 24 hours.

2 Stir Bloody Mary mixture to recombine, then serve in chilled collins glasses filled with ice, garnishing individual portions as desired.

Smoky Peach Sangria

SERVES 4 to 6

TOTAL TIME 1 hour, plus 1 hour chilling

Why This Recipe Works A pitcher of sangria adds punch to any outdoor party. This summertime version combines white wine and smoked peaches. After you muddle the peaches in wine and peach liqueur, the mixture macerates in the fridge (up to a whole day ahead for make-ahead ease). A quick run through a strainer before serving removes the solids, leaving behind a smoky, peachy party in a glass.

- 1 cup wood chips
- 4 peaches (3 halved, 1 sliced thin)
- 3 ounces peach liqueur
- 1 (750-ml) bottle dry white wine, such as Sauvignon Blanc or Pinot Grigio

  Mint leaves, optional

1 Using large piece of heavy-duty aluminum foil, wrap chips in 8 by 4½-inch foil packet. (Make sure chips do not poke holes in sides or bottom of packet. If using gas, make sure there are no more than 2 layers of foil on bottom of packet.) Cut 2 evenly spaced 2-inch slits in top of packet.

2A For a charcoal grill Open bottom vent completely. Light large chimney starter half filled with charcoal briquettes (3 quarts). When top coals are partially covered with ash, pour into steeply banked pile against side of grill. Place wood chip packet on coals. Set cooking grate in place, cover, and open lid vent completely. Heat grill until hot and wood chips are smoking, about 5 minutes.

2B For a gas grill Remove cooking grate and place wood chip packet directly on primary burner. Set cooking grate in place; turn all burners to high; cover; and heat grill until hot and wood chips are smoking, 15 to 25 minutes. Leave primary burner on high and turn off other burner(s).

3 Clean and oil cooking grate. Grill peach halves, cut side down, on cooler side of grill, covered, until tender, about 20 minutes.

4 Transfer peach halves to large bowl and add peach liqueur. Using muddler or potato masher, muddle peaches until broken down and all juice is expressed, about 30 seconds. Stir in wine, cover, and refrigerate until mixture is chilled and flavors meld, at least 1 hour or up to 24 hours.

5 Strain mixture through fine-mesh strainer set over serving pitcher or large container, pressing on solids to extract as much liquid as possible; discard solids. Keep sangria chilled in refrigerator until ready to serve. Serve sangria in glasses filled with ice, garnishing individual portions with peach slices and mint leaves, if desired.

Flare Trade

Smoker Heat and maintain smoker temperature of 275 to 300 degrees following manufacturer's guidelines and tips on page 15. Place peach halves in center of smoker grate and proceed with step 3.

2 Both Hands Needed

Smoked Turkey Club Panini

SERVES 4   **TOTAL TIME** 40 minutes

⅓ cup mayonnaise

⅓ cup oil-packed sun-dried tomatoes, rinsed, patted dry, and minced, plus ¼ cup tomato packing oil

8 (½-inch-thick) slices crusty bread

8 slices bacon

8 ounces thinly sliced Swiss cheese

8 ounces thinly sliced smoked turkey (see page 206)

1 ounce (1 cup) baby arugula

Why This Recipe Works Using a plancha, a sheet pan, and a cast-iron skillet, you can create first-rate panini outdoors. A combination of bold, zesty sun-dried tomatoes and mayonnaise makes a deeply flavorful condiment that complements smoked turkey (deli turkey also works well), bacon, and Swiss cheese. Brushing some of the tomato oil onto the bread boosts flavor and ensures crispy, golden-edged sandwiches. The plancha allows for all the components to be cooked quickly, starting with the bacon. Since picking up the plancha to pour off the bacon fat is impractical (not to mention dangerous), you'll use tongs and paper towels to wipe the cooking surface clean. When choosing bread, look for a wide loaf of rustic bread that will yield big slices. You will need a 10- or 12-inch cast-iron skillet and a cast-iron plancha measuring at least 20 by 10 inches.

1   Combine mayonnaise and tomatoes in bowl. Brush tomato oil on 1 side of bread slices. Flip slices over and spread mayonnaise mixture on second side; set aside. Lightly spray underside of rimmed baking sheet with vegetable oil spray and set aside, oiled side up.

2A   For a charcoal grill Open bottom vent completely. Light large chimney starter three-quarters filled with charcoal briquettes (4½ quarts). When top coals are partially covered with ash, pour evenly over grill. Set cooking grate in place, center plancha on grill, cover, and open lid vent completely. Heat grill with plancha until hot, about 5 minutes.

2B   For a gas grill Turn all burners to high; cover; and heat grill until hot, about 15 minutes. Center plancha on grill, cover, and heat for 5 more minutes. Turn all burners to medium-high.

3   Add bacon to plancha in single layer and cook until crispy, 3 to 5 minutes, flipping as needed. Transfer bacon to paper towel-lined plate. Using tongs, clean plancha with paper towels.

4   Assemble 4 sandwiches by layering ingredients as follows between prepared bread slices (with mayonnaise mixture inside sandwiches): half of Swiss, turkey, bacon, arugula, and remaining Swiss. Press gently on sandwiches to set.

Flare Trade

Flat-Top Grill Turn all burners to medium-high and heat griddle until hot, about 10 minutes. Leave all burners on medium-high. Clean griddle and proceed with step 3.

Open Fire Prepare medium-hot single-level fire in open-fire grill. Set cooking grate at least 6 inches from coals and flames, place plancha on cooking grate, and heat plancha until hot, about 5 minutes. Proceed with step 3.

5 Place sandwiches on plancha. Center prepared baking sheet, oiled side down, on top of sandwiches. Center 10- or 12-inch cast-iron skillet on sheet and cook until bread is golden and crisp on first side, about 4 minutes.

Using 2 spatulas, flip sandwiches, replace sheet and skillet, and cook until second side is golden and crisp and cheese is melted, about 4 minutes. Serve immediately.

Grilled Red Curry Chicken Sandwiches with Spicy Slaw

SERVES 4   **TOTAL TIME** 30 minutes

2 tablespoons plus 2 teaspoons fish sauce, divided

2 tablespoons vegetable oil

2 tablespoons packed brown sugar

4 teaspoons red curry paste, divided

¼ teaspoon pepper

8 (3- to 4-ounce) chicken cutlets, ½ inch thick, trimmed

½ cup mayonnaise

1 tablespoon lime juice

1 (11-ounce) bag green coleslaw mix

4 (6-inch) Italian sub rolls, split lengthwise, toasted on grill if desired

Why This Recipe Works Minimal prep and cooking means these sandwiches are an awesome choice for your next cookout, campout, or backyard meal. Red curry paste and fish sauce deliver big flavor with little effort to both the chicken marinade and the coleslaw dressing. The slaw, made with time-saving store-bought coleslaw mix, adds cool, fresh crunch when tucked into toasty sub rolls along with the grilled chicken cutlets. If chicken cutlets are unavailable, you can make your own by halving four 6- to 8-ounce boneless, skinless chicken breasts horizontally and pounding them to a ½-inch thickness. If you like a bit of extra heat, serve with sriracha or your favorite hot sauce.

1   Whisk 2 tablespoons fish sauce, oil, sugar, 2 teaspoons curry paste, and pepper together in bowl. Add chicken and toss to coat.

2   Whisk mayonnaise, lime juice, remaining 2 teaspoons fish sauce, and remaining 2 teaspoons curry paste together in large bowl. Add coleslaw mix and toss to combine. Season with salt and pepper to taste; set aside.

3A   **For a charcoal grill** Open bottom vent completely. Light large chimney starter filled with charcoal briquettes (6 quarts). When top coals are partially covered with ash, pour evenly over grill. Set cooking grate in place, cover, and open lid vent completely. Heat grill until hot, about 5 minutes.

3B   **For a gas grill** Turn all burners to high; cover; and heat grill until hot, about 15 minutes. Leave all burners on high.

4   Clean and oil cooking grate. Grill cutlets until lightly browned and register 160 degrees, about 4 minutes per side. Divide cutlets and slaw evenly among rolls. Serve.

Flare Trade

Flat-Top Grill Turn all burners to medium-high and heat griddle until hot, about 10 minutes. Turn all burners to high. Clean griddle and proceed with step 4.

Open Fire Prepare hot single-level fire in open-fire grill. Set cooking grate at least 6 inches from coals and flames and heat grill until hot, about 5 minutes. Proceed with step 4.

Philly-Style Cheesesteaks

SERVES 4   **TOTAL TIME** 40 minutes, plus 1 hour freezing

2 pounds skirt steak, trimmed and cut with grain into 3-inch-wide strips

2 tablespoons vegetable oil

1 onion, chopped fine

¼ cup grated Parmesan cheese

½ teaspoon table salt

⅛ teaspoon pepper

8 slices white American cheese (8 ounces)

4 (8-inch) Italian sub rolls, split lengthwise, toasted on grill if desired

Why This Recipe Works With a plancha on your grill, you don't need to travel any farther than your backyard to enjoy a Philly cheesesteak. Its flat surface gets the beef and onion beautifully browned and provides plenty of room for shingling slices of cheese over separate mounds of filling for easy portioning. The best cut of beef for a homemade version of this iconic sandwich is skirt steak: Its thin profile and open-grained texture make for easy slicing, especially when the steak is briefly frozen first. As for the cheese choice, we're partial to melty, gooey American cheese, with a little Parmesan mixed into the meat to add a welcome sharpness. If you're a provolone loyalist, by all means substitute that for the American cheese. Top these sandwiches with chopped pickled hot peppers, griddled or sautéed mushrooms or bell peppers, sweet relish, or hot sauce. You will need a cast-iron plancha measuring at least 20 by 10 inches.

1   Place steak pieces on large plate or baking sheet and freeze until very firm, about 1 hour.

2   Using sharp knife, shave steak pieces as thin as possible against grain. Mound meat on cutting board and chop coarse with knife 10 to 20 times.

3A   For a charcoal grill Open bottom vent completely. Light large chimney starter three-quarters filled with charcoal briquettes (4½ quarts). When top coals are partially covered with ash, pour evenly over grill. Set cooking grate in place, center plancha on grill, cover, and open lid vent completely. Heat grill with plancha until hot, about 5 minutes.

3B   For a gas grill Turn all burners to high; cover; and heat grill until hot, about 15 minutes. Center plancha on grill, cover, and heat for 5 more minutes. Turn all burners to medium-high.

4   Heat oil on plancha until just smoking. Add meat and onion in even layer and cook without stirring until well browned on 1 side, 4 to 6 minutes. Stir and continue to cook until meat is no longer pink, 2 to 4 minutes. Transfer meat mixture to colander set in large bowl. Drain excess moisture from meat.

Flare Trade

Flat-Top Grill Turn all burners to medium-high and heat griddle until hot, about 10 minutes. Leave all burners on medium-high. Clean griddle and proceed with step 4, reducing heat to low in step 5.

Open Fire Prepare medium-hot single-level fire in open-fire grill. Set cooking grate at least 6 inches from coals and flames, place plancha on cooking grate, and heat plancha until hot, about 5 minutes. Proceed with step 4.

5 Return meat mixture to plancha (discard any liquid in bowl) and add Parmesan, salt, and pepper. Heat, stirring constantly, until meat is warmed through, 1 to 2 minutes. Reduce heat to medium (if using gas). Divide mixture evenly into 4 individual portions the length of rolls. Shingle 2 slices of American cheese over each portion. Cover and let cheese melt, about 1 minute. Center rolls cut side down over each portion of meat. Using spatula, scoop under each portion of meat and flip meat and roll to create filled sandwich. Serve immediately.

Grilled Beer Brats and Onions

SERVES 6 to 8   **TOTAL TIME** 1 hour

2	pounds onions, sliced into ½-inch-thick rounds
3	tablespoons vegetable oil
1¼	teaspoons pepper, divided
3	cups beer
⅔	cup Dijon mustard
1	teaspoon sugar
1	teaspoon caraway seeds
2	pounds bratwurst (8 to 12 sausages)
8-12	(6-inch) Italian sub rolls, split lengthwise, toasted on grill if desired

Why This Recipe Works A tailgating favorite, these sturdy sandwiches of meaty, beer-soaked bratwurst and savory-sweet grilled onions are easy and delicious enough to enjoy anytime, not just in a parking lot at halftime. The sausages marinate in the beer and seasonings in a disposable pan, picking up flavor while the grill heats up. Grilling the onions before adding them to the pan contributes nice char flavor to the sausages as they braise on the grill, and Dijon mustard adds brightness and body. After the braise, just lay the sausages directly on the cooking grate for a final crisping to give them good color and a great sear. Light-bodied lagers work best here. Depending on the size of your grill, you may need to cook the onions in two batches in step 3. You will need a 13 by 9-inch disposable aluminum roasting pan.

1   Push toothpick horizontally through each onion round to keep rings intact while grilling. Brush onion rounds with oil and sprinkle with ¼ teaspoon pepper; set aside. Combine beer, mustard, sugar, caraway seeds, and remaining 1 teaspoon pepper in disposable pan, then add sausages in single layer.

2A   **For a charcoal grill** Open bottom vent completely. Light large chimney starter filled with charcoal briquettes (6 quarts). When top coals are partially covered with ash, pour evenly over grill. Set cooking grate in place, cover, and open lid vent completely. Heat grill until hot, about 5 minutes.

2B   **For a gas grill** Turn all burners to high; cover; and heat grill until hot, about 15 minutes. Leave all burners on high.

3   Clean and oil cooking grate. Grill onions until lightly charred on both sides, 6 to 10 minutes, flipping as needed. Remove toothpicks from onion rounds, transfer onions to pan with sausages, put pan on cooking grate, cover grill, and cook for 15 minutes.

4   Move pan to 1 side of grill. Transfer sausages directly to grill and brown on all sides, about 5 minutes. Transfer sausages to platter and tent with aluminum foil. Continue to cook onion mixture in pan, uncovered, until sauce is slightly thickened, about 5 minutes. Serve sausages and onions on rolls, spooning sauce over.

Flare Trade

Flat-Top Grill Turn all burners to medium-high and heat griddle until hot, about 10 minutes. Leave all burners on medium-high. Clean griddle and proceed with step 3.

Open Fire Prepare hot single-level fire in open-fire grill. Set cooking grate at least 6 inches from coals and flames and heat grill until hot, about 5 minutes. Proceed with step 3.

Grilled Pork Bánh Mì

SERVES 4   TOTAL TIME 1 hour

½ cup unseasoned rice vinegar

3 tablespoons sugar

1 carrot, peeled and cut into 2-inch-long matchsticks

1 (6-inch) piece daikon radish, peeled and cut into 2-inch-long matchsticks

¼ cup fish sauce, divided

2 tablespoons sriracha, divided

¾ cup mayonnaise

1 (1-pound) pork tenderloin, trimmed

2 teaspoons five-spice powder

1 (24-inch) baguette, cut into four 6-inch pieces and split horizontally, toasted on grill if desired

½ English cucumber, halved lengthwise and sliced thin

1 cup fresh cilantro leaves

Why This Recipe Works The most traditional versions of the Vietnamese sandwich called bánh mì feature grilled pork and pâté layered in a baguette and topped with pickled vegetables, fresh herbs, and various condiments. This homage, which is made with grilled pork tenderloin seasoned with five-spice powder and a spicy mayo for slathering on the bread, brings the essence of this classic street food to your backyard. To make the quick pickles, toss carrot and daikon radish in a mixture of rice vinegar, sugar, sriracha, and fish sauce, which gives the vegetables a sweet-spicy-salty flavor. You can prep the remaining ingredients while the pickles marinate, and the sandwiches come together quickly after that. You can substitute six red radishes for the daikon, if desired.

1   Combine vinegar and sugar in bowl and microwave until sugar dissolves, about 1½ minutes. Add carrot, daikon, 2 tablespoons fish sauce, and 1 tablespoon sriracha to bowl and toss to combine. Let sit for 15 minutes, then drain and set aside. Meanwhile, whisk mayonnaise, remaining 2 tablespoons fish sauce, and remaining 1 tablespoon sriracha together in second bowl; set aside. Rub pork with five-spice powder.

2A   For a charcoal grill Open bottom vent completely. Light large chimney starter filled with charcoal briquettes (6 quarts). When top coals are partially covered with ash, pour evenly over grill. Set cooking grate in place, cover, and open lid vent completely. Heat grill until hot, about 5 minutes.

2B   For a gas grill Turn all burners to high; cover; and heat grill until hot, about 15 minutes. Leave all burners on high.

3   Clean and oil cooking grate. Grill pork (covered if using gas) until browned on all sides and pork registers 135 to 140 degrees, 12 to 14 minutes. Transfer to cutting board, tent with aluminum foil, and let rest for 5 minutes.

4   Slice pork thin against grain. Spread mayonnaise mixture evenly on cut sides of baguette pieces. Divide pickled vegetables, pork, cucumber, and cilantro evenly among baguette bottoms, close sandwiches, and serve.

Flare Trade

Open Fire Prepare hot single-level fire in open-fire grill. Set cooking grate at least 6 inches from coals and flames and heat grill until hot, about 5 minutes. Proceed with step 3.

Grilled Arayes with Parsley-Cucumber Salad

SERVES 4 to 6   **TOTAL TIME** 1 hour

1 cup plain Greek yogurt

½ cup minced fresh mint

2 tablespoons tahini

1 tablespoon grated lemon zest plus ¼ cup juice (2 lemons), divided

½ cup extra-virgin olive oil, divided

2¼ teaspoons table salt, divided

3 cups fresh parsley leaves

1 English cucumber, halved lengthwise and sliced thin

4 ounces feta cheese, sliced thin

½ cup walnuts, toasted and chopped coarse

¼ cup pomegranate seeds

1 onion, cut into 1-inch pieces

1 cup fresh cilantro leaves

1 tablespoon ground coriander

1 tablespoon ground cumin

1 tablespoon paprika

1½ teaspoons pepper

½ teaspoon cayenne pepper

¼ teaspoon ground cinnamon

2 pounds ground lamb

4 (8-inch) pitas

Why This Recipe Works Laced with herbs and warm spices, these Middle Eastern pressed and grilled lamb sandwiches are a street food favorite and all-around flavor bomb. The meat mixture is packed with seasoning: traditional cumin, coriander, and onion, as well as lemon zest, cayenne, and paprika. As the sandwiches cook, the lamb releases fat and juices into the bread, which help it crisp up over the grill's heat. The bright yogurt-tahini sauce and an herb-based salad make this a meal. You can substitute 85 percent lean ground beef for the ground lamb, if desired. This recipe works best with ¼-inch-thick pitas that are fresh and pliable.

1   Whisk yogurt, mint, tahini, 1 tablespoon lemon juice, 2 tablespoons oil, and ⅛ teaspoon salt together in bowl. Set sauce aside.

2   Whisk 2 tablespoons oil, 1 tablespoon lemon juice, and ⅛ teaspoon salt together in large bowl. Add parsley and cucumber and toss to coat. Transfer to serving platter and top with feta, walnuts, and pomegranate seeds. Set salad aside.

3   Pulse onion and cilantro in food processor until finely chopped, 10 to 12 pulses, scraping down sides of bowl as needed. Transfer mixture to large bowl. Stir in remaining ¼ cup oil, lemon zest and remaining 2 table-spoons juice, coriander, cumin, paprika, remaining 2 teaspoons salt, pepper, cayenne, and cinnamon. Add lamb and gently knead with your hands until thoroughly combined.

4   Using kitchen shears, cut around circumference of each pita and separate into 2 halves. Place 4 thicker halves on counter, interior side up. Divide lamb mixture into 4 equal portions and place 1 portion in center of each pita half. Using spatula, gently spread lamb mixture into even layer, leaving ½-inch border. Top each lamb portion with 1 thinner pita half. Press each sandwich firmly until lamb mixture spreads to ¼ inch from edge of pita. Transfer sandwiches to large plate, cover with plastic wrap, and set aside.

5A   For a charcoal grill Open bottom vent completely. Light large chimney starter two-thirds filled with charcoal briquettes (4 quarts). When top coals are partially covered with ash, pour evenly over grill. Set cooking grate in place, cover, and open lid vent completely. Heat grill until hot, about 5 minutes.

5B **For a gas grill** Turn all burners to high; cover; and heat grill until hot, about 15 minutes. Turn all burners to medium-high.

6 Clean and oil cooking grate. Grill sandwiches, covered, until first side is evenly browned and edges are starting to crisp, 7 to 10 minutes, moving sandwiches as needed to ensure even cooking. Flip sandwiches, cover, and continue to cook until second side is evenly browned and edges are crispy, 7 to 10 minutes longer. Transfer sandwiches to cutting board and cut each into quarters. Transfer sandwiches to platter and serve with sauce and salad.

Flare Trade

Open Fire Prepare medium-hot single-level fire in open-fire grill. Set cooking grate at least 6 inches from coals and flames and heat grill until hot, about 5 minutes. Proceed with step 6.

Grilled Halloumi Wraps

SERVES 4   **TOTAL TIME** 1 hour

1 red onion, halved and sliced thin

3 tablespoons red wine vinegar

1 tablespoon ground sumac

¾ teaspoon table salt, divided

2 tablespoons lemon juice

1 garlic clove, minced

½ cup plain Greek yogurt

1 large red bell pepper

4 (8-inch) pitas

12 ounces halloumi cheese, sliced crosswise ½ inch thick

1 tablespoon extra-virgin olive oil

¼ teaspoon red pepper flakes

2 ounces (2 cups) baby arugula

Why This Recipe Works Firm and easy to brown, halloumi cheese is a total natural on the grill. In these wraps, the cheese's salty richness is offset by crisp sumac-spiked onion, smoky-sweet grilled bell pepper, and peppery arugula. While the cheese and peppers cook, you'll steam some moistened pitas in a foil packet on the cooler side of the grill so that they'll be soft and flexible when it comes time to wrap. For a yogurt spread that's garlicky without being harsh, stir the garlic into the lemon juice to deactivate its alliinase before the yogurt is whisked in. The saltiness of halloumi varies; for the best results, select a product that has less than 260 milligrams of sodium per serving.

1   Stir onion, vinegar, sumac, and ¼ teaspoon salt in medium bowl until well combined and set aside. Whisk lemon juice, garlic, and ¼ teaspoon salt together in small bowl. Whisk in yogurt until smooth.

2   Slice ½ inch from top and bottom of bell pepper. Gently remove stem from top. Twist and pull out core, using knife to loosen at edges if necessary. Cut slit down 1 side of bell pepper. Turn bell pepper skin side down and gently press so it opens to create long strip. Slide knife along insides to remove remaining ribs and seeds.

3   Lightly moisten 2 pitas with water. Sandwich remaining pitas between moistened pitas and wrap tightly in lightly greased heavy-duty aluminum foil.

4A   For a charcoal grill   Open bottom vent completely. Light large chimney starter filled with charcoal briquettes (6 quarts). When top coals are partially covered with ash, pour evenly over half of grill. Set cooking grate in place, cover, and open lid vent completely. Heat grill until hot, about 5 minutes.

4B   For a gas grill   Turn all burners to high; cover; and heat grill until hot, about 15 minutes. Leave primary burner on high and turn off other burner(s).

5   Clean and oil cooking grate. Arrange halloumi slices and bell pepper, skin side up, on hotter side of grill. Cook, covered, until first side of cheese and bell pepper are lightly browned, 3 to 5 minutes. Using tongs, flip halloumi and bell pepper and continue to cook until second side of cheese and bell pepper are lightly browned, 3 to 5 minutes.

Flare Trade

Open Fire   Prepare hot half-grill fire in open-fire grill. Set cooking grate at least 6 inches from coals and flames and heat grill until hot, about 5 minutes. Proceed with step 5.

6 Meanwhile, place packet of pitas on cooler side of grill. Flip occasionally to heat, about 5 minutes. Transfer halloumi and bell pepper to cutting board. Cut bell pepper into ½-inch pieces and transfer to second small bowl. Add oil, pepper flakes, and remaining ¼ teaspoon salt and toss to combine.

7 Lay each warm pita on 12-inch square of foil or parchment paper. Spread each pita with one-quarter of yogurt mixture. Place one-quarter of halloumi in middle of each pita. Top with pepper, onion, and arugula. Drizzle with any remaining onion liquid. Roll pita into cylinder. Wrap in foil and cut in half. Serve.

Eggplant and Mozzarella Panini

SERVES 4   **TOTAL TIME** 45 minutes

10 ounces eggplant, ends trimmed, cut crosswise into ¾-inch-thick rounds

12 ounces plum tomatoes, halved and seeded

5 tablespoons extra-virgin olive oil, divided

½ teaspoon table salt, divided

¼ teaspoon pepper, divided

8 (½-inch-thick) slices crusty bread

½ cup coarsely chopped fresh basil

1 tablespoon red wine vinegar

2 garlic cloves, minced

8 ounces fresh mozzarella cheese, sliced thin

Flare Trade

Flat-Top Grill Turn all burners to medium-high and heat griddle until hot, about 10 minutes. Leave all burners on medium-high. Clean griddle and proceed with step 3.

Open Fire Prepare medium-hot single-level fire in open-fire grill. Set cooking grate at least 6 inches from coals and flames and heat grill until hot, about 5 minutes. Proceed with step 3.

Why This Recipe Works With a simple ingredient list that highlights garden-fresh eggplant and tomatoes, melty mozzarella, and fragrant basil, these panini are sure to become a summertime favorite. Placed directly on the grill grate, the eggplant slices cook through without turning greasy, and halved plum tomatoes become nicely charred. Mashing the grilled tomatoes with red wine vinegar and chopped basil makes a quick, chunky sauce to layer with the eggplant and slices of fresh mozzarella. The sandwiches become crisp and toasty when pressed between a hot plancha and a baking sheet weighted with a cast-iron skillet. You will need a 10- or 12-inch cast-iron skillet and a cast-iron plancha measuring at least 20 by 10 inches.

1   Brush eggplant and tomatoes with 3 tablespoons oil and sprinkle with ¼ teaspoon salt and ⅛ teaspoon pepper. Brush remaining 2 tablespoons oil evenly over 1 side of each slice of bread; set aside. Lightly spray underside of rimmed baking sheet with vegetable oil spray and set aside, oiled side up.

2A   For a charcoal grill Open bottom vent completely. Light large chimney starter three-quarters filled with charcoal briquettes (4½ quarts). When top coals are partially covered with ash, pour evenly over grill. Set cooking grate in place, cover, and open lid vent completely. Heat grill until hot, about 5 minutes.

2B   For a gas grill Turn all burners to high; cover; and heat grill and until hot, about 15 minutes. Turn all burners to medium-high.

3   Clean and oil cooking grate. Grill eggplant and tomatoes (covered if using gas) until eggplant is browned and tender and tomatoes are slightly charred, 4 to 5 minutes per side. Transfer tomatoes to bowl and mash with fork. Stir in basil, vinegar, garlic, remaining ¼ teaspoon salt, and remaining ⅛ teaspoon pepper.

4   Assemble 4 sandwiches by layering ingredients as follows between prepared bread slices (with oiled sides outside sandwiches): half of mozzarella, tomato sauce, eggplant, and remaining mozzarella. Press gently on sandwiches to set.

5 Center plancha on now-empty grill. Cover and heat plancha for 5 minutes. Place sandwiches on plancha. Center prepared baking sheet, oiled side down, on top of sandwiches. Center 10- or 12-inch cast-iron skillet on sheet and cook until bread is golden and crisp on first side, about 3 minutes. Using 2 spatulas, flip sandwiches, replace sheet and skillet, and cook until second side is golden and crisp and cheese is melted, about 3 minutes. Serve immediately.

Grilled Turkey Burgers with Spinach and Feta

SERVES 4   **TOTAL TIME** 50 minutes

1¼   pounds ground turkey

2   ounces (2 cups) baby spinach, chopped

2   ounces feta cheese, crumbled (½ cup)

2   tablespoons unsalted butter, melted and cooled

2   teaspoons minced fresh dill

1   garlic clove, minced

¼   teaspoon pepper

½   teaspoon table salt

4   hamburger buns, toasted on grill if desired

Why This Recipe Works The smoky, flame-kissed flavor imparted by the grill transforms mild-mannered turkey burgers into a welcome alternative to beef. But for superlative burgers, you've got to give the patties a little boost with some flavorful add-ins before they hit the heat. Melted butter and feta cheese provide richness and flavor while also helping to prevent the burgers from drying out. Baby spinach adds color and textural interest, and fresh dill and minced garlic seal the deal. One of our favorite techniques when making burger patties is to press a divot into the center of each patty before cooking, which keeps the burger flat as it cooks. You can use ground chicken instead of turkey; just be sure to avoid ground chicken breast or ground turkey breast (also labeled 99 percent fat-free). Creating nonstick conditions for the grill grate is key here (see page 9) so these patties don't stick. Serve with your favorite burger toppings.

1   Break ground turkey into small pieces in large bowl. Add spinach, feta, melted butter, dill, garlic, and pepper and gently knead with your hands until well combined. Divide turkey mixture into 4 equal portions, then gently shape each portion into ¾-inch-thick patty. Using your fingertips, press center of each patty down until about ½ inch thick, creating slight divot.

2A   **For a charcoal grill** Open bottom vent completely. Light large chimney starter three-quarters filled with charcoal briquettes (4½ quarts). When top coals are partially covered with ash, pour evenly over grill. Set cooking grate in place, cover, and open lid vent completely. Heat grill until hot, about 5 minutes.

2B   **For a gas grill** Turn all burners to high; cover; and heat grill until hot, about 15 minutes. Turn all burners to medium-high.

3   Clean and oil cooking grate. Sprinkle patties with salt. Grill patties (covered if using gas), divot side up, until well browned on first side and meat easily releases from grill, 4 to 6 minutes. Flip patties and continue to cook until browned on second side and meat registers 160 degrees, 5 to 7 minutes. Transfer burgers to platter and let rest for 5 minutes. Serve burgers on buns.

Flare Trade

Flat-Top Grill Turn all burners to medium-high and heat griddle until hot, about 10 minutes. Leave all burners on medium-high. Clean griddle and proceed with step 3.

Open Fire Prepare medium-hot single-level fire in open-fire grill. Set cooking grate at least 6 inches from coals and flames and heat grill until hot, about 5 minutes. Proceed with step 3.

Variations

Grilled Turkey Burgers with Miso and Ginger
Omit spinach, feta, salt, and pepper. Whisk 2 tablespoons
miso paste and 1 tablespoon water in bowl until combined.
Add miso mixture to turkey with melted butter. Substitute
1 teaspoon grated fresh ginger for dill and 2 minced
scallions for garlic.

**Grilled Turkey Burgers with Herbs
and Goat Cheese**
Omit spinach and garlic. Substitute ¾ cup crumbled
goat cheese for feta. Add 1 large minced shallot and
2 tablespoons minced fresh parsley to turkey with
melted butter.

Smashed Burgers

SERVES 2   **TOTAL TIME** 40 minutes

Sauce

- 2 tablespoons mayonnaise
- 1 tablespoon minced shallot
- 1½ teaspoons finely chopped dill pickles plus ½ teaspoon brine
- 1½ teaspoons ketchup
- ⅛ teaspoon sugar
- ⅛ teaspoon pepper

Burgers

- 2 hamburger buns
- 8 ounces 80 percent lean ground beef
- 2 tablespoons vegetable oil
- ¼ teaspoon kosher salt
- ⅛ teaspoon pepper
- 4 slices American cheese (4 ounces)

Flare Trade

Flat-Top Grill Turn all burners to medium-high and heat griddle until hot, about 10 minutes. Leave all burners on medium-high. Clean griddle and proceed with step 4.

Why This Recipe Works Thin and crispy-edged, these smashed burgers outshine any fast-food option. Firmly pressing the meat with a small saucepan makes it spread and stick uniformly to the plancha, which helps guarantee deep browning. The small patties cook through quickly; sandwiching a slice of American cheese between two patties helps them stick together while acting like a rich cheese sauce. A creamy, tangy burger sauce adds more richness. Top the burgers with lettuce and tomato and nestle them in soft burger buns for a classic burger joint experience. You can use 85 percent lean ground beef, but 90 percent lean will produce a dry burger. We strongly prefer Kraft Singles here for their meltability. To serve four, double the sauce and burger ingredients but use the same amount of oil. Transfer the first four cooked burgers to a wire rack set in a rimmed baking sheet, add the cheese, and keep warm (on the grill if there's room) while cooking the remaining four burgers. You will need a cast-iron plancha measuring at least 20 by 10 inches.

1 **For the sauce** Stir all ingredients together in bowl.

2 **For the burgers** Spread 1 tablespoon sauce on cut side of each bun top; set aside. Divide beef into 4 equal pieces (2 ounces each); form into loose, rough balls (do not compress).

3A **For a charcoal grill** Open bottom vent completely. Light large chimney starter three-quarters filled with charcoal briquettes (4½ quarts). When top coals are partially covered with ash, pour evenly over grill. Set cooking grate in place, center plancha on grill, cover, and open lid vent completely. Heat grill with plancha until hot, about 5 minutes.

3B **For a gas grill** Turn all burners to high; cover; and heat grill until hot, about 15 minutes. Center plancha on grill, cover, and heat for an additional 5 minutes. Turn all burners to medium-high.

4 Heat oil on plancha until just smoking. Place beef balls about 3 inches apart on plancha. Use bottom of greased saucepan to firmly smash each ball until 4 to 4½ inches in diameter. Sprinkle patties with salt and pepper. Cook until at least three-quarters of each patty is no longer pink on top, about 2 minutes. Use thin metal spatula to loosen patties from plancha. Flip patties and cook for 15 seconds. Transfer to platter. Transfer 1 burger to each bun bottom and top each with 1 slice American cheese; repeat with remaining burgers and cheese. Cap with prepared bun tops. Serve immediately.

Grilled Smokehouse Barbecue Burgers

SERVES 4   **TOTAL TIME** 45 minutes, plus 30 minutes chilling

Coleslaw

- 3 cups shredded green cabbage
- 2 tablespoons sugar, plus extra for seasoning
- 1 teaspoon table salt
- 1 carrot, peeled and shredded
- 2 tablespoons cider vinegar, plus extra for seasoning
- 1 tablespoon vegetable oil
- ⅛ teaspoon celery seeds
- ⅛ teaspoon pepper

Burgers

- 2 pounds 85 percent lean ground beef
- 2 teaspoons garlic powder
- 2 teaspoons onion powder
- 3 tablespoons barbecue sauce, plus extra for serving
- 2 cups wood chips
- ½ teaspoon table salt
- ¼ teaspoon pepper
- 4 large hamburger buns, toasted on grill if desired

Why This Recipe Works If you love beef infused with bold, smoky barbecue flavor, these burgers are for you. A generous 2 cups of wood chips on the grill creates smoke that thoroughly permeates the meat; soaking the chips mellows the effect so the flavor is strong but not overpowering. These burgers are supersized, which allows them to absorb more smoke as they cook through than smaller burgers would, and incorporating a few tablespoons of bottled barbecue sauce into the ground beef adds an extra blast of flavor. Sweet and tangy coleslaw makes a fresh topping; finish with a drizzle of your favorite barbecue sauce and you've got all the flavors of a smokehouse in one bite. Wood chunks are not recommended for this recipe.

1 **For the coleslaw** Toss cabbage with sugar and salt in large bowl. Cover and microwave, stirring occasionally, until cabbage is partially wilted and has reduced in volume by about one-third, about 2 minutes. Transfer cabbage to salad spinner and spin until excess liquid has been removed. Return cabbage to now-empty bowl, add carrot, vinegar, oil, celery seeds, and pepper, and toss to combine. Season with salt and sugar to taste. Refrigerate until well chilled, at least 30 minutes or up to 4 hours.

2 **For the burgers** Break ground beef into small pieces and spread into even layer on rimmed baking sheet. Sprinkle with garlic powder and onion powder and drizzle with barbecue sauce. Using 2 forks, gently toss beef mixture to combine. Divide beef mixture into 4 equal portions, then gently shape each portion into 1-inch-thick patty. Using your fingertips, press center of each patty down until about ½ inch thick, creating slight divot.

3 Using large piece of heavy-duty aluminum foil, wrap chips in 8 by 4½-inch foil packet. (Make sure chips do not poke holes in sides or bottom of packet. If using gas, make sure there are no more than 2 layers of foil on bottom of packet.) Cut 2 evenly spaced 2-inch slits in top of packet.

4A **For a charcoal grill** Open bottom vent halfway. Light large chimney starter filled with charcoal briquettes (6 quarts). When top coals are partially covered with ash, pour evenly over grill. Place wood chip packet on coals. Set cooking grate in place, cover, and open lid vent halfway. Heat grill until hot and wood chips are smoking, about 5 minutes.

4B For a gas grill Remove cooking grate and place wood chip packet directly on primary burner. Set cooking grate in place; turn all burners to high; cover; and heat grill until hot and wood chips are smoking, 15 to 25 minutes. Leave all burners on high.

5 Clean and oil cooking grate. Sprinkle patties with salt and pepper. Grill patties divot side up, covered, until well browned on first side, 2 to 4 minutes. Flip patties and continue to cook until browned on second side and meat registers 120 to 125 degrees (for medium-rare) or 130 to 135 degrees (for medium), 3 to 5 minutes.

6 Transfer burgers to platter and let rest for 5 minutes. Toss coleslaw to recombine. Serve burgers on buns, topped with coleslaw, passing extra barbecue sauce separately.

Flare Trade

Open Fire Omit wood chip packet. Prepare hot single-level fire in open-fire grill. Set cooking grate at least 6 inches from coals and flames and heat grill until hot, about 5 minutes. Proceed with step 5.

Grind-Your-Own Sirloin Burgers

SERVES 4   **TOTAL TIME** 45 minutes, plus 1 hour freezing

1½ pounds sirloin steak tips, trimmed and cut into ½-inch chunks

4 tablespoons unsalted butter, cut into ¼-inch pieces

1¾ teaspoons kosher salt, divided

1⅛ teaspoons pepper, divided

4 hamburger buns, toasted on grill if desired

Why This Recipe Works There's one surefire way to get a burger with a craggy charred crust, a rich beefy taste, and an interior so juicy and tender that it practically falls apart at the slightest pressure: Grind your own meat. A food processor makes it easy; just trim excess fat, cut the meat into ½-inch pieces, freeze it for about 30 minutes to firm it up so that the blades cut it cleanly, and process it in small batches to ensure an even grind. Steak tips (sometimes called flap meat) are the way to go here: They're beefy, decently tender, and require little trimming. The final trick to these burgers: After pressing a divot into the patties to prevent burger bulge, freeze the patties briefly before grilling. By the time they've thawed at their centers, enough crust has developed to hold together the tender interior. When tossing the salt and pepper with the ground meat and shaping the patties, take care not to overwork the meat or the burgers will become dense. Serve with your favorite toppings. You will need a 13 by 9-inch disposable aluminum roasting pan.

1   Place beef chunks and butter on large plate in single layer. Freeze until meat is very firm and starting to harden around edges but is still pliable, about 30 minutes.

2   Place one-quarter of meat and one-quarter of butter cubes in food processor and pulse until finely ground into pieces the size of rice grains, 15 to 20 pulses, stopping and redistributing meat around bowl as necessary to ensure beef is evenly ground. Transfer meat to baking sheet. Repeat grinding with remaining 3 batches of meat and butter. Spread mixture into even layer on baking sheet and inspect carefully, discarding any long strands of gristle or large chunks of hard meat, fat, or butter.

3   Sprinkle ¾ teaspoon salt and 1 teaspoon pepper over meat and, using 2 forks, gently toss to combine. Divide beef mixture into 4 portions, then gently shape each portion into ¾-inch-thick patty about 4½ inches in diameter. Using your fingertips, press center of each patty down until about ¼ inch thick, creating slight divot. Transfer patties to platter and freeze for 30 to 45 minutes.

Flare Trade

Flat-Top Grill Turn all burners to medium-high and heat griddle until hot, about 15 minutes. Turn all burners to high. Clean griddle and proceed with step 5, increasing cooking range to 3 to 7 minutes per side.

Open Fire Prepare hot single-level fire in open-fire grill. Set cooking grate at least 6 inches from coals and flames and heat grill until hot, about 5 minutes. Proceed with step 5.

4A For a charcoal grill Using skewer, poke 12 holes in bottom of disposable pan. Open bottom vent completely and place disposable pan in center of grill. Light large chimney starter two-thirds filled with charcoal briquettes (4 quarts). When top coals are partially covered with ash, pour into disposable pan. Set cooking grate in place, cover, and open lid vent completely. Heat grill until hot, about 5 minutes.

4B For a gas grill Turn all burners to high; cover; and heat grill until hot, about 15 minutes. Leave all burners on high.

5 Clean and oil cooking grate. Sprinkle patties with remaining ½ teaspoon salt and remaining ⅛ teaspoon pepper. Grill patties divot side up (directly over coals if using charcoal), without moving them, until browned and meat easily releases from grill, 4 to 7 minutes. Flip burgers and continue to grill until browned on second side and meat registers 120 to 125 degrees (for medium-rare) or 130 to 135 degrees (for medium), 4 to 7 minutes.

6 Transfer burgers to plate and let rest for 5 minutes. Transfer burgers to buns and serve.

Grilled Green Chile and Chorizo Cheeseburgers

SERVES 4   **TOTAL TIME** 50 minutes

12 ounces ground pork

12 ounces Mexican-style chorizo sausage, casings removed

1 teaspoon table salt, divided

1 teaspoon pepper, divided

½ onion, sliced into ½-inch-thick rounds

1 Anaheim chile, stemmed, halved, and seeded

1 jalapeño chile, stemmed, halved, and seeded

1 garlic clove, minced

3 ounces Monterey Jack cheese, shredded (¾ cup)

4 hamburger buns, toasted on grill if desired

¼ cup mayonnaise

1 cup shredded iceberg lettuce

Why This Recipe Works This burger uses two types of pork as well as two types of chiles for ultimate fire-roasted flavor. Our southwestern topping combines a mild Anaheim chile and a hot jalapeño for slightly sweet and satisfyingly spicy results. For intense smoky flavor, cook the chiles along with some onion on the grill; once they develop a delicious char, chop them and combine them with a little garlic to create the chunky chile topping. Layer it on top of the patties after you flip them and then top it all with shredded Monterey Jack and let the cheese melt; this method helps the topping stick to the burgers instead of sliding out the side of the bun. Use fresh Mexican-style chorizo here, not the dry-cured Spanish version. Traditional New Mexican chile burgers use Hatch chiles; although they were too difficult for us to track down, feel free to substitute them for the jalapeño and Anaheim if you can find them. For more heat, include the jalapeño ribs and seeds.

1 Combine pork and chorizo in bowl. Form pork mixture into 8 equal balls, then press into ¾-inch-thick patties about 4 inches in diameter. Using your fingertips, press center of each patty down until about ½ inch thick, creating slight divot. Sprinkle patties with ¾ teaspoon salt and ¾ teaspoon pepper. Push toothpick horizontally through each onion round to keep rings intact while grilling.

2A For a charcoal grill Open bottom vent completely. Light large chimney starter filled with charcoal briquettes (6 quarts). When top coals are partially covered with ash, pour evenly over grill. Set cooking grate in place, cover, and open lid vent completely. Heat grill until hot, about 5 minutes.

2B For a gas grill Turn all burners to high; cover; and heat grill until hot, about 15 minutes. Leave all burners on high.

3 Clean and oil cooking grate. Grill Anaheim, jalapeño, and onion until vegetables are lightly charred and tender, 4 to 8 minutes, flipping as needed. Transfer vegetables to bowl, cover, and let sit for 5 minutes. Remove skins from chiles and discard; remove toothpicks from onion rounds.

Flare Trade

Flat-Top Grill Turn all burners to medium-high and heat griddle until hot, about 15 minutes. Turn all burners to high. Clean griddle and proceed with step 3.

Open Fire Prepare hot single-level fire in open-fire grill. Set cooking grate at least 6 inches from coals and flames and heat grill until hot, about 5 minutes. Proceed with step 3.

4 Chop chiles and onion. Combine chiles and onion with garlic, remaining ¼ teaspoon salt, and remaining ¼ teaspoon pepper in bowl; set aside.

5 Grill patties divot side up, covered, until well browned on first side, about 5 minutes. Flip patties and top each with 1 tablespoon chile mixture and 2 tablespoons Monterey Jack. Continue to grill, covered, until cheese is melted and patties are browned on second side and register 160 degrees, about 5 minutes. Transfer to platter, arranging burgers in stacks of two. Let rest for 5 minutes.

6 Spread 1 tablespoon mayonnaise on each bun top. Place 1 burger stack on each bun bottom, followed by ¼ cup lettuce and bun top. Serve.

Grilled Harissa Lamb Burgers

SERVES 4   **TOTAL TIME** 40 minutes

3 tablespoons mayonnaise

2 tablespoons harissa, divided

1 tablespoon minced fresh mint

1½ teaspoons grated lemon zest, divided

1½ pounds ground lamb

½ teaspoon pepper, divided

1 red onion, sliced into ½-inch-thick rounds

1 tablespoon vegetable oil

½ teaspoon table salt

4 hamburger buns, toasted on grill if desired

1 cup baby arugula

Why This Recipe Works With its earthy flavor and tender texture—and with a simple charred onion topping that grills right alongside the patty—lamb might just become your new favorite choice for burgers. Lamb's distinctive taste pairs well with the bold flavor of harissa, a traditional North African condiment with irresistibly complex chile flavor. Cool, creamy mayonnaise provides a rich base for the spicy harissa-spiked sauce, and a blast of fresh mint and lemon zest balances out the harissa's heat. The red color of the harissa makes these burgers look rarer than they actually are, so be sure to use an instant-read thermometer to accurately gauge doneness.

1   Combine mayonnaise, 1 tablespoon harissa, mint, and ½ teaspoon lemon zest in bowl and season with salt and pepper to taste; cover and refrigerate until ready to serve.

2   Break ground lamb into small pieces in large bowl. Add remaining 1 tablespoon harissa, remaining 1 teaspoon lemon zest, and ¼ teaspoon pepper and gently knead with your hands until well combined. Divide lamb mixture into 4 portions, then gently shape each portion into ¾-inch-thick patty. Using your fingertips, press center of each patty down until about ½ inch thick, creating slight divot.

3   Push toothpick horizontally through each onion round to keep rings intact while grilling. Brush onion rounds with oil.

4A   For a charcoal grill Open bottom vent completely. Light large chimney starter filled with charcoal briquettes (6 quarts). When top coals are partially covered with ash, pour evenly over grill. Set cooking grate in place, cover, and open lid vent completely. Heat grill until hot, about 5 minutes.

4B   For a gas grill Turn all burners to high; cover; and heat grill until hot, about 15 minutes. Leave all burners on high.

5   Clean and oil cooking grate. Place onion rounds on grill and cook (covered if using gas) until softened and lightly charred, 3 to 6 minutes per side. Transfer to bowl as onion rounds finish cooking and cover to keep warm.

Flare Trade

Flat-Top Grill Turn all burners to medium-high and heat griddle until hot, about 15 minutes. Turn all burners to high. Clean griddle and proceed with step 5, cooking onions and burgers at same time.

Open Fire Prepare hot single-level fire in open-fire grill. Set cooking grate at least 6 inches from coals and flames and heat grill until hot, about 5 minutes. Proceed with step 5.

6 Meanwhile, sprinkle patties with salt and remaining ¼ teaspoon pepper. Grill patties, divot side up, until well browned on first side, 2 to 4 minutes. Flip patties and continue to cook until browned on second side and meat registers 120 to 125 degrees (for medium-rare) or 130 to 135 (for medium), 2 to 5 minutes. Transfer burgers to platter and let rest for 5 minutes.

7 Remove toothpicks from onion rounds and separate into rings. Spread mayonnaise mixture on bun tops. Serve burgers on buns, topped with onion and arugula.

Salmon Burgers with Asparagus and Lemon-Herb Sauce

SERVES 4   **TOTAL TIME** 45 minutes

6 tablespoons mayonnaise, divided

2 scallions, minced, divided

3 tablespoons chopped fresh parsley, divided

1 tablespoon lemon juice

1 slice hearty white sandwich bread, torn into 1-inch pieces

1 pound skinless salmon fillets, cut into 1-inch pieces

1 tablespoon Dijon mustard

2 teaspoons capers, rinsed and minced

¾ teaspoon table salt, divided

⅛ teaspoon plus ½ teaspoon pepper, divided

1 pound asparagus, trimmed

1 teaspoon extra-virgin olive oil

4 hamburger buns, toasted on grill if desired

1 small head Bibb lettuce, leaves separated

Thinly sliced tomato

Why This Recipe Works Salmon burgers can be delicate, but don't let that stop you from cooking them on the grill. Fresh bread crumbs and a little mayo help bind the patties together while still letting the salmon flavor shine. A food processor makes quick work of chopping the fish, and chilling the burgers briefly firms them up so they're less prone to breakage. A tart, herbal sauce of lemon, scallions, and parsley mixed with mayo tops these rich burgers. Spears of asparagus, grilled until lightly caramelized, make an appealing side that you can also eat with your hands. Use asparagus that is at least ½ inch thick near the base; pencil-thin asparagus cannot withstand the heat and will overcook. Be sure to use raw salmon, not cooked or canned salmon. To help the burgers slide easily on and off the grill, use a metal spatula coated with vegetable oil spray. Creating nonstick conditions for the grill grate is key here (see page 9).

1   Whisk ¼ cup mayonnaise, half of scallions, 1 tablespoon parsley, and lemon juice together in bowl. Season with salt and pepper to taste; set aside for serving.

2   Pulse bread in food processor to fine crumbs, about 4 pulses; transfer to large bowl. Working in 2 batches, pulse salmon in now-empty food processor until coarsely ground, about 4 pulses; transfer to bowl with bread crumbs and toss to combine. Add mustard, capers, remaining 2 tablespoons mayonnaise, remaining scallions, remaining 2 tablespoons parsley, ¼ teaspoon salt, and ⅛ teaspoon pepper and gently fold into salmon mixture until well combined.

3   Divide salmon mixture into 4 equal portions and gently pack into 1-inch-thick patties, about 3½ inches wide. Place patties on parchment paper–lined baking sheet and refrigerate for at least 15 minutes. Meanwhile, toss asparagus with oil, ¼ teaspoon salt, and ¼ teaspoon pepper.

4A   For a charcoal grill Open bottom vent completely. Light large chimney starter filled with charcoal briquettes (6 quarts). When top coals are partially covered with ash, pour evenly over grill. Set cooking grate in place, cover, and open lid vent completely. Heat grill until hot, about 5 minutes.

4B **For a gas grill** Turn all burners to high; cover; and heat grill until hot, about 15 minutes. Leave all burners on high.

5 Clean and oil cooking grate. Sprinkle patties with remaining ¼ teaspoon salt and remaining ¼ teaspoon pepper. Grill patties and asparagus until patties are well browned and salmon registers 125 degrees (for medium-rare) and asparagus is just tender and caramelized, 4 to 10 minutes, flipping both halfway through cooking (move asparagus as needed to ensure even cooking). Transfer patties and asparagus to platter.

6 Arrange burgers on bun bottoms and top with lettuce, tomato slices, lemon-herb sauce, and bun tops. Serve with asparagus.

Flare Trade

Flat-Top Grill Turn all burners to medium-high and heat griddle until hot, about 15 minutes. Turn all burners to high. Clean griddle and proceed with step 5.

Open Fire Prepare hot single-level fire in open-fire grill. Set cooking grate at least 6 inches from coals and flames and heat grill until hot, about 5 minutes. Proceed with step 5.

Grilled Portobello Burgers with Goat Cheese and Arugula

SERVES 4   **TOTAL TIME** 45 minutes

4 portobello mushroom caps
   (4 to 5 inches in diameter),
   gills removed

1 large red onion, sliced into
   ½-inch-thick rounds

3 tablespoons plus 1 teaspoon
   extra-virgin olive oil, divided

2 garlic cloves, minced

2 teaspoons minced fresh thyme

¼ teaspoon table salt

¼ teaspoon pepper

2 ounces goat cheese,
   crumbled (½ cup)

1 cup baby arugula

¼ teaspoon balsamic vinegar

4 hamburger buns,
   toasted on grill if desired

   Thinly sliced tomato

Why This Recipe Works When the king of mushrooms meets the grill, magic happens as its texture softens and its earthy, rich flavor deepens. Layer this portobello burger with tangy goat cheese and peppery arugula, top it off with a tomato slice and smoky grilled onion, and you have a meatless burger with an irresistible combination of tastes and textures. Mushroom gills can sometimes have an off taste; scrape them out to avoid a muddy flavor. Lightly scoring the smooth side of the mushroom with a crosshatch pattern expedites the release of excess moisture and tenderizes the caps, making them easier to bite into.

1   Cut ¹⁄₁₆-inch-deep slits on top side of mushroom caps, spaced ½ inch apart, in crosshatch pattern. Push toothpick horizontally through each onion round to keep rings intact while grilling. Brush onion rounds with 1 tablespoon oil. Combine garlic, thyme, salt, pepper, and 2 tablespoons oil in bowl; set aside.

2A   For a charcoal grill Open bottom vent completely. Light large chimney starter three-quarters filled with charcoal briquettes (4½ quarts). When top coals are partially covered with ash, pour evenly over grill. Set cooking grate in place, cover, and open lid vent completely. Heat grill until hot, about 5 minutes.

2B   For a gas grill Turn all burners to high; cover; and heat grill until hot, about 15 minutes. Turn all burners to medium-high.

3   Clean and oil cooking grate. Grill onion and mushrooms, gill side down, (covered if using gas) until onion and mushrooms are lightly charred and beginning to soften, 8 to 12 minutes, flipping onion as needed, and flipping mushrooms halfway and brushing with oil-garlic mixture. Sprinkle mushrooms with goat cheese and let cheese melt, about 2 minutes. As they finish cooking, transfer mushrooms and onion to platter and tent with aluminum foil.

4 Toss arugula with vinegar and remaining 1 teaspoon oil in bowl and season with salt and pepper to taste. Remove toothpicks from onion rounds and separate into rings. Place arugula and mushroom caps on bun bottoms. Top with tomato, onion, and bun tops. Serve.

Flare Trade

Flat-Top Grill Turn all burners to medium-high and heat griddle until hot, about 10 minutes. Leave all burners on medium-high. Clean griddle and proceed with step 3.

Open Fire Prepare medium-hot single-level fire in open-fire grill. Set cooking grate at least 6 inches from coals and flames and heat grill until hot, about 5 minutes. Proceed with step 3.

Grilled Chicken Tacos with Salsa Verde

SERVES 4   **TOTAL TIME** 45 minutes, plus 30 minutes chilling

¼ cup vegetable oil, divided

3 tablespoons lime juice (2 limes), divided, plus lime wedges for serving

2 tablespoons water

1 teaspoon plus pinch sugar, divided

2¼ teaspoons table salt, divided

½ teaspoon pepper

5 garlic cloves, minced, divided

1½ pounds boneless, skinless chicken breasts, trimmed and pounded to ¾-inch thickness

1 onion, sliced into ½-inch-thick rounds

1 jalapeño chile, stemmed, halved, and seeded

1 pound tomatillos, husks and stems removed, rinsed well and dried, divided

12 (6-inch) corn tortillas

½ cup chopped fresh cilantro

1 avocado, halved, pitted, and cut into ½-inch pieces (optional)

4 radishes, trimmed and sliced thin (optional)

Why This Recipe Works Lightly charred boneless chicken breasts accompanied by a piquant salsa verde are at the heart of this go-to taco-night meal that you can cook entirely on the grill. Because it's paired with such flavorful elements, the chicken needs just a brief stint in a lime-garlic marinade before being grilled over a hot fire. A little salt and sugar in the marinade keeps the chicken moist as it cooks and enhances its flavor. There's plenty of room on the grill to add a bit of char to the salsa vegetables: tomatillos, onion, and jalapeño. Putting the salsa together is as simple as pulsing the grilled vegetables with additional raw tomatillos, cilantro, lime juice, and garlic. Toast the corn tortillas on the grill until they develop a toasty, popcorn-like aroma, and then wrap them tightly in foil to stay warm and soft. Set all the components out with avocado and sliced radishes so everyone can assemble their own tacos.

1   Whisk 3 tablespoons oil, 1 tablespoon lime juice, water, 1 teaspoon sugar, 1½ teaspoons salt, pepper, and half of garlic together in medium bowl. Add chicken to marinade, toss to coat, cover, and refrigerate, turning occasionally, for 30 minutes.

2   Push toothpick horizontally through each onion round to keep rings intact while grilling. Brush onion, jalapeño, and half of tomatillos with remaining 1 tablespoon oil and sprinkle with ¼ teaspoon salt. Halve remaining tomatillos; set aside. Remove chicken from marinade, let excess marinade drip off, and transfer to plate.

3A   For a charcoal grill Open bottom vent completely. Light large chimney starter filled with charcoal briquettes (6 quarts). When top coals are partially covered with ash, pour evenly over grill. Set cooking grate in place, cover, and open lid vent completely. Heat grill until hot, about 5 minutes.

3B   For a gas grill Turn all burners to high; cover; and heat grill until hot, about 15 minutes. Leave all burners on high.

4   Clean and oil cooking grate. Grill chicken and oiled vegetables, (covered if using gas), turning as needed, until chicken is well browned and registers 160 degrees and vegetables are lightly charred and soft, 10 to 15 minutes. Transfer chicken and vegetables to cutting board and tent with aluminum foil.

5 Working in batches, grill tortillas, turning as needed, until lightly charred, 30 to 60 seconds per side; wrap tightly in foil to keep soft.

6 Remove toothpicks from onion rounds. Chop grilled vegetables coarse, then pulse with cilantro, remaining 2 tablespoons lime juice, remaining pinch sugar, remaining ½ teaspoon salt, remaining garlic, and remaining tomatillos in food processor until slightly chunky, 16 to 18 pulses. Slice chicken thin on bias. Serve with tortillas; lime wedges; tomatillo sauce; avocado, if using; and radishes, if using.

Flare Trade

Flat-Top Grill Turn all burners to medium-high and heat griddle until hot, about 10 minutes. Turn all burners to high. Clean griddle and proceed with step 4. Clean griddle again before heating tortillas.

Open Fire Prepare hot single-level fire in open-fire grill. Set cooking grate at least 6 inches from coals and flames and heat grill until hot, about 5 minutes. Proceed with step 4.

Tacos al Carbón

SERVES 4   **TOTAL TIME** 45 minutes

3 tablespoons extra-virgin olive oil, divided

2 teaspoons minced canned chipotle chile in adobo sauce, plus 1 teaspoon adobo sauce, divided

2 teaspoons kosher salt, divided

¾ teaspoon ground cumin

1 (1½- to 1¾-pound) flank steak

2 jalapeño chiles

20 scallions

12 (6-inch) corn tortillas

1½ tablespoons lime juice, plus more to taste, plus lime wedges for serving

Fresh cilantro leaves

Mexican crema

Why This Recipe Works Tacos al carbón feature meat (usually steak) seasoned with a marinade or spices, cooked over a live fire, tucked into soft corn tortillas, and topped with garnishes such as charred scallions and lime juice. Thin, beefy flank steak cooks quickly and has lots of surface area for holding flavor, in this case a spicy, smoky paste made with chipotle chiles in adobo sauce. Dividing the steak to separate the thinner portions from the thicker ones lets you cook all the meat just the way you want it. Frequent flipping helps the top and bottom shrink at about the same rate so the steaks stay flat and brown evenly. The scallions and jalapeños for the salsa pick up some flavor from the meat as they grill. Once the grate is clear, the corn tortillas can be toasted on the hotter side of the grill. This steak's grill flavor is created when some of the fat and juices land on the fire and create small, controlled flare-ups, so choose a steak that has some visible fat deposits. Sour cream can be substituted for the crema, if desired.

1 Combine 1 tablespoon oil, chipotle, 1½ teaspoons salt, and cumin in bowl. Trim fat deposits on steak to ⅛-inch thickness. Cut steak lengthwise (with grain) into three 2- to 3-inch-wide strips. Rub steaks all over with chipotle mixture and transfer to rimmed baking sheet.

2A **For a charcoal grill** Open bottom vent completely. Light large chimney starter mounded with charcoal briquettes (7 quarts). When top coals are partially covered with ash, pour evenly over half of grill. Set cooking grate in place, cover, and open lid vent completely. Heat grill until hot, about 5 minutes.

2B **For a gas grill** Turn all burners to high; cover; and heat grill until hot, about 15 minutes. Turn off 1 burner (if using grill with more than 2 burners, turn off burner farthest from primary burner) and leave other burner(s) on high.

3 Clean and oil cooking grate. Arrange steak and jalapeños on hotter side of grill. Cook steak and jalapeños (covered if using gas), flipping every 2 minutes, until meat is well browned and registers 120 to 125 degrees (for medium-rare) or 130 to 135 degrees (for medium) and jalapeños' skins are blistered and charred in spots, 7 to 12 minutes. Transfer steak to cutting board and tent with aluminum foil. Transfer jalapeños to medium bowl and cover tightly.

4 Grill scallions on hotter side of grill until greens are well charred on 1 side, 1 to 2 minutes. Flip scallions, arranging so that greens are on cooler side while white and pale green parts are on hotter side. Continue to cook until whites are well charred, 1 to 2 minutes. Transfer to bowl with jalapeños and cover tightly.

5 Working in batches, grill tortillas on hotter side of grill, turning as needed, until lightly charred, 30 to 60 seconds per side; wrap tightly in foil to keep soft.

6 Without peeling, stem and seed jalapeños and reserve seeds. Chop jalapeños fine, chop scallions coarse, and transfer to bowl. Stir in remaining 2 tablespoons oil, lime juice, adobo sauce, and remaining ½ teaspoon salt. Season with lime juice, salt, and jalapeño seeds to taste. Slice steak thin against grain and transfer to serving platter. Serve, passing scallion salsa, tortillas, lime wedges, cilantro, and crema separately.

Flare Trade

Flat-Top Grill Turn all burners to medium-high and heat griddle until hot, about 10 minutes. Turn all burners to high. Clean griddle and proceed with step 3, cooking scallions at same time as steak and jalapeños and flipping as needed for even char. Clean griddle again before heating tortillas.

Open Fire Prepare hot half-grill fire in open-fire grill. Set cooking grate at least 6 inches from coals and flames and heat grill until hot, about 5 minutes. Proceed with step 3.

Tacos al Pastor

SERVES 8 to 10   **TOTAL TIME** 2 hours, plus 1 hour chilling

1½ ounces dried guajillo chiles, stemmed

1 ounce dried ancho chiles, stemmed

½ cup cider vinegar

½ cup pineapple juice

1 tablespoon table salt

4 garlic cloves, peeled

1 tablespoon dried oregano

2 teaspoons ground cumin

1½ teaspoons pepper

½ teaspoon ground cinnamon

1 (2½-pound) boneless pork butt roast, trimmed

1 pineapple, peeled, quartered lengthwise, and cored, 3 quarters set aside for another use

24 (6-inch) corn tortillas

Finely chopped onion

Fresh cilantro leaves

Lime wedges

Flare Trade

Open Fire Prepare hot half-grill fire in open-fire grill. Set cooking grate at least 6 inches from coals and flames and heat grill until hot, about 5 minutes. Proceed with step 5, cooking pork for 1 hour to 1½ hours, checking browning of pork often and moving pieces as needed to ensure even char.

Why This Recipe Works Tacos al pastor boast a long history and an irresistible combination of spicy-sweet flavors designed to satisfy a hungry crowd. Traditionally, thin slices of marinated pork are layered on a rotating spit and roasted in front of an open flame; this recipe uses boneless pork butt roast, cut into thick "steaks," to make cooking the tacos a backyard-friendly event. First, the pork marinates in a potent paste of toasted guajillo and ancho chiles, garlic, pineapple juice, vinegar, and oregano. Next, the pork cooks slowly over indirect heat, ensuring moist and tender meat, and then the steaks get a final sear over a hot fire to char the outer edges. Lightly grilled pineapple adds sweet juiciness, while raw onion, cilantro, and lime punch things up. Slice the meat extra-thin to mimic the original, serve it with corn tortillas, and watch it disappear. Note that 1½ ounces guajillos is about six chiles; 1 ounce anchos is about two chiles.

1   Using kitchen shears, cut guajillos and anchos in half lengthwise and discard seeds and stems. Cut guajillos and anchos into 1-inch pieces. Place guajillos and anchos in 12-inch skillet and cook over medium heat, stirring often, until fragrant and darkened slightly, about 6 minutes. Immediately transfer guajillos and anchos to bowl and cover with hot water. Let sit until soft, about 5 minutes.

2   Using slotted spoon, lift guajillos and anchos from water and transfer to blender; discard soaking water. Add vinegar, pineapple juice, salt, garlic, oregano, cumin, pepper, and cinnamon and process until smooth, about 1 minute, scraping down sides of blender jar as needed. Set aside ¼ cup marinade.

3   Cut pork crosswise into approximate 1½-inch-thick steaks. Transfer pork to 1-gallon zipper-lock bag. Add remaining marinade to bag with pork. Seal bag and turn to distribute marinade evenly. Refrigerate for at least 1 hour or up to 24 hours.

4A   For a charcoal grill Open bottom vent completely. Light large chimney starter filled with charcoal briquettes (6 quarts). When top coals are partially covered with ash, pour evenly over half of grill. Set cooking grate in place, cover, and open lid vent completely. Heat grill until hot, about 5 minutes.

4B **For a gas grill** Turn all burners to high; cover; and heat grill until hot, about 15 minutes. Adjust primary burner to medium-high and turn off other burners. (Adjust burner as needed to maintain grill temperature of 350 degrees.)

5 Clean and oil cooking grate. Remove pork from marinade and place on cooler side of grill. Cover and cook until pork registers 150 degrees, about 50 minutes for charcoal or 1 hour 5 minutes to 1 hour 10 minutes for gas.

6 Brush tops of steaks with 2 tablespoons reserved marinade. Flip steaks, marinade side down, onto hotter side of grill. Brush second side of steaks with remaining 2 tablespoons reserved marinade. Place pineapple on hotter side of grill next to steaks. Cook, uncovered for charcoal and covered for gas, until pork is well charred and registers 175 degrees, 6 to 8 minutes per side for charcoal or 12 to 15 minutes per side for gas. Cook pineapple until warmed through, flipping as needed, about 10 minutes. Transfer pork and pineapple to wire rack set in rimmed baking sheet, tent with aluminum foil, and let rest for 15 minutes.

7 Working in batches, grill tortillas on hotter side of grill, turning as needed, until lightly charred, 30 to 60 seconds per side; wrap tightly in foil to keep soft. Transfer pork and pineapple to carving board and slice thin. Season with salt to taste. Divide pork and pineapple evenly among tortillas. Top tacos with onion and cilantro. Serve with lime wedges.

Grilled Swordfish Tacos

SERVES 6   **TOTAL TIME** 1¼ hours, plus 30 minutes chilling

3 tablespoons vegetable oil, divided

1 tablespoon ancho chile powder

2 teaspoons chipotle chile powder

1 teaspoon dried oregano

1 teaspoon ground coriander

2 garlic cloves, minced

1 teaspoon table salt

2 tablespoons tomato paste

½ cup orange juice

6 tablespoons lime juice (3 limes), divided, plus lime wedges for serving

2 pounds skinless swordfish steaks, 1 inch thick, cut lengthwise into 1-inch-wide strips

1 pineapple, peeled, quartered lengthwise, cored, and each quarter halved lengthwise

1 jalapeño chile

18 (6-inch) corn tortillas

1 red bell pepper, stemmed, seeded, and cut into ¼-inch pieces

2 tablespoons minced fresh cilantro, plus extra for serving

½ head iceberg lettuce (4½ ounces), cored and sliced thin

1 avocado, halved, pitted, and sliced thin

Why This Recipe Works For bold fish tacos, fire up the grill. Sturdy swordfish steaks, cut into strips, hold up better to being flipped on the grill than flaky options such as cod. Coat the strips with a flavor-packed paste featuring ancho and chipotle chile powders, oregano, and a touch of citrus juice to develop deep charring over the fire. Refreshing grilled pineapple salsa, creamy avocado, and crisp lettuce complete these tacos and offer a satisfying array of flavors, textures, and temperatures. Mahi-mahi, tuna, and halibut fillets are all suitable substitutes for the swordfish; buy 1-inch-thick fillets and cut them in a similar fashion to the swordfish. Creating nonstick conditions for the grill grate is key here (see page 9).

1   Heat 2 tablespoons oil, ancho chile powder, and chipotle chile powder in 8-inch skillet over medium heat, stirring constantly, until fragrant and some bubbles form, 2 to 3 minutes. Add oregano, coriander, garlic, and salt and continue to cook until fragrant, about 30 seconds longer. Add tomato paste and, using spatula, mash tomato paste with spice mixture until combined, about 20 seconds. Stir in orange juice and 2 tablespoons lime juice. Cook, stirring constantly, until thoroughly mixed and reduced slightly, about 2 minutes. Transfer chile mixture to large bowl and let cool for 15 minutes.

2   Add swordfish to bowl with chile mixture and stir gently with rubber spatula to coat fish. Cover and refrigerate for at least 30 minutes or up to 2 hours.

3A   For a charcoal grill Open bottom vent completely. Light large chimney starter mounded with charcoal briquettes (7 quarts). When top coals are partially covered with ash, pour evenly over grill. Set cooking grate in place, cover, and open lid vent completely. Heat grill until hot, about 5 minutes.

3B   For a gas grill Turn all burners to high; cover; and heat grill until hot, about 15 minutes. Leave all burners on high.

4   Clean and oil cooking grate. Brush both sides of pineapple with remaining 1 tablespoon oil. Grill swordfish, pineapple, and jalapeño until they have begun to brown, 3 to 5 minutes. Using thin spatula, flip fish, pineapple, and jalapeño. Cover and continue to cook until second sides of pineapple and jalapeño are browned and swordfish registers 140 degrees, 3 to 5 minutes. Transfer fish

to large platter, flake into pieces, and tent with aluminum foil. Transfer pineapple and jalapeño to cutting board.

5   Working in batches, grill tortillas, turning as needed, until lightly charred, 30 to 60 seconds per side; wrap tightly in foil to keep soft.

6   When cool enough to handle, chop pineapple and jalapeño fine. Transfer to medium bowl and stir in bell pepper, cilantro, and remaining ¼ cup lime juice. Season with salt to taste. Top tortillas with flaked fish, pineapple salsa, lettuce, and avocado. Serve with lime wedges and extra cilantro.

Flare Trade

Flat-Top Grill   Turn all burners to medium-high and heat griddle until hot, about 10 minutes. Leave all burners on medium-high. Clean griddle and proceed with step 4. Clean griddle again before heating tortillas.

Open Fire   Prepare medium-hot single-level fire in open-fire grill. Set cooking grate at least 6 inches from coals and flames and heat grill until hot, about 5 minutes. Proceed with step 4.

Smoked Salmon Tacos

SERVES 4 **TOTAL TIME** 1 hour, plus 4 hours chilling

Salmon

- 1 **cup packed brown sugar for salting**
- ¼ **cup kosher salt for salting**
- 1 **tablespoon granulated garlic**
- 1 **(2-pound) center-cut, skin-on salmon fillet, about 1½ inches thick**
- 1 **cup wood chips**
- 2 **tablespoons apricot preserves**
- 1 **tablespoon water**

Tacos

- 12 **(6-inch) flour tortillas**
- ½ **cup mayonnaise**
- ¼ **cup spicy brown mustard**
- 2 **teaspoons lemon juice**
- ¼ **teaspoon ground cumin**
- 1 **small Granny Smith apple, peeled and chopped fine**
- 1 **small celery rib, chopped fine**
- 1 **small carrot, peeled and shredded**
- 3 **ounces (3 cups) mesclun**

Flare Trade

Smoker Heat and maintain smoker temperature of 250 to 275 degrees following manufacturer's guidelines and tips on page 15. Clean and oil smoker grate, then center salmon on grate. Proceed with step 5.

Why This Recipe Works Once you taste the sweet-smoky fish, creamy mustard sauce, and crunchy slaw in these creative California-style tacos, you'll forget how unexpected they sound as taco ingredients. An apricot glaze heightens the salmon's appealing sweetness. Green apple, celery, and carrot come together as a crisp, satisfying slaw, while spicy brown mustard punches up the sauce. If using Arctic char or wild salmon, cook the fillets until they reach 130 degrees (for medium) and start checking for doneness early. If you can find them, applewood chips impart the best flavor to the fish; however, hickory chips are widely available and work fine here. To ensure even cooking, buy a whole center-cut salmon fillet and cut it into four equal pieces. Note that the seasoned fillets must be refrigerated for at least 4 hours before grilling. Creating nonstick conditions for the grill grate is key here (see page 9). If you'd like to use wood chunks when using a charcoal grill, substitute one medium wood chunk for the wood chip packet

1 **For the salmon** Combine sugar, salt, and granulated garlic in bowl. Cut salmon crosswise into 4 equal fillets. Transfer salmon and sugar mixture to 1-gallon zipper-lock bag. Press out air, seal bag, and turn to evenly coat salmon with sugar mixture. Refrigerate for at least 4 hours or up to 24 hours.

2 Using large piece of heavy-duty aluminum foil, wrap chips in 8 by 4½-inch foil packet. (Make sure chips do not poke holes in sides or bottom of packet. If using gas, make sure there are no more than 2 layers of foil on bottom of packet.) Cut 2 evenly spaced 2-inch slits in top of packet.

3 Remove salmon from sugar mixture; discard mixture. Rinse excess sugar mixture from salmon and pat salmon dry with paper towels. Whisk preserves and water together in small bowl; microwave until mixture is fluid, about 30 seconds.

4A **For a charcoal grill** Open bottom vent completely. Light large chimney starter one-third filled with charcoal briquettes (2 quarts). When top coals are partially covered with ash, pour evenly over half of grill. Place wood chip packet on coals. Set cooking grate in place, cover, and open lid vent completely. Heat grill until hot and wood chips are smoking, about 5 minutes.

4B **For a gas grill** Remove cooking grate and place wood chip packet directly on primary burner. Set cooking grate in place; turn all burners to high; cover; and heat grill until hot and wood chips are smoking,

15 to 25 minutes. Turn primary burner to medium and turn off other burner(s). (Adjust primary burner as needed to maintain grill temperature between 250 and 275 degrees.)

5 Clean and oil cooking grate. Brush tops and sides of salmon fillets evenly with apricot mixture. Place fillets, skin side down, on cooler side of grill with thicker ends facing fire. Cover grill (position lid vent over salmon if using charcoal) and cook until centers of fillets register 135 degrees (for medium-well), 28 to 35 minutes. Transfer salmon to plate, tent with aluminum foil, and let rest for 5 minutes. (If skin sticks to cooking grate, insert fish spatula between skin and fillet to separate and lift fillet from skin.)

6 Working in batches, grill tortillas on hotter side of grill, turning as needed, until lightly charred, 30 to 60 seconds per side; wrap tightly in foil to keep soft.

7 **For the tacos** Meanwhile, whisk mayonnaise, mustard, lemon juice, and cumin together in bowl. Combine apple, celery, and carrot in second bowl.

8 Remove and discard salmon skin. Flake salmon into bite-size pieces and season with salt to taste. Divide salmon evenly among tortillas, about ⅓ cup per tortilla. Serve, topping each taco with desired amounts of mesclun, mayonnaise mixture, and apple mixture.

Breakfast Burritos with Black Beans and Chorizo

SERVES 4   **TOTAL TIME** 1 hour

Chipotle Sour Cream

- ¼ cup sour cream
- 2 tablespoons minced canned chipotle chile in adobo sauce
- 2 teaspoons lime juice
- 1 garlic clove, minced
- ¼ teaspoon cayenne pepper
- ¼ teaspoon table salt

Burritos

- 2 tablespoons vegetable oil, divided
- ½ onion, chopped fine
- ¼ teaspoon table salt
- 1 (15-ounce) can black beans, rinsed
- ⅓ cup water
- ¼ cup chopped pickled jalapeños (optional)
- 8 ounces Mexican-style chorizo sausage, casings removed
- 8 large eggs, beaten
- 3 ounces sharp cheddar cheese, shredded (¾ cup)
- 4 (10-inch) flour tortillas

Why This Recipe Works Grilled burritos for breakfast? You bet. Stoke a fire first thing in the morning and enjoy breakfast al fresco. And if you've got your outdoor prep station set up (see page 24), you can assemble the burritos outside as well. The fillings of beans and cheesy chorizo with eggs are made in rapid succession in a cast-iron skillet and then folded into grill-warmed tortillas along with a zesty chipotle sour cream. Grilled seam side down and brushed with oil, the burritos hold together nicely while turning golden brown. Use fresh Mexican-style chorizo, not the dry-cured Spanish version. For less spice, omit the cayenne and reduce the chipotle chile to 1 tablespoon. You will need a 12-inch cast-iron skillet .

1 **For the chipotle sour cream** Stir all ingredients together in bowl; set aside.

2A **For a charcoal grill** Open bottom vent completely. Light large chimney starter filled with charcoal briquettes (6 quarts). When top coals are partially covered with ash, pour evenly over grill. Set cooking grate in place, cover, and open lid vent completely. Heat grill until hot, about 5 minutes.

2B **For a gas grill** Turn all burners to high; cover; and heat grill until hot, about 15 minutes. Leave all burners on high.

3 **For the burritos** Center 12-inch cast-iron skillet on cooking grate, cover, and heat skillet for 5 minutes. Heat 1 tablespoon oil in skillet until shimmering. Add onion and salt and cook until softened, about 5 minutes. Stir in beans and water and cook until beans are heated through and liquid begins to thicken, 2 to 4 minutes. Off heat, using potato masher or fork, mash beans until about half are broken down. Transfer bean mixture to bowl; stir in jalapeño, if using; and cover to keep warm. Wipe skillet clean with paper towels.

4 Cook chorizo in now-empty skillet centered on grill, breaking up meat with spatula until well browned, 5 to 8 minutes. Add eggs and, using spatula, constantly and firmly scrape along bottom and sides of skillet until eggs begin to clump and spatula leaves trail on bottom of skillet, about 2 minutes. Off heat, gently fold eggs until clumped and wet, about 30 seconds. Fold in cheddar and cover to keep warm.

5 Using tongs, warm 2 tortillas at a time on grill until warm and pliable, about 10 seconds per side.

6 Arrange tortillas on work surface. Spread 1½ tablespoons chipotle sour cream across bottom third of each tortilla, leaving 1-inch border. Divide black bean mixture and egg mixture evenly over chipotle sour cream. Working with 1 burrito at a time, fold sides of tortilla over filling, then fold up bottom of tortilla and roll tightly around filling.

7 Brush burritos with remaining 1 tablespoon oil and place burritos seam side down on cooking grate. Grill until crisp and golden, about 30 seconds per side. Serve.

Flare Trade

Open Fire Prepare hot single-level fire in open-fire grill. Set cooking grate at least 6 inches from coals and flames and heat grill until hot, about 5 minutes. Proceed with step 3.

3 Weeknight Dinners

2 ounces blue cheese, crumbled (½ cup)

6 tablespoons extra-virgin olive oil, divided

3 tablespoons red wine vinegar

2 teaspoons table salt, divided

1 teaspoon pepper, divided

3 romaine lettuce hearts (6 ounces each), halved lengthwise

2 ripe but firm avocados, halved and pitted

4 (6- to 8-ounce) boneless, skinless chicken breasts, trimmed and pounded to ¾-inch thickness

8 ounces cherry tomatoes, halved

4 hard-cooked large eggs, halved

6 slices bacon, cooked and crumbled (½ cup)

1 tablespoon chopped fresh chives

Why This Recipe Works Time spent over live fire deepens the flavor of avocados and romaine lettuce to give this classic salad a smoky outdoor twist. You can prep most of the other ingredients—the blue cheese dressing, hard-cooked eggs, and crispy bacon—ahead, if you like, which makes mealtime cooking and assembly a snap. You'll grill boneless, skinless chicken breasts first; while they rest, it's time for the lettuce and avocados to pick up some browning over the fire. Slice the chicken and arrange it on a platter with the lettuce, avocados, eggs, bacon, and juicy cherry tomatoes; spoon the chunky, cheesy dressing over everything; and you've got an outdoor summertime meal that's as impressive as it is easy.

1   Combine blue cheese, ¼ cup oil, vinegar, ½ teaspoon salt, and ¼ teaspoon pepper in bowl; set aside. Brush remaining 2 tablespoons oil onto cut sides of lettuce and avocados and sprinkle with ½ teaspoon salt and ½ teaspoon pepper. Pat chicken dry with paper towels and sprinkle with remaining 1 teaspoon salt and remaining ¼ teaspoon pepper.

2A   **For a charcoal grill** Open bottom vent completely. Light large chimney starter filled with charcoal briquettes (6 quarts). When top coals are partially covered with ash, pour evenly over grill. Set cooking grate in place, cover, and open lid vent completely. Heat grill until hot, about 5 minutes.

2B   **For a gas grill** Turn all burners to high; cover; and heat grill until hot, about 15 minutes. Leave all burners on high.

3   Clean and oil cooking grate. Grill chicken until browned and registers 160 degrees, 10 to 14 minutes, flipping as needed. Transfer chicken to cutting board and tent with aluminum foil. Grill lettuce and avocados, cut sides down, until charred in spots, about 2 minutes. Transfer to cutting board.

4   Using spoon, scoop avocado flesh from skin. Cut lettuce in half lengthwise. Slice chicken ¾ inch thick. Arrange lettuce, avocados, chicken, tomatoes, and eggs on serving platter. Top salad with bacon and drizzle with dressing. Sprinkle with chives. Serve.

Flare Trade

Open Fire Prepare hot single-level fire in open-fire grill. Set cooking grate at least 6 inches from coals and flames and heat grill until hot, about 5 minutes. Proceed with step 3.

Grilled Garam Masala Chicken, Tomatoes, and Naan with Chutney

SERVES 4   TOTAL TIME 50 minutes

- 2 pounds ripe but firm tomatoes, cored and halved along equator
- ¼ cup extra-virgin olive oil, divided
- 1 teaspoon table salt, divided
- ½ teaspoon pepper, divided
- 4 naans
- 5 teaspoons garam masala, divided
- 4 (6- to 8-ounce) boneless, skinless chicken breasts, trimmed and pounded to ¾-inch thickness
- ¼ cup mango chutney, plus extra for serving

Why This Recipe Works Reaching for tomatoes might not be your first instinct when firing up the grill, but a little time over the flames transforms these late-summer beauties into much more than a simple sandwich layer. The grill brings the halved tomatoes' juices to the surface, creating a top-notch saucy situation once they're cut into. Sweet-tangy mango chutney spread over the grilled chicken mingles with the juicy charred tomatoes. Naan, topped with olive oil and garam masala before a brief stint on the grill, is ideal for scooping up every last bit of sauce.

1   Toss tomatoes with 1 tablespoon oil, ½ teaspoon salt, and ¼ teaspoon pepper in bowl. Let sit for at least 15 minutes or up to 1 hour.

2   Meanwhile, brush naans with 2 tablespoons oil and sprinkle with 2 teaspoons garam masala. Pat chicken dry with paper towels, rub all over with remaining 1 tablespoon oil, and sprinkle with remaining ½ teaspoon salt, remaining ¼ teaspoon pepper, and remaining 1 tablespoon garam masala.

3A   For a charcoal grill Open bottom vent completely. Light large chimney starter filled with charcoal briquettes (6 quarts). When top coals are partially covered with ash, pour evenly over grill. Set cooking grate in place, cover, and open lid vent completely. Heat grill until hot, about 5 minutes.

3B   For a gas grill Turn all burners to high; cover; and heat grill until hot, about 15 minutes. Leave all burners on high.

4   Clean and oil cooking grate. Grill chicken (covered if using gas) until browned and registers 160 degrees, 10 to 14 minutes, flipping as needed. Transfer chicken to serving platter and top with mango chutney. Tent with aluminum foil and let rest while grilling tomatoes and naans.

5   Add tomatoes, cut sides down, and naans to now-empty grill and grill (covered if using gas) until tomatoes are charred, beginning to soften, and juices bubble and naans are lightly charred, 4 to 6 minutes per side for tomatoes and about 1 minute per side for naan. Transfer tomatoes and naans to platter with chicken as they finish cooking. Serve chicken, tomatoes, and naans with extra mango chutney.

Flare Trade

Open Fire Prepare hot single-level fire in open-fire grill. Set cooking grate at least 6 inches from coals and flames and heat grill until hot, about 5 minutes. Proceed with step 4.

Grilled Pesto Chicken with Cucumber and Cantaloupe Salad

SERVES 4   **TOTAL TIME** 1¼ hours

4 cups fresh basil leaves

¾ cup plus 2 tablespoons extra-virgin olive oil, divided

5 garlic cloves, peeled

6½ teaspoons lemon juice, divided

1¼ teaspoons table salt, divided

¾ teaspoon pepper, divided

2 ounces Parmesan cheese, grated (1 cup)

4 (12-ounce) bone-in split chicken breasts, trimmed

1 cup ½-inch cantaloupe pieces

¼ English cucumber, halved lengthwise and sliced thin crosswise (1 cup)

2 ounces feta cheese, crumbled (½ cup)

2 tablespoons chopped fresh mint

Flare Trade

Open Fire Prepare hot half-grill fire in open-fire grill. Set cooking grate at least 6 inches from coals and flames and heat grill until hot, about 5 minutes. Grill chicken on cooler side of grill, turning and moving as needed to ensure even browning, until chicken registers 160 degrees, 30 to 40 minutes.

Why This Recipe Works Pesto is rightly used for so much more than pasta, and here it's the defining flavor in a vibrant grilled chicken dish. But how do you infuse the chicken with enough basil and garlic flavor so that these elements still shine after their stint over the flames? The answer starts with homemade pesto, which has a stronger, fresher flavor than store-bought. The potent blend is divided and used in three ways: stuffed into pockets cut in each bone-in breast, added to a marinade, and made into a sauce to serve with the chicken after it's grilled. A minty salad of cucumber and cantaloupe with crumbled feta makes a cooling, easy side.

1 Process basil, ½ cup oil, garlic, 1½ tablespoons lemon juice, ¾ teaspoon salt, and ⅛ teaspoon pepper in food processor until smooth, about 1 minute, scraping down bowl as needed. Remove ¼ cup pesto from processor and reserve for marinating chicken. Add Parmesan to pesto in processor and pulse until incorporated, about 3 pulses. Remove ¼ cup Parmesan pesto from processor and reserve for stuffing chicken. Add ¼ cup oil to Parmesan pesto in processor and pulse until combined, about 3 pulses; set aside for saucing cooked chicken.

2 Starting on thick side of breast closest to breastbone, cut horizontal pocket in each breast, stopping ½ inch from edge so halves remain attached. Season chicken, inside and out, with remaining ½ teaspoon salt and ½ teaspoon pepper. Place 1 tablespoon Parmesan pesto reserved for stuffing in pocket of each breast. Evenly space 2 pieces of 12-inch-long kitchen twine beneath each breast and tie to secure; trim excess twine. Rub stuffed breasts all over with pesto reserved for marinating; set aside.

3 Meanwhile, whisk remaining 2 tablespoons oil, remaining 2 teaspoons lemon juice, and remaining ⅛ teaspoon pepper in large bowl. Add cantaloupe, cucumber, feta, and mint and toss to combine; set aside.

4A For a charcoal grill Open bottom vent completely. Light large chimney starter filled with charcoal briquettes (6 quarts). When top coals are partially covered with ash, pour evenly over half of grill. Set cooking grate in place, cover, and open lid vent completely. Heat grill until hot, about 5 minutes.

4B For a gas grill Turn all burners to high; cover; and heat grill until hot, about 15 minutes. Turn all burners to medium-high. (Adjust burners as needed to maintain grill temperature of 350 degrees.)

5 Clean and oil cooking grate. Grill chicken skin side up (over cooler side if using charcoal), covered, until chicken registers 160 degrees, 25 to 35 minutes.

6 Flip chicken skin side down. If using charcoal, slide chicken to hotter side of grill. Cover and cook until well browned, 5 to 10 minutes. Transfer chicken to platter, tent with aluminum foil, and let rest for 5 minutes. Remove twine from chicken and carve meat from bone. Serve chicken with cucumber salad, passing Parmesan pesto sauce separately.

Grilled Chicken Thighs with Butternut Squash and Cilantro Vinaigrette

SERVES 4   **TOTAL TIME** 45 minutes

½ cup vegetable oil, divided

2 tablespoons Thai red curry paste

2 teaspoons grated lime zest, divided, plus 2 tablespoons juice

1 teaspoon table salt, divided

¼ teaspoon plus ⅛ teaspoon pepper, divided

8 (3- to 5-ounce) boneless, skinless chicken thighs, trimmed

2 pounds butternut squash, peeled, halved lengthwise, seeded, and sliced crosswise ½ inch thick

2 cups fresh cilantro leaves

Why This Recipe Works If you've never grilled butternut squash, you're missing out: This winter squash is simply fantastic with a bit of char. Half-inch-thick slices are easy to maneuver on the grill, and you might be surprised to learn that they cook through in the same amount of time it takes for curry paste–rubbed chicken thighs to get perfectly browned. (The boneless chicken and squash half-moons also cook quickly and easily, without burning, on a flat-top grill.) A drizzle of bright cilantro-lime vinaigrette offsets the sweetness of the squash and the richness of the chicken thighs, and is the only finishing touch you'll need.

1 Whisk 2 tablespoons oil, curry paste, 1 teaspoon lime zest, ½ teaspoon salt, and ¼ teaspoon pepper together in large bowl. Add chicken and toss to coat. Toss squash with 2 tablespoons oil, ¼ teaspoon salt, and remaining ⅛ teaspoon pepper in second bowl.

2 Pulse cilantro, remaining 1 teaspoon lime zest, lime juice, remaining ¼ cup oil, and remaining ¼ teaspoon salt in food processor until cilantro is finely chopped, 6 to 8 pulses, scraping down sides of bowl as needed.

3A For a charcoal grill Open bottom vent completely. Light large chimney starter filled with charcoal briquettes (6 quarts). When top coals are partially covered with ash, pour evenly over grill. Set cooking grate in place, cover, and open lid vent completely. Heat grill until hot, about 5 minutes.

3B For a gas grill Turn all burners to high; cover; and heat grill until hot, about 15 minutes. Turn all burners to medium-high.

4 Clean and oil cooking grate. Grill chicken and squash (covered if using gas) until both are well browned and tender and chicken registers 175 degrees, 16 to 20 minutes, flipping as needed for even browning. Transfer chicken and squash to serving platter. Serve chicken and squash with cilantro vinaigrette.

Flare Trade

Flat-Top Grill Turn all burners to medium-high and heat griddle until hot, about 10 minutes. Leave all burners on medium-high. Clean griddle and proceed with step 4.

Sweet and Tangy Barbecue Chicken Thighs with Sweet Potatoes and Scallions

SERVES 4   **TOTAL TIME** 1½ hours

1½ pounds sweet potatoes, unpeeled, sliced into ½-inch-thick rounds

1 teaspoon table salt, divided

1 teaspoon pepper, divided

2 tablespoons plus 1 teaspoon extra-virgin olive oil, divided

12 scallions, trimmed

8 (5- to 7-ounce) bone-in chicken thighs, trimmed

¾ cup ketchup

3 tablespoons molasses

1 tablespoon cider vinegar

1 teaspoon hot sauce

⅛ teaspoon liquid smoke (optional)

Flare Trade

Open Fire Prepare hot half-grill fire in open-fire grill. Set cooking grate at least 6 inches from coals and flames and heat grill until hot, about 5 minutes. Grill chicken on cooler side, turning and moving as needed to ensure even browning, until chicken registers 175 degrees, 35 to 45 minutes. Move chicken to hotter side, brush with ¼ cup sauce, flip, and cook until browned, 1 to 2 minutes. Brush with ¼ cup sauce, flip, and cook until well browned, 1 to 2 minutes. Transfer chicken to cooler side and proceed with step 5.

Why This Recipe Works Bone-in chicken brushed with tangy barbecue sauce is a classic, but for perfectly crisp skin and succulent chicken, hold the sauce—at least at first. This tried-and-true cooking method starts chicken thighs unadorned over indirect heat to get a jump on cooking before you give them a first coat; after more cooking, they're ready for intense heat and another lacquering of sauce. Thick rounds of parcooked sweet potatoes make a substantial side; flip them often while grilling to brown them just right. Chopped grilled scallions, tossed with the cooked sweet potatoes, add savory notes and pops of green.

1   Toss potatoes with 1 tablespoon water, ½ teaspoon salt, and ½ teaspoon pepper in bowl. Cover and microwave until tender, 6 to 10 minutes, stirring halfway; drain well and toss with 2 tablespoons oil. Toss scallions with remaining 1 teaspoon oil. Pat chicken dry with paper towels and sprinkle with remaining ½ teaspoon salt and remaining ½ teaspoon pepper. Combine ketchup; molasses; vinegar; hot sauce; and liquid smoke, if using, in bowl. Season with salt and pepper to taste.

2A   For a charcoal grill Open bottom vent halfway. Light large chimney starter mounded with charcoal briquettes (7 quarts). When top coals are partially covered with ash, pour evenly over half of grill. Set cooking grate in place, cover, and open lid vent halfway. Heat grill until hot, about 5 minutes.

2B   For a gas grill Turn all burners to high; cover; and heat grill until hot, about 15 minutes. Leave primary burner on high and turn off other burner(s). (Adjust primary burner as needed to maintain grill temperature between 400 and 450 degrees; if using 3-burner grill, adjust primary burner and second burner.)

3   Clean and oil cooking grate. Place chicken, skin side down, on cooler side of grill. Cover and cook for 20 minutes. Rearrange chicken, keeping skin side down, so that pieces that were closest to edge of grill are now closer to heat source and vice versa. Brush chicken with ¼ cup sauce, cover, and continue to cook until chicken registers 175 degrees, 15 to 20 minutes longer.

4   Move chicken to hotter side of grill, keeping skin side down, and cook until skin is lightly charred, about 5 minutes. Flip chicken skin side up and brush with ¼ cup sauce. Cook until flesh side is lightly browned, 1 to 2 minutes. Transfer chicken to cooler side of grill to keep warm while cooking potatoes and scallions.

5   Add potatoes and scallions to hotter side of grill and cook (covered if using gas) until lightly charred on both sides, about 3 to 5 minutes per side. Transfer scallions to cutting board, let cool slightly, and cut into 1-inch pieces. Toss scallions with sweet potatoes and serve with chicken, passing remaining ½ cup sauce separately.

Paprika and Lime–Rubbed Chicken with Grilled Vegetable Succotash

SERVES 4 **TOTAL TIME** 55 minutes

12 ounces cherry tomatoes

1 red onion, sliced into ½-inch-thick rounds

3 ears corn, husks and silk removed

¼ cup extra-virgin olive oil, divided

1 teaspoon table salt, divided

¾ teaspoon pepper, divided

1 tablespoon plus ½ teaspoon smoked hot paprika, divided

4 teaspoons grated lime zest, divided, plus 2 tablespoons juice (2 limes), plus lime wedges for serving

1½ teaspoons packed dark brown sugar

1 teaspoon ground cumin

3 pounds bone-in chicken pieces (split breasts cut in half crosswise, drumsticks, and/or thighs), trimmed

3 tablespoons minced fresh cilantro, divided

2 garlic cloves, minced

1 (15-ounce) can butter beans, rinsed

Why This Recipe Works Smoked paprika, lime zest, and cumin flavor a spice rub that coats bone-in chicken parts. Cooking the chicken on the cooler side of the grill avoids flare-ups while still giving it great flavor and char. Ears of corn, onion rounds, and skewered cherry tomatoes soften and pick up grill flavor over the hotter side while the chicken cooks. After chopping the onions and cutting the corn off the cobs, you'll toss the vegetables with a simple dressing that includes more lime zest and paprika to reinforce the flavors of the chicken, plus some cilantro. Creamy, mild canned butter beans round out the grilled succotash. You will need four 12-inch metal skewers.

1 Thread tomatoes onto four 12-inch metal skewers. Push toothpick horizontally through each onion round to keep rings intact while grilling. Brush corn, onion, and tomato skewers with 2 tablespoons oil and sprinkle with ½ teaspoon salt and ¼ teaspoon pepper.

2 Combine 1 tablespoon paprika, 1 tablespoon lime zest, sugar, cumin, remaining ½ teaspoon salt, and remaining ½ teaspoon pepper together in large bowl. Pat chicken dry with paper towels, transfer to bowl with spice mixture, and stir to coat evenly.

3A For a charcoal grill Open bottom vent completely. Light large chimney starter filled with charcoal briquettes (6 quarts). When top coals are partially covered with ash, pour two-thirds evenly over half of grill, then pour remaining coals over other half of grill. Set cooking grate in place, cover, and open lid vent completely. Heat grill until hot, about 5 minutes.

3B For a gas grill Turn all burners to high; cover; and heat grill until hot, about 15 minutes. Leave primary burner on high and turn other burner(s) to low.

4 Clean and oil cooking grate. Place chicken, skin side down, on cooler side of grill. Cover and cook until skin is well browned and slightly charred, breasts register 160 degrees, and drumsticks/thighs register 175 degrees, 20 to 30 minutes, flipping and rearranging as needed so all pieces get equal exposure to heat source. Transfer chicken pieces to serving platter as they finish cooking, tent with aluminum foil, and let rest.

5   While chicken cooks, place corn, onion, and tomato skewers on hotter side of grill. Cook vegetables covered, flipping as needed, until tomato skins blister, about 2 minutes, and corn and onion are lightly charred, 8 to 10 minutes. Transfer to cutting board as they finish cooking.

6   Remove toothpicks from onion rings. Chop grilled onion and cut corn kernels from cobs. Whisk remaining 1 teaspoon lime zest, lime juice, 2 tablespoons cilantro, garlic, remaining ½ teaspoon paprika, and remaining 2 tablespoons oil together in large bowl. Add beans, tomatoes, chopped onion, and corn to bowl and toss to combine. Season with salt and pepper to taste. Sprinkle remaining 1 tablespoon cilantro over chicken. Serve with succotash and lime wedges.

Flare Trade

Open Fire   Prepare hot half-grill fire in open-fire grill. Set cooking grate at least 6 inches from coals and flames and heat grill until hot, about 5 minutes. Proceed with step 4, extending cooking time to 40 to 50 minutes.

Stir-Fried Cumin Beef

SERVES 4   TOTAL TIME 45 minutes

1 tablespoon water

¼ teaspoon baking soda

1 pound flank steak, trimmed, cut with grain into 2- to 2½-inch-wide strips, each strip sliced against grain ¼ inch thick

¼ cup vegetable oil, divided

4 garlic cloves, minced

1 tablespoon grated fresh ginger

1 tablespoon cumin seeds, ground

2 teaspoons Sichuan chili powder

1¼ teaspoons Sichuan peppercorns, ground

½ teaspoon table salt, divided

1 tablespoon Shaoxing wine or dry sherry

1 tablespoon soy sauce

2 teaspoons molasses

½ teaspoon cornstarch

½ small onion, sliced thin

2 tablespoons coarsely chopped fresh cilantro

Why This Recipe Works Stir-frying and cooking outdoors isn't an either/or proposition. Take your wok outside, where the powerful heat generated by corralled charcoal encourages amazing browning on this cumin beef with aromatic garlic and onion, lightly glossed in a soy-based glaze. A quick soak in a baking soda solution keeps the thin strips of steak tender as they cook. As for the spices, grinding whole cumin seeds and Sichuan peppercorns releases vibrant compounds that give the dish plenty of fragrance, while Sichuan chili powder adds heat. You'll stir-fry the beef until its juices reduce to a clingy fond, and then toss in the garlic and onion at the end, so the onion retains a light crunch. You can substitute 1 tablespoon ground cumin for the cumin seeds. If you can't find Sichuan chili powder, gochugaru (Korean red pepper flakes) are a good substitute. Another alternative is 1¾ teaspoons of ancho chile powder plus ¼ teaspoon of cayenne pepper. There is no substitute for Sichuan peppercorns. You will need a 13 by 9-inch disposable aluminum roasting pan. A 12-inch cast-iron skillet can be used in place of the wok.

1 Combine water and baking soda in medium bowl. Add beef and toss to coat. Let sit at room temperature for 5 minutes. While beef rests, combine 2 tablespoons oil, garlic, and ginger in small bowl. Combine cumin, chili powder, Sichuan peppercorns, and ¼ teaspoon salt in second small bowl. Add Shaoxing wine, soy sauce, molasses, cornstarch, and remaining ¼ teaspoon salt to beef mixture. Toss until well combined.

2 Using skewer, poke 12 holes in bottom of disposable pan. Open bottom vent of charcoal grill completely and place disposable pan in center. Light large chimney starter three-quarters filled with charcoal briquettes (4½ quarts). When top coals are partially covered with ash, pour into disposable pan. Set cooking grate in place, cover, and open lid vent completely. Heat grill until hot, about 5 minutes.

3 Center 14-inch flat-bottomed carbon-steel wok on cooking grate over coals. Heat 1 tablespoon oil in wok until just smoking. Using tongs, add half of beef mixture and toss slowly but constantly until exuded meat juices have evaporated and meat begins to sizzle, 2 to 6 minutes. Transfer to clean bowl. Repeat with remaining 1 tablespoon oil and remaining beef mixture.

4   Add garlic mixture to now-empty wok and cook, stirring constantly, until fragrant, 15 to 30 seconds. Add onion and cook, tossing slowly but constantly with tongs, until onion begins to soften, 1 to 2 minutes. Return beef to wok and toss to combine. Sprinkle cumin mixture over beef and toss until onion takes on pale orange color. Transfer to serving platter, sprinkle with cilantro, and serve immediately.

Flare Trade

Gas Grill   Turn all burners to high; cover; and heat grill until hot, about 15 minutes. Leave all burners on high. Center 12-inch cast-iron skillet on cooking grate and proceed with step 3.

Open Fire   Prepare hot single-level fire in open-fire grill. Set cooking grate at least 6 inches from coals and flames and heat grill until hot, about 5 minutes. Proceed with step 3.

Grilled Steak Fajitas

¾ cup pineapple juice

½ cup plus 1 tablespoon vegetable oil, divided

¼ cup soy sauce

3 garlic cloves, minced

2 pounds skirt steak, trimmed and cut crosswise into 6 equal pieces

3 yellow, red, orange, or green bell peppers

1 large red onion, sliced into ½-inch-thick rounds

1 teaspoon table salt, divided

½ teaspoon pepper, divided

12 (6-inch) flour tortillas

1 tablespoon chopped fresh cilantro

Why This Recipe Works Grilling accentuates the bold flavors of fajitas and suits their casual presentation: tender steak nestled into soft flour tortillas along with onions and colorful bell peppers. Skirt steak, the classic choice, has big beefy flavor, and a marinade of soy sauce, garlic, and sweet-tangy pineapple juice amps up the meatiness even more. Cooking the steak to medium or medium-well means that it's firmer and thus easier to eat when combined with the vegetables. You'll char the bell peppers and onion over a hot fire and then move them to a pan on the cooler side of the grill to steam before tossing them with some marinade. Wrapping the tortillas in foil makes it easy to warm them gently on the grill. Serve with pico de gallo, Charred Guacamole (page 32), sour cream, and lime wedges. You will need a 13 by 9-inch disposable aluminum roasting pan.

1 Whisk pineapple juice, ½ cup oil, soy sauce, and garlic together in bowl. Reserve ¼ cup marinade. Transfer remaining 1¼ cups marinade to 1-gallon zipper-lock bag. Add steak, press out air, seal bag, and turn to distribute marinade. Refrigerate until ready to grill.

2 Using paring knife, cut around stems of bell peppers and remove cores and seeds. Push toothpick horizontally through each onion round to keep rings intact while grilling. Brush bell peppers and onion evenly with remaining 1 tablespoon oil and sprinkle with ¼ teaspoon salt and ¼ teaspoon pepper. Wrap tortillas in aluminum foil; set aside.

3A For a charcoal grill Open bottom vent completely. Light large chimney starter filled with charcoal briquettes (6 quarts). When top coals are partially covered with ash, pour evenly over half of grill. Set cooking grate in place, cover, and open lid vent completely. Heat grill until hot, about 5 minutes.

3B For a gas grill Turn all burners to high; cover; and heat grill until hot, about 15 minutes. Leave primary burner on high and turn other burner(s) to low.

4 Clean and oil cooking grate. Remove steak from marinade and pat dry with paper towels; discard marinade. Sprinkle steak with remaining ¾ teaspoon salt and remaining ¼ teaspoon pepper. Place bell peppers and onion on hotter side of grill and place tortilla packet on cooler side of grill. Cook (covered if using gas) until vegetables are charred and tender, 8 to 13 minutes, flipping and moving as needed for even cooking, and until tortillas are warmed through, about 10 minutes, flipping halfway through cooking.

5 Remove tortillas from grill; keep wrapped and set aside. Transfer vegetables to disposable pan, cover pan tightly with foil, and place on cooler side of grill. (If using gas, cover grill and allow hotter side to reheat for 5 minutes.) Place steak on hotter side of grill and cook (covered if using gas) until charred and meat registers 135 to 140 degrees (for medium to medium-well), 2 to 4 minutes per side. Transfer steak to cutting board and tent with foil. Remove disposable pan from grill.

6 Carefully remove foil from disposable pan (steam may escape). Slice bell peppers into thin strips. Remove toothpicks from onion rounds and separate rings. Return vegetables to disposable pan and toss with cilantro and reserved marinade. Season with salt and pepper to taste. Slice steak thin against grain. Transfer steak and vegetables to serving platter. Serve with warmed tortillas.

Flare Trade

Flat-Top Grill Turn all burners to medium-high and heat griddle until hot, about 10 minutes. Leave all burners on medium-high. Clean griddle. Halve and thinly slice bell peppers and onion and toss with 1 tablespoon oil, ¼ teaspoon salt, and ¼ teaspoon pepper. Arrange vegetables over half of griddle and cook, tossing frequently, until well browned, 7 to 10 minutes. Cook steak on open side of griddle until meat registers 135 to 140 degrees, 2 to 4 minutes per side. Turn all burners to medium. Heat tortillas on griddle, turning as needed, until charred, 30 to 60 seconds per side; wrap in foil. Assemble fajitas as directed in step 6.

Grilled Steak Tips, Broccoli, and Red Onion with Anchovy-Garlic Butter

SERVES 4   **TOTAL TIME** 45 minutes

- 6 tablespoons unsalted butter
- 3 anchovy fillets, rinsed and minced
- 3 garlic cloves, minced
- ¼ teaspoon red pepper flakes
- 1 tablespoon lemon juice
- 2 pounds sirloin steak tips, trimmed and cut into 1-inch chunks
- 2 teaspoons table salt, divided
- 1 teaspoon pepper, divided
- ¼ cup extra-virgin olive oil, divided
- 2 tablespoons water
- 1 pound broccoli crowns, cut into 3-inch wedges
- 1 red onion, sliced into ½-inch-thick rounds
- 2 tablespoons minced fresh chives

Why This Recipe Works Steak tips are a beloved New England choice for fast grilling, and here you'll dress them up with vegetables and a bistro-inspired butter sauce. Threaded onto skewers, the tips get beautifully charred over the fire. Brushing oil onto onion rounds prevents them from sticking to the grate as they cook. Wedges of broccoli are tossed in a mixture of oil and water; the water turns to steam on the grill, an ingenious little trick to help evenly cook the broccoli. The grilled elements are all tied together with an umami-rich sauce flavored with garlic, anchovies, lemon, and pepper flakes. You will need four 12-inch metal skewers.

1 Cook butter, anchovies, garlic, and pepper flakes in small saucepan over medium heat, stirring frequently until garlic turns straw-colored, about 4 minutes. Off heat, whisk in lemon juice. Cover to keep warm and set aside.

2 Pat beef dry with paper towels and sprinkle with 1 teaspoon salt and ½ teaspoon pepper. Thread beef onto four 12-inch metal skewers. Whisk 3 tablespoons oil, water, ¾ teaspoon salt, and remaining ½ teaspoon pepper together in large bowl. Add broccoli wedges to oil mixture and toss to coat. Push toothpick horizontally through each onion round to keep rings intact while grilling. Brush onion rounds with remaining 1 tablespoon oil and sprinkle with remaining ¼ teaspoon salt.

3A For a charcoal grill Open bottom vent completely. Light large chimney starter filled with charcoal briquettes (6 quarts). When top coals are partially covered with ash, pour evenly over grill. Set cooking grate in place, cover, and open lid vent completely. Heat grill until hot, about 5 minutes.

3B For a gas grill Turn all burners to high; cover; and heat grill until hot, about 15 minutes. Leave all burners on high.

4 Clean and oil cooking grate. Grill beef, broccoli, and onion until meat is charred and registers 120 to 125 degrees (for medium-rare) and vegetables are crisp-tender and browned, 10 to 12 minutes, flipping as needed. Remove toothpicks from onion rounds. Sprinkle beef and vegetables with chives. Serve with butter sauce.

Flare Trade

Open Fire Prepare hot single-level fire in open-fire grill. Set cooking grate at least 6 inches from coals and flames and heat grill until hot, about 5 minutes. Proceed with step 4.

1 tablespoon ground cumin

1½ teaspoons table salt, divided

½ teaspoon pepper

¾ teaspoon chili powder, divided

1 (1½- to 2-pound) flank steak, 1 inch thick, trimmed

¼ cup mayonnaise

¼ cup grated Pecorino Romano cheese

2 tablespoons minced fresh cilantro

1 tablespoon lime juice, plus lime wedges for serving

1 garlic clove, minced

4 ears corn, husks and silk removed

Why This Recipe Works Steak and corn is a quintessential summertime meal, and this take on it bursts with creamy, spicy, zesty flavors. Rubbing the steak with cumin and chili powder reinforces the smoky quality that the meat picks up on the grill. You'll brush the cheesy elote sauce (which uses Pecorino rather than the traditional cotija cheese) on the corn both before grilling to promote browning and after the corn comes off the grill. Slicing the flank steak against the grain before serving (that is, perpendicular to the orientation of the muscle fibers) makes this relatively tough cut much more tender.

1   Combine cumin, 1 teaspoon salt, pepper, and ½ teaspoon chili powder in bowl. Pat steak dry with paper towels and sprinkle with spice mixture. Combine mayonnaise, Pecorino, cilantro, lime juice, garlic, remaining ½ teaspoon salt, and remaining ¼ teaspoon chili powder in separate bowl. Set aside.

2A   **For a charcoal grill** Open bottom vent completely. Light large chimney starter filled with charcoal briquettes (6 quarts). When top coals are partially covered with ash, pour evenly over grill. Set cooking grate in place, cover, and open lid vent completely. Heat grill until hot, about 5 minutes.

2B   **For a gas grill** Turn all burners to high; cover; and heat grill until hot, about 15 minutes. Leave all burners on high.

3   Clean and oil cooking grate. Grill steak until charred and meat registers 120 to 125 degrees (for medium-rare), 8 to 12 minutes, flipping as needed. Transfer to cutting board and tent with aluminum foil.

4   Brush corn with half of mayonnaise mixture. Grill corn, turning often, until well browned on all sides, about 12 minutes. Transfer to serving platter and brush with remaining mayonnaise mixture. Cut corn in half and slice steak on bias against grain. Serve with lime wedges.

Flare Trade

Open Fire Prepare hot single-level fire in open-fire grill. Set cooking grate at least 6 inches from coals and flames and heat grill until hot, about 5 minutes. Proceed with step 3.

Steak and Vegetables

SERVES 4   TOTAL TIME 1 hour

3 tablespoons unsalted butter, melted

2 tablespoons soy sauce

2 garlic cloves, minced

2 (1-pound) boneless rib-eye steaks, 1½ to 1¾ inches thick, trimmed

2 tablespoons plus 2 teaspoons vegetable oil, divided

1¼ teaspoons white pepper, divided

1 teaspoon table salt, divided

2 zucchini (8 ounces each), halved lengthwise and sliced ¾ inch thick

2 onions, cut into ¾-inch pieces

6 ounces shiitake mushrooms, stemmed and halved if small or quartered if large

2 tablespoons mirin, divided

Why This Recipe Works The cast-iron plancha, with its seasoned nonstick surface and superior heat retention, is the perfect piece of equipment to create a hibachi-like experience on the grill. And rib-eye steak is a great cut of beef for this cooking method. It's very flavorful, with lots of marbling and a smooth, fine texture, and its generous thickness allows for a beautiful crust. To avoid overcrowding the food and thus steaming it, batch cooking is the way to go here. The steak is cooked first and then the vegetables are cooked in two batches, where they pull double duty by absorbing the flavorful drippings and helping to clean up the plancha. A flavorful finishing sauce made with umami-heavy soy sauce and sweet mirin is added in the last few minutes of cooking the vegetables. You will need a cast-iron plancha measuring at least 20 by 10 inches.

1 Combine melted butter, soy sauce, and garlic in bowl; set aside. Pat steaks dry with paper towels. Rub steaks with 2 teaspoons oil and sprinkle with 1 teaspoon white pepper and ¾ teaspoon salt. In large bowl, toss zucchini, onions, mushrooms, remaining ¼ teaspoon white pepper, and remaining ¼ teaspoon salt with remaining 2 tablespoons oil. Set steaks and vegetables aside.

2A **For a charcoal grill** Open bottom vent completely. Light large chimney starter filled with charcoal briquettes (6 quarts). When top coals are partially covered with ash, pour evenly over grill. Set cooking grate in place, center plancha on grill, cover, and open lid vent completely. Heat grill with plancha until hot, about 5 minutes.

2B **For a gas grill** Turn all burners to high and heat grill until hot, about 15 minutes. Center plancha on grill, cover, and heat for an additional 5 minutes. Leave all burners on high.

3 Add steaks to plancha and cook, flipping steaks every 2 minutes, until well browned and meat registers 120 to 125 degrees (for medium-rare), 10 to 13 minutes. Transfer steaks to carving board, tent with aluminum foil, and let rest.

4 While steaks rest, add half of mixed vegetables to hot plancha. Pat vegetables into even layer and cook, without stirring, until beginning to brown, about 3 minutes. Stir and continue to cook 2 minutes longer.

Flare Trade

Flat-Top Grill Turn all burners to medium-high and heat griddle until hot, about 10 minutes. Leave all burners on medium-high. Clean griddle, then cook steaks and vegetables on griddle together, following cooking times as directed in recipe.

Pour 1 tablespoon mirin and 1 tablespoon soy-garlic butter over vegetables, stir to combine, and cook until liquid has evaporated and vegetables are well browned, about 2 minutes longer. Transfer cooked vegetables to serving platter. Repeat cooking process with remaining vegetables, remaining 1 tablespoon mirin, and 1 tablespoon soy-garlic butter.

5 Slice steaks ¼ inch thick and transfer to serving platter with vegetables. Drizzle steaks with remaining soy-garlic butter. Serve.

Grilled Strip Steak and Potatoes with Blue Cheese Butter

SERVES 4   **TOTAL TIME** 35 minutes

4 tablespoons unsalted butter, softened

3 tablespoons crumbled blue cheese

2 tablespoons minced fresh chives

1 garlic clove, minced

1 teaspoon table salt, divided

½ teaspoon pepper, divided

1½ pounds small (1- to 2-inch-wide) red or yellow potatoes, unpeeled, halved

2 tablespoons extra-virgin olive oil, divided

2 (1-pound) strip steaks, 1 inch thick, trimmed

Why This Recipe Works When the family is craving meat and potatoes but you're craving being outdoors, this superfast recipe steps up to the plate. Strip steaks need just a little salt and pepper and 10 minutes over a hot fire to taste their best. Skewered parcooked potatoes turn tender and browned in the amount of time it takes for the steaks to cook. A quick blue cheese–garlic butter evokes classic steakhouse flavors; dollop some of it on the just-grilled steak and toss the rest with the potatoes for wall-to-wall flavor. You will need four 12-inch metal skewers.

1   Mash butter with blue cheese, chives, garlic, ¼ teaspoon salt, and ⅛ teaspoon pepper with fork in large bowl until combined; set blue cheese butter aside until ready to serve. Toss potatoes with 1 tablespoon olive oil, ¼ teaspoon salt, and ⅛ teaspoon pepper in bowl. Microwave, covered, until potatoes offer slight resistance when poked with tip of paring knife, about 6 minutes, stirring halfway through. Drain if necessary, then toss with remaining 1 tablespoon oil. Thread potatoes onto four 12-inch metal skewers.

2A   For a charcoal grill Open bottom vent completely. Light large chimney starter filled with charcoal briquettes (6 quarts). When top coals are partially covered with ash, pour evenly over grill. Set cooking grate in place, cover, and open lid vent completely. Heat grill until hot, about 5 minutes.

2B   For a gas grill Turn all burners to high; cover; and heat grill until hot, about 15 minutes. Leave all burners on high.

3   Clean and oil cooking grate. Pat steaks dry with paper towels and sprinkle with remaining ½ teaspoon salt and remaining ¼ teaspoon pepper. Grill steaks and potatoes (covered if using gas) until meat registers 120 to 125 degrees (for medium-rare) and potatoes are lightly charred and tender, 8 to 16 minutes, flipping as needed.

4   Transfer steaks to cutting board, dollop with half of reserved blue cheese butter, tent with aluminum foil, and let rest. Slide potatoes off skewers into bowl with remaining garlic butter and toss to coat. Slice steaks ½ inch thick. Serve with potatoes.

Flare Trade

Open Fire Prepare hot single-level fire in open-fire grill. Set cooking grate at least 6 inches from coals and flames and heat grill until hot, about 5 minutes. Proceed with step 3.

Bún Chả

SERVES 4 to 6   **TOTAL TIME** 1 hour

Noodles and Salad

- 8   ounces rice vermicelli

- 1   head Boston lettuce (8 ounces), torn into bite-size pieces

- 1   English cucumber, peeled, quartered lengthwise, seeded, and sliced thin on bias

- 1   cup fresh cilantro leaves and stems

- 1   cup fresh mint leaves, torn if large

Sauce

- 1   small Thai chile, stemmed and minced

- 3   tablespoons sugar, divided

- 1   garlic clove, minced

- ⅔   cup hot water

- 5   tablespoons fish sauce

- ¼   cup lime juice (2 limes)

Pork Patties

- 1   large shallot, minced

- 1   tablespoon fish sauce

- 1½   teaspoons sugar

- ½   teaspoon baking soda

- ½   teaspoon pepper

- 1   pound ground pork

Why This Recipe Works Vietnamese bún chả —a vibrant mix of grilled pork patties; cool, tender greens; and springy rice vermicelli, all united by a potent sauce—makes an ideal meal on a hot summer night. You can easily prepare the noodles, greens, and sauce ahead of time, if you like. The pork patties need only a brief grilling time; mixing baking soda into the ground pork raises the meat's pH, helping the patties stay moist and brown well. Briefly soaking the grilled patties in the sauce further flavors them and, in turn, infuses the sauce with grill flavor. Serve the noodles, salad, sauce, and pork patties separately so everyone can combine components to their taste. We prefer the more delicate springiness of vermicelli made from 100 percent rice flour to those that include a secondary starch. Use the cilantro leaves and the thin, delicate stems, not the thicker ones close to the roots. For a less spicy sauce, use only half the Thai chile.

1 **For the noodles and salad** Bring 4 quarts water to boil in large pot. Stir in noodles and cook until tender, 4 to 12 minutes. Drain noodles and rinse under cold running water until cool. Drain noodles very well, spread on large plate, and let stand at room temperature to dry. Arrange lettuce, cucumber, cilantro, and mint separately on large serving platter and refrigerate until needed.

2 **For the sauce** Meanwhile, using mortar and pestle (or on cutting board using flat side of chef's knife), mash Thai chile, 1 tablespoon sugar, and garlic to fine paste. Transfer to medium bowl and add hot water, fish sauce, lime juice, and remaining 2 tablespoons sugar. Stir until sugar is dissolved; set aside.

3 **For the pork patties** Combine shallot, fish sauce, sugar, baking soda, and pepper in medium bowl. Add pork and mix until well combined. Shape pork mixture into 12 patties, each about 2½ inches wide and ½ inch thick.

4A **For a charcoal grill** Open bottom vent completely. Light large chimney starter filled with charcoal briquettes (6 quarts). When top coals are partially covered with ash, pour evenly over half of grill. Set cooking grate in place, cover, and open lid vent completely. Heat grill until hot, about 5 minutes.

4B For a gas grill Turn all burners to high; cover; and heat grill until hot, about 15 minutes. Leave all burners on high.

5 Clean and oil cooking grate. Grill patties (directly over coals if using charcoal; covered if using gas) until well charred and meat registers 160 degrees, 3 to 4 minutes per side. Transfer patties to bowl with sauce and gently toss to coat. Let stand for 5 minutes.

6 Transfer patties to serving plate, reserving sauce. Serve noodles, salad, sauce, and pork patties separately.

Flare Trade

Flat-Top Grill Turn all burners to medium-high and heat griddle until hot, about 10 minutes. Turn all burners to high. Clean griddle and proceed with step 5.

Open Fire Prepare hot single-level fire in open-fire grill. Set cooking grate at least 6 inches from coals and flames and heat grill until hot, about 5 minutes. Proceed with step 5.

Grilled Sausages and Polenta with Arugula Salad

1 ounce Parmesan cheese, grated (½ cup)

⅓ cup extra-virgin olive oil

2 tablespoons red wine vinegar

1 teaspoon minced fresh rosemary

1 garlic clove, minced

¼ teaspoon table salt

⅛ teaspoon pepper

1 (18-ounce) tube precooked polenta, sliced ½ inch thick

1½ pounds sweet or hot Italian sausage (6 to 8 links), pricked all over with fork

12 ounces cherry tomatoes, halved

5 ounces (5 cups) baby arugula

Flare Trade

Flat-Top Grill Turn all burners to medium-high and heat griddle until hot, about 10 minutes. Leave all burners on medium-high. Clean griddle and proceed with step 3.

Open Fire Prepare hot single-level fire in open-fire grill. Set cooking grate at least 6 inches from coals and flames and heat grill until hot, about 5 minutes. Proceed with step 3.

Why This Recipe Works For a speedy dinner off the grill, this combo of grilled Italian sausages and sliced polenta delivers with hearty, satisfying flavors. A rosemary and Parmesan vinaigrette flavors grilled slabs of convenient precooked polenta and also dresses a quick arugula and tomato salad. Handle the polenta minimally once it's on the grill; to avoid sticking, let the polenta char lightly before trying to turn it, and use a metal fish spatula. Use your favorite Italian sausages—they need no special treatment save for poking them with a fork so they don't burst while browning over the hot fire. Avoid using pregrated Parmesan cheese here, as it will not dissolve properly in the dressing.

1 Whisk Parmesan, oil, vinegar, rosemary, garlic, salt, and pepper together in large bowl. Brush 3 tablespoons of dressing over polenta; reserve remaining dressing for grilled polenta and salad.

2A **For a charcoal grill** Open bottom vent completely. Light large chimney starter filled with charcoal briquettes (6 quarts). When top coals are partially covered with ash, pour evenly over grill. Set cooking grate in place, cover, and open lid vent completely. Heat grill until hot, about 5 minutes.

2B **For a gas grill** Turn all burners to high; cover; and heat grill until hot, about 15 minutes. Leave all burners on high.

3 Clean and oil cooking grate. Grill sausages and polenta until sausages and polenta are lightly charred on all sides, and sausages are no longer pink in center and register 160 degrees, about 6 minutes, flipping as needed. (Handle polenta gently to avoid breaking.) Transfer sausages and polenta to serving platter.

4 Drizzle polenta with 2 tablespoons reserved dressing. Add tomatoes and arugula to remaining dressing and toss to coat; season with salt and pepper to taste. Serve sausages and polenta with salad.

Fried Rice with Ham, Gai Lan, and Mushrooms

SERVES 4 to 6   **TOTAL TIME** 1 hour

2 tablespoons Chinese black vinegar or sherry vinegar

4 teaspoons soy sauce

1 tablespoon Shaoxing wine or dry sherry

1 tablespoon hoisin sauce

1 tablespoon packed brown sugar

¼ teaspoon white pepper

6 scallions, white and green parts separated and sliced thin

¼ cup plus 1 teaspoon vegetable oil, divided

2 garlic cloves, minced

12 ounces gai lan, trimmed

2 large eggs

¼ teaspoon table salt

8 ounces shiitake mushrooms, stemmed and sliced ¼ inch thick

4 ounces ham steak, cut into ½-inch pieces (¾ cup)

4 cups cooked jasmine rice, room temperature

Why This Recipe Works Since restaurant wok burners use plenty of fire to achieve delicately smoky flavor, it makes sense that this technique translates to outdoor stir-frying at home—even when it comes to delightfully unexpected choices such as fried rice. Simply corral the coals in the center of the cooking area for concentrated high heat. Guidelines for great fried rice remain the same: Use dry (not sticky) cooked rice and stir-fry the elements in batches, combining them just before serving. Cooking the gai lan leaves and stems separately ensures fully cooked but still crisp stems and vibrantly green leaves. Shiitake mushrooms add an umami punch, and a complex vinegar-based sauce ties everything together. We prefer jasmine rice, but you can use any long-grain white rice. If gai lan is unavailable you can substitute broccoli. You will need a 13 by 9-inch disposable aluminum roasting pan. A 12-inch cast-iron skillet can be used in place of the wok.

1   Whisk vinegar, soy sauce, Shaoxing wine, hoisin, sugar, and white pepper in small bowl until sugar has dissolved; set aside. Combine scallion whites, 2 tablespoons oil, and garlic in second small bowl; set aside.

2   Trim leaves from bottom 3 inches of gai lan stalks; reserve. Cut tops (leaves and florets) from stalks and cut into 1-inch pieces. Quarter stalks lengthwise if more than 1 inch in diameter, or halve stalks lengthwise if less than 1 inch in diameter. Keep leaves and tops separate from stalks. Beat eggs and salt in bowl until well combined; set aside.

3   Using skewer, poke 12 holes in bottom of disposable pan. Open bottom vent of charcoal grill completely and place disposable pan in center. Light large chimney starter three-quarters filled with charcoal briquettes (4½ quarts). When top coals are partially covered with ash, pour into disposable pan. Set cooking grate in place, cover, and open lid vent completely. Heat grill until hot, about 5 minutes.

4   Center 14-inch flat-bottomed carbon-steel wok on cooking grate over coals. Heat 2 teaspoons oil in wok until just smoking. Add mushrooms and gai lan leaves and tops. Cook, tossing vegetables slowly but constantly, until mushrooms are softened and gai lan leaves and tops are completely

wilted, 3 to 5 minutes. Add ham and cook, stirring frequently, until ham is warmed through, about 1 minute; transfer to large bowl.

5 Heat 1 tablespoon oil in now-empty wok until shimmering. Add eggs and cook, stirring frequently, until eggs just form cohesive mass, 30 seconds to 1 minute (eggs will not be completely dry). Transfer to bowl with vegetables and break up any large egg curds.

6 Heat remaining 2 teaspoons oil in now-empty wok until just smoking. Add gai lan stalks and ¼ cup water (water will sputter); cover; and cook, covered with wok lid, until bright green, about 5 minutes. Uncover and continue to cook, tossing slowly but constantly, until water has evaporated and stalks are crisp-tender, 1 to 3 minutes; transfer to bowl with egg and vegetable mixture.

7 Add scallion-white mixture to now-empty wok and cook, mashing mixture into pan, until fragrant, about 30 seconds. Add rice (breaking up clumps with spoon), vinegar mixture, cooked vegetable-egg mixture, and scallion greens. Cook, tossing slowly but constantly, until mixture is evenly coated and heated through, 3 to 7 minutes. Serve immediately.

Flare Trade

Gas Grill Turn all burners to high; cover; and heat grill until hot, about 15 minutes. Leave all burners on high. Center 12-inch cast-iron skillet on cooking grate and proceed with step 4.

Open Fire Prepare hot single-level fire in open-fire grill. Set cooking grate at least 6 inches from coals and flames and heat grill until hot, about 5 minutes. Proceed with step 4.

Grilled Pork Chops with Plums

SERVES 4   TOTAL TIME 30 minutes

- 2 tablespoons extra-virgin olive oil
- 1 tablespoon lemon juice
- 4 plums, halved and pitted
- 2 tablespoons packed brown sugar, divided
- 1½ teaspoons ground coriander
- ½ teaspoon table salt
- ½ teaspoon ground ginger
- ¼ teaspoon pepper
- 4 (6-ounce) bone-in pork rib or center-cut chops, ½ inch thick, trimmed
- 3 ounces (3 cups) baby arugula

Why This Recipe Works This weeknight-friendly, warm-weather riff on pork roast with prunes pairs quick-grilling pork chops with juicy ripe plums—one of late summer's finest fruits. The pork chops are sprinkled with a savory-sweet spice mixture of coriander, ginger, salt, and pepper, plus a bit of brown sugar to play off the sweetness of the plums. It takes just a few minutes on the grill for these thin-cut chops to cook through and pick up great grill marks, while the bit of extra fat from the bone keeps the meat juicy. While the chops rest, the halved plums get a quick turn over the heat and emerge with concentrated sweetness, making an ideal accompaniment to the tender pork chops.

1   Whisk oil and lemon juice together in medium bowl; set aside dressing. Rub cut sides of plums with 1 tablespoon sugar. Combine coriander, salt, ground ginger, pepper, and remaining 1 tablespoon sugar in small bowl. Pat pork dry with paper towels and sprinkle all over with spice mixture.

2A   For a charcoal grill Open bottom vent completely. Light large chimney starter filled with charcoal briquettes (6 quarts). When top coals are partially covered with ash, pour evenly over grill. Set cooking grate in place, cover, and open lid vent completely. Heat grill until hot, about 5 minutes.

2B   For a gas grill Turn all burners to high; cover; and heat grill until hot, about 15 minutes. Leave all burners on high.

3   Clean and oil cooking grate. Grill pork until browned and meat registers 140 to 145 degrees, 2 to 3 minutes per side. Transfer to serving platter, tent with aluminum foil, and let rest for 10 minutes. Meanwhile, grill plums until caramelized and tender, about 3 minutes per side.

4   Add plums and arugula to bowl with dressing and toss to combine. Transfer to serving platter with pork. Serve.

Flare Trade

Open Fire Prepare hot single-level fire in open-fire grill. Set cooking grate at least 6 inches from coals and flames and heat grill until hot, about 5 minutes. Proceed with step 3.

Grilled Pork Tenderloin with Pineapple-Lentil Salad

SERVES 4   **TOTAL TIME** 1 hour

Pork

- ½ teaspoon table salt
- ¾ teaspoon sugar
- ¼ teaspoon ground cumin
- ¼ teaspoon chipotle chile powder
- 1 (1-pound) pork tenderloin, trimmed

Salad

- ½ pineapple, peeled, cored, and cut lengthwise into 6 wedges
- 1 poblano chile, stemmed, seeded, and quartered
- 2 tablespoons extra-virgin olive oil, divided
- 1 (15-ounce) can lentils, rinsed
- ½ cup fresh cilantro leaves
- 2 tablespoons lime juice, plus lime wedges for serving
- ¼ cup pepitas, toasted

Flare Trade

Open Fire Prepare hot half-grill fire in open-fire grill. Set cooking grate at least 6 inches from coals and flames and heat grill until hot, about 5 minutes. Proceed with step 3.

Why This Recipe Works The charred-yet-sweet fruitiness that grilled pineapple adds to a lentil salad makes a delicious counterpoint to a smoky, perfectly grilled pork tenderloin, made ultrasavory with a cumin and chipotle chile powder rub. Once the spiced tenderloin is browned, grill the pineapple and a poblano chile and then combine the two with fresh cilantro leaves, lime juice, a bit of the reserved spice rub, and the lentils. A final sprinkling of pepitas adds a bit of crunch. Any variety of canned lentils will work in this recipe.

1   **For the pork** Combine salt, sugar, cumin, and chile powder in small bowl. Reserve ½ teaspoon spice mixture for salad. Pat tenderloin dry with paper towels. Rub remaining spice mixture evenly over surface of tenderloin. Refrigerate while preparing grill.

2A   **For a charcoal grill** Open bottom vent completely. Light large chimney starter filled with charcoal briquettes (6 quarts). When top coals are partially covered with ash, pour evenly over half of grill. Set cooking grate in place, cover, and open lid vent completely. Heat grill until hot, about 5 minutes.

2B   **For a gas grill** Turn all burners to high; cover; and heat grill until hot, about 15 minutes. Leave primary burner on high and turn off other burner(s).

3   Clean and oil cooking grate. Place tenderloin on hotter side of grill. Cover and cook, turning tenderloin every 2 minutes, until well browned on all sides, about 8 minutes.

4   **For the salad** Brush pineapple and poblano with 1 tablespoon oil. Move tenderloin to cooler side of grill (6 to 8 inches from heat source) and place pineapple and poblano on hotter side of grill. Cover and cook until pineapple and poblano are charred and softened, 8 to 10 minutes, and pork registers 135 to 140 degrees, 12 to 17 minutes, turning tenderloin every 5 minutes and flipping pineapple and poblano as needed. Transfer pineapple, poblano, and tenderloin to cutting board. Tent tenderloin with aluminum foil and let rest for 5 minutes.

5 Chop pineapple and poblano. Transfer to large bowl and add remaining 1 tablespoon oil, lentils, cilantro, lime juice, and reserved spice mixture and toss gently to combine. Season with salt and pepper to taste. Sprinkle with pepitas. Slice tenderloin ½ inch thick and serve with salad and lime wedges.

Tuscan Pork Ribs with Grilled Radicchio

SERVES 4 to 6   **TOTAL TIME** 1 hour

3   heads radicchio (10 ounces each), quartered

½   cup extra-virgin olive oil, divided

1½   teaspoons table salt, divided

1¼   teaspoons pepper, divided

2   (2½- to 3-pound) racks St. Louis–style spareribs, trimmed, membrane removed, and each rack cut into 2-rib sections

2   garlic cloves, minced

1   teaspoon finely chopped fresh rosemary

2   tablespoons lemon juice

Why This Recipe Works Ribs in an hour? This isn't a dream. Tuscan ribs, or rosticciana, differ from American barbecued ribs in that there's no heady spice mixture or in-your-face sauce. Instead of low-and-slow cooking, they are quickly grilled to create a crispy exterior and satisfying chewy interior. St. Louis–style spareribs offer bold, meaty flavor, and it's easy to peel the tough, papery membranes from the racks. Cutting the ribs into two-rib sections creates more surface area for fast, flavorful browning, and salting them prior to grilling ensures that they cook up juicy. Use the still-hot fire to grill wedges of radicchio. The vinaigrette, though slightly nontraditional, provides a bright contrast to the ribs' richness and elevates the radicchio. When portioning the meat into two-rib sections, start at the thicker end of the rack. If you are left with a three-rib piece at the tapered end, grill it as such. Take the temperature of the meat between the bones.

1   Place radicchio on rimmed baking sheet, brush with 3 tablespoons oil, and sprinkle with ½ teaspoon salt and ¼ teaspoon pepper. Pat ribs dry with paper towels. Rub evenly on both sides with remaining 1 teaspoon salt and place on wire rack set in rimmed baking sheet. Let sit at room temperature for 15 minutes or up to 1 hour. Brush meat side of ribs with 1 tablespoon oil and sprinkle with remaining 1 teaspoon pepper.

2   Combine remaining ¼ cup oil, garlic, and rosemary in small bowl and microwave until fragrant and just starting to bubble, about 30 seconds. Whisk in lemon juice and set aside.

3A   For a charcoal grill Open bottom vent completely. Light large chimney starter filled with charcoal briquettes (6 quarts). When top coals are partially covered with ash, pour evenly over grill. Set cooking grate in place, cover, and open lid vent completely. Heat grill until hot, about 5 minutes.

3B   For a gas grill Turn all burners to high; cover; and heat grill until hot, about 15 minutes. Turn all burners to medium-high.

Flare Trade

Open Fire Prepare hot single-level fire in open-fire grill. Set cooking grate at least 6 inches from coals and flames and heat grill until hot, about 5 minutes. Proceed with step 4.

4 Clean and oil cooking grate. Place ribs meat side down on grill. Cover and cook until ribs are spotty brown with light but defined grill marks, 4 to 6 minutes. Flip ribs and cook, covered, until second side is spotty brown, 4 to 6 minutes, moving ribs as needed to ensure even browning. Flip again and cook, covered, until meat side is deeply browned and charred and thick ends of ribs register 175 to 185 degrees, 4 to 6 minutes. Transfer ribs to cutting board, tent with aluminum foil, and let rest for 10 minutes. While ribs rest, grill radicchio (covered if using gas), turning every 1½ minutes, until edges are browned and wilted but centers are still slightly firm, about 5 minutes. Transfer radicchio to serving platter.

5 Cut ribs between bones and serve with radicchio, passing vinaigrette separately.

Lamb and Summer Vegetable Kebabs with Grilled Focaccia

1 small loaf focaccia bread, halved and cut crosswise into 1-inch-thick slices

5 tablespoons extra-virgin olive oil, divided, plus extra for drizzling

2 pounds boneless leg of lamb, trimmed and cut into 1½-inch pieces

¼ cup minced fresh mint, divided

2 teaspoons minced fresh rosemary, divided

¾ teaspoon table salt, divided

½ teaspoon pepper, divided

2 garlic cloves, minced

2 small yellow summer squash (12 ounces), halved lengthwise and cut into 1-inch-thick half moons

2 red bell peppers, stemmed, seeded, and cut into 1½-inch pieces

2 red onions, cut into 1-inch pieces

1 lemon, halved

Why This Recipe Works The smoke of the grill does wonders for the grassy, slightly earthy flavor of lamb. Skewered chunks of lamb seasoned with mint and rosemary go on the hotter side of a two-level fire to brown and cook through (we prefer medium doneness in this recipe), while summer squash, red bell peppers, and red onions go onto separate skewers to pick up light char over the cooler side. It's a cinch to also grill store-bought focaccia for mopping up the delicious lamb and vegetable juices. Squeeze the grilled lemon halves over everything. If you have long, thin pieces of meat, roll or fold them into approximate 1½-inch cubes before skewering. You will need six 12-inch metal skewers.

1   Brush focaccia slices with 2 tablespoons oil. Combine lamb, 2 tablespoons mint, 1 teaspoon rosemary, ½ teaspoon salt, and ¼ teaspoon pepper in large bowl and toss to coat. Thread lamb tightly onto two 12-inch metal skewers; set aside.

2   Whisk remaining 2 tablespoons mint, remaining 1 teaspoon rosemary, remaining 3 tablespoons oil, garlic, remaining ¼ teaspoon salt, and remaining ¼ teaspoon pepper in large bowl. Add squash, bell pepper, and onion to bowl and toss to coat. In alternating pattern of squash, bell pepper, and 3 pieces onion, thread vegetables onto four 12-inch metal skewers.

3A   For a charcoal grill Open bottom vent completely. Light large chimney starter filled with charcoal briquettes (6 quarts). When top coals are partially covered with ash, pour two-thirds evenly over half of grill, then pour remaining coals over other half of grill. Set cooking grate in place, cover, and open lid vent completely. Heat grill until hot, about 5 minutes.

3B   For a gas grill Turn all burners to high; cover; and heat grill until hot, about 15 minutes. Leave primary burner on high and turn other burner(s) to medium.

4   Clean and oil cooking grate. Place lamb skewers on hotter side of grill and place vegetable skewers and lemon halves on cooler side of grill. Cook (covered if using gas), turning skewers every 3 to 4 minutes, until lamb is

well browned and registers 130 to 135 degrees (for medium) and vegetable skewers are tender and lightly charred, 8 to 12 minutes. Transfer to serving platter as skewers finish cooking and tent with aluminum foil.

5 Grill focaccia on now-empty hotter side of grill until lightly browned, 1 to 2 minutes per side. Transfer to second platter and drizzle with extra oil. Slide lamb and vegetables off skewers onto plates and serve with grilled lemon.

Flare Trade

Open Fire Prepare hot single-level fire in open-fire grill. Set cooking grate at least 6 inches from coals and flames and heat grill until hot, about 5 minutes. Grill lamb skewers and vegetable skewers, turning skewers every 3 to 4 minutes. Grill lemon halves and focaccia until lightly browned, 1 to 2 minutes per side.

Grilled Lamb Shoulder Chops with Zucchini and Corn Salad

SERVES 4   **TOTAL TIME** 1 hour

½ cup extra-virgin olive oil, divided

3 garlic cloves, minced, divided

1 teaspoon table salt, divided

¾ teaspoon pepper, divided

4 (8- to 12-ounce) lamb shoulder chops (blade or round bone), ¾ to 1 inch thick, trimmed

⅛ teaspoon red pepper flakes

2 ears corn, husks and silk removed

1½ pounds zucchini, sliced lengthwise into ½-inch-thick planks

2 tablespoons chopped fresh basil

4 teaspoons lemon juice

2 ounces feta cheese, crumbled (½ cup)

Flare Trade

Open Fire Prepare medium-hot single-level fire in open-fire grill. Set cooking grate at least 6 inches from coals and flames and heat grill until hot, about 5 minutes. Proceed with step 4. Grill chops, turning and moving as needed to ensure even browning.

Why This Recipe Works If you ever feel like you're in a bit of a rut when it comes to choosing which meat to grill, inexpensive lamb shoulder chops are a fun way to mix things up. They're a great match for the grill because their distinctive gutsy flavor holds up beautifully to the smoke. A simple marinade of olive oil, garlic, salt, and pepper infuses the chops with flavor. Ears of corn and planks of zucchini get brushed with a similar marinade (plus red pepper flakes for some kick); once grill-charred, they become the stars of a summery salad that gets a punch from fresh basil, lemon juice, and feta. We like our lamb shoulder chops cooked to medium, as this cut can be tough if cooked any less than that.

1   Whisk 3 tablespoons oil, one-third of garlic, ½ teaspoon salt, and ½ teaspoon pepper together in 13 by 9-inch baking dish. Add lamb chops to marinade and turn to coat.

2   Whisk pepper flakes, remaining 5 tablespoons oil, remaining garlic, remaining ½ teaspoon salt, and remaining ¼ teaspoon pepper together in large bowl. Brush corn with 1 tablespoon oil mixture. Add zucchini to remaining oil mixture in bowl and toss to coat.

3A   For a charcoal grill Open bottom vent completely. Light large chimney starter three-quarters filled with charcoal briquettes (4½ quarts). When top coals are partially covered with ash, pour evenly over grill. Set cooking grate in place, cover, and open lid vent completely. Heat grill until hot, about 5 minutes.

3B   For a gas grill Turn all burners to high; cover; and heat grill until hot, about 15 minutes. Turn all burners to medium-high.

4   Clean and oil cooking grate. Transfer corn and zucchini to grill, reserving remaining oil mixture in bowl. Grill corn and zucchini (covered if using gas), turning corn every 2 to 3 minutes until kernels are lightly charred all over, 10 to 15 minutes total, and zucchini is well browned and tender, 5 to 7 minutes per side; transfer corn and zucchini to cutting board. Turn all burners to high if using gas.

5 Grill chops, covered, until browned and meat registers 130 to 135 degrees (for medium), 4 to 6 minutes per side. Transfer chops to serving platter, tent with aluminum foil, and let rest.

6 Cut kernels from cobs. Slice zucchini on bias ½ inch thick. Add vegetables to bowl with reserved oil mixture. Add basil and lemon juice to vegetables and toss to combine. Season with salt and pepper to taste. Transfer salad to serving platter and sprinkle feta over top. Serve with lamb chops.

Grilled Shrimp, Corn, and Avocado Salad

SERVES 4   **TOTAL TIME** 50 minutes

2 ripe but firm avocados, halved and pitted

6 tablespoons extra-virgin olive oil, divided

3 ears corn, husks and silk removed

1 teaspoon table salt, divided

1 teaspoon pepper, divided

2 pounds jumbo shrimp, (16 to 20 per pound) peeled and deveined

2 teaspoons grated lime zest (2 limes), limes halved

3 romaine lettuce hearts (6 ounces each), halved lengthwise and chopped

Why This Recipe Works Grill-charred fresh corn and sweet jumbo shrimp are a favorite light summertime meal, combined here with crisp romaine hearts in a dinner salad. Grilled avocados take the flavor to a whole new level: Imagine that buttery, grassy flavor you're used to, but crisped and smoky. Lime on the grill is also a slam dunk, with a caramelized flavor element that adds nuance to its acidity and makes for a superstar salad dressing. Extra-large shrimp (21 to 25 per pound) can be substituted for jumbo shrimp; reduce the total cooking time in step 4 by about 1 minute. Creating nonstick conditions for the grill grate is key here (see page 9). You will need four 12-inch metal skewers.

1 Rub cut sides of avocados with 1 teaspoon oil. Rub corn all over with 2 teaspoons oil and sprinkle with ½ teaspoon salt and ½ teaspoon pepper. Thread shrimp tightly onto four 12-inch metal skewers, alternating direction of heads and tails. Pat shrimp dry with paper towels, then brush with 1 tablespoon oil and sprinkle with ¼ teaspoon salt and ¼ teaspoon pepper.

2A For a charcoal grill Open bottom vent completely. Light large chimney starter filled with charcoal briquettes (6 quarts). When top coals are partially covered with ash, pour evenly over grill. Set cooking grate in place, cover, and open lid vent completely. Heat grill until hot, about 5 minutes.

2B For a gas grill Turn all burners to high; cover; and heat grill until hot, about 15 minutes. Leave all burners on high.

3 Clean and oil cooking grate. Grill corn (covered if using gas) until charred on all sides, 10 to 13 minutes, turning as needed. Transfer to cutting board. Grill avocados and lime halves (covered if using gas), cut sides down, until lightly charred, about 2 minutes. Transfer to cutting board with corn and let cool slightly, about 5 minutes.

4 Meanwhile, grill shrimp (covered if using gas) until lightly charred and opaque throughout, about 4 minutes, flipping halfway through grilling. Using tongs, slide shrimp off skewers into clean bowl and toss with 1 tablespoon oil and lime zest; set aside.

Flare Trade

Flat-Top Grill Turn all burners to medium-high and heat griddle until hot, about 10 minutes. Leave all burners on medium-high. Clean griddle and proceed with step 3.

Open Fire Prepare hot single-level fire in open-fire grill. Set cooking grate at least 6 inches from coals and flames and heat grill until hot, about 5 minutes. Proceed with step 3.

5 Scoop flesh from charred avocado halves and cut into 1-inch pieces. Cut kernels from cobs. Juice limes to yield ¼ cup. Whisk lime juice, remaining 3 tablespoons oil, remaining ¼ teaspoon salt, and remaining ¼ teaspoon pepper together in large bowl. Add romaine, avocado, corn, and shrimp to dressing and toss gently to combine. Season with salt and pepper to taste. Serve.

Grilled Shrimp Skewers with Chili Crisp and Napa Cabbage Slaw

SERVES 4 **TOTAL TIME** 40 minutes

2 pounds jumbo shrimp (16 to 20 per pound), peeled and deveined

¼ cup vegetable oil, divided

¼ teaspoon pepper

¼ cup chili crisp, plus extra for serving

2 tablespoons white wine vinegar

½ teaspoon table salt

1 small head napa cabbage (1½ pounds), cored and sliced thin

4 scallions, sliced thin on bias

1 cup fresh cilantro leaves

¼ cup salted dry-roasted peanuts, chopped

Why This Recipe Works Chili crisp, aka lao gan ma, or "godmother sauce," is a spicy Chinese condiment often used as a dipping sauce for dumplings or as a sauce for noodles, rice, or stir-fried greens. It's also magical when applied to sweet, briny grilled shrimp fresh off the grill. The skewered, grilled, and seasoned shrimp get an easy-prep side: a refreshing slaw of napa cabbage, scallions, and cilantro with dry-roasted peanuts for salty crunch. This fast seasonal dinner deserves a top spot in your outdoor cooking rotation. Creating nonstick conditions for the grill grate is key here (see page 9). You will need four 12-inch metal skewers.

1 Thread shrimp tightly onto four 12-inch metal skewers, alternating direction of heads and tails. Pat shrimp dry with paper towels, then brush with 1 tablespoon oil and sprinkle with pepper.

2A **For a charcoal grill** Open bottom vent completely. Light large chimney starter mounded with charcoal briquettes (7 quarts). When top coals are partially covered with ash, pour evenly over grill. Set cooking grate in place, cover, and open lid vent completely. Heat grill until hot, about 5 minutes.

2B **For a gas grill** Turn all burners to high; cover; and heat grill until hot, about 15 minutes. Leave all burners on high.

3 Clean and oil cooking grate. Grill shrimp (covered if using gas) until lightly charred and opaque throughout, about 4 minutes, flipping halfway through grilling. Using tongs, slide shrimp off skewers onto serving platter and brush with chili crisp.

4 Whisk remaining 3 tablespoons oil, vinegar, and salt together in large bowl. Add cabbage, scallions, and cilantro and toss to coat. Season with salt and pepper to taste. Sprinkle with peanuts and serve with shrimp, passing extra chili crisp separately.

Flare Trade

Open Fire Prepare hot single-level fire in open-fire grill. Set cooking grate at least 6 inches from coals and flames and heat grill until hot, about 5 minutes. Proceed with step 3.

Grilled Tuna Steaks with Cucumber-Mint Farro Salad

SERVES 4   **TOTAL TIME** 1 hour

1½ cups whole farro

1 teaspoon table salt, divided, plus salt for cooking farro

6 tablespoons extra-virgin olive oil, divided

2 tablespoons lemon juice

2 tablespoons plain Greek yogurt

¼ teaspoon pepper, divided

1 English cucumber, halved lengthwise, seeded, and sliced ¼ inch thick

6 ounces cherry tomatoes, halved

2 ounces (2 cups) baby arugula

3 tablespoons chopped fresh mint

2 teaspoons honey

1 teaspoon water

2 (8- to 12-ounce) skinless tuna steaks, 1 inch thick, halved crosswise

Why This Recipe Works While cooking your entire meal on the grill has major appeal, there's also something to be said for a side dish that you can assemble ahead in the kitchen: At mealtime, a quick and easy grill stint gets you to the finish line. Here, chewy farro is punctuated by crisp cucumber, juicy tomatoes, and peppery arugula. A creamy yogurt dressing makes the salad a cooling complement to the honey-brushed grill-seared tuna. We prefer the flavor and texture of whole farro; pearl farro can be used, but the texture may be softer. Do not use quick-cooking or presteamed farro. The cooking time for farro can vary greatly across brands, so begin to check for doneness after 10 minutes. We prefer our tuna served rare or medium-rare. If you like it cooked medium, use the timing for medium-rare, then tent the steaks with aluminum foil for 5 minutes. Creating nonstick conditions for the grill grate is key here (see page 9).

1   Bring 4 quarts water to boil in Dutch oven. Add farro and 1 tablespoon salt and cook until grains are tender with slight chew, 15 to 30 minutes. Drain farro, spread evenly on rimmed baking sheet, and let cool, about 10 minutes.

2   Whisk 3 tablespoons oil, lemon juice, yogurt, ½ teaspoon salt, and ⅛ teaspoon pepper together in large bowl. Add drained farro, cucumber, tomatoes, arugula, and mint and toss gently to combine. Season with salt and pepper to taste; set aside.

3   Whisk remaining 3 tablespoons oil, honey, water, remaining ½ teaspoon salt, and remaining ⅛ teaspoon pepper together in bowl. Pat tuna dry with paper towels and generously brush with oil-honey mixture.

4A   For a charcoal grill Open bottom vent completely. Light large chimney starter filled with charcoal briquettes (6 quarts). When top coals are partially covered with ash, pour evenly over half of grill. Set cooking grate in place, cover, and open lid vent completely. Heat grill until hot, about 5 minutes.

4B   For a gas grill Turn all burners to high; cover; and heat grill until hot, about 15 minutes. Leave all burners on high.

5 Clean and oil cooking grate. Place tuna on grill (on hotter side if using charcoal) and cook (covered if using gas) until grill marks form and bottom is opaque, 1 to 3 minutes. Flip tuna and cook until opaque at perimeter and center is translucent red when checked with tip of paring knife and registers 110 degrees (for rare), about 1½ minutes; or until opaque at perimeter and reddish pink at center and registers 125 degrees (for medium-rare), about 3 minutes. Serve tuna with farro salad.

Flare Trade

Flat-Top Grill Turn all burners to medium-high and heat griddle until hot, about 10 minutes. Turn all burners to high. Clean griddle and proceed with step 5.

Open Fire Prepare hot single-level fire in open-fire grill. Set cooking grate at least 6 inches from coals and flames and heat grill until hot, about 5 minutes. Proceed with step 5.

Grilled Swordfish with Potatoes and Salsa Verde

SERVES 4   **TOTAL TIME** 40 minutes

1½ pounds small (1- to 2-inch-wide) red or yellow potatoes, unpeeled, halved

⅓ cup extra-virgin olive oil, divided

1¾ teaspoons plus ⅛ teaspoon table salt, divided

⅛ teaspoon plus ¾ teaspoon pepper, divided

2 (1-pound) skinless swordfish steaks, 1 to 1½ inches thick, halved crosswise

½ cup minced fresh parsley

2 tablespoons capers, rinsed and minced

2 teaspoons finely grated lemon zest plus 4 teaspoons juice

2 anchovy fillets, rinsed and minced

1 garlic clove, minced

Why This Recipe Works Keeping it simple translates to impressive results when you build your outdoor meal around a proven winner such as thick, meaty swordfish steaks. A punchy Italian-style salsa verde with parsley, capers, and lemon complements the rich swordfish. Skewered small potatoes cook quickly and easily on the grill; microwaving the potatoes before grilling keeps them from burning on the grate before cooking through. If swordfish isn't available, you can substitute halibut. Creating nonstick conditions for the grill grate is key here (see page 9). You will need four 12-inch metal skewers.

1 Toss potatoes with 1 tablespoon oil, ¼ teaspoon salt, and ⅛ teaspoon pepper in bowl. Microwave, covered, until potatoes offer slight resistance when pierced with tip of paring knife, about 6 minutes, stirring halfway through. Drain if necessary, then toss with additional 1 tablespoon oil. Thread potatoes onto four 12-inch metal skewers.

2 Brush swordfish pieces with 1 tablespoon oil and sprinkle with 1½ teaspoons salt and ½ teaspoon pepper. Combine parsley, capers, lemon zest and juice, anchovies, garlic, remaining oil, remaining ⅛ teaspoon salt, and remaining ¼ teaspoon pepper in bowl; set aside salsa verde.

3A For a charcoal grill Open bottom vent completely. Light large chimney starter filled with charcoal briquettes (6 quarts). When top coals are partially covered with ash, pour evenly over grill. Set cooking grate in place, cover, and open lid vent completely. Heat grill until hot, about 5 minutes.

3B For a gas grill Turn all burners to high; cover; and heat grill until hot, about 15 minutes. Leave all burners on high.

4 Clean and oil cooking grate. Grill swordfish and potatoes until swordfish is browned on both sides and registers 130 degrees, and potatoes are well browned and tender, 8 to 12 minutes, flipping both halfway through grilling. Transfer to serving platter as swordfish and potatoes finish cooking. Serve swordfish and potatoes with salsa verde.

Flare Trade

Open Fire Prepare hot single-level fire in open-fire grill. Set cooking grate at least 6 inches from coals and flames and heat grill until hot, about 5 minutes. Proceed with step 4.

Grilled Caesar Salad with Salmon

SERVES 4   **TOTAL TIME** 1 hour

Dressing

⅓ cup buttermilk

3 tablespoons mayonnaise

2 tablespoons lemon juice

2 tablespoons water

3 anchovy fillets, rinsed, patted dry, and minced

2 garlic cloves, minced

2 teaspoons Dijon mustard

1 teaspoon Worcestershire sauce

2 tablespoons extra-virgin olive oil

1 ounce Parmesan cheese, grated (½ cup), plus extra for serving

Salad

1 (2- to 2¼-pound) center-cut, skin-on salmon fillet, about 1½ inches thick

Vegetable oil spray

½ teaspoon table salt

¼ teaspoon pepper

3 romaine lettuce hearts (6 ounces each), halved lengthwise

1 (5-inch) piece baguette, sliced 1-inch thick on bias

Why This Recipe Works The grill excels at transforming ordinary salad components—in this case, romaine lettuce, bread, and salmon fillet—into something quite extraordinary by adding a slightly smoky, charred flavor. The salmon cooks over the hot side of the fire while the romaine hearts char and the baguette slices turn golden over a medium-hot fire. Some unconventional Caesar ingredients—buttermilk, mayonnaise, and Dijon mustard—make a light, tangy dressing that complements this grilled seafood version of the classic salad. Cut the bread on an extreme bias for larger pieces that are easy to handle on the grill. Creating nonstick conditions for the grill grate is key here (see page 9).

1 **For the dressing** Process buttermilk, mayonnaise, lemon juice, water, anchovies, garlic, mustard, and Worcestershire in blender until smooth, about 30 seconds. With blender running, add oil in steady stream until incorporated. Transfer dressing to bowl. Stir Parmesan into dressing. Season with salt and pepper to taste; set aside.

2 **For the salad** Trim away and discard thinner bottom 1 inch of salmon to make salmon more consistent thickness. Cut salmon crosswise into 4 equal fillets and pat dry with paper towels.

3A **For a charcoal grill** Open bottom vent completely. Light large chimney starter filled with charcoal briquettes (6 quarts). When top coals are partially covered with ash, pour two-thirds evenly over half of grill, then pour remaining coals over other half of grill. Set cooking grate in place, cover, and open lid vent completely. Heat grill until hot, about 5 minutes.

3B **For a gas grill** Turn all burners to high; cover; and heat grill until hot, about 15 minutes. Leave primary burner on high and turn other burner(s) to medium.

4 Clean and oil cooking grate. Away from grill, lightly spray salmon with oil spray and sprinkle with salt and pepper. Lightly spray romaine hearts and bread with oil spray. Place fillets on grill, flesh side down and perpendicular to grate bars, on hotter side of grill, spaced about 3 inches apart. Cover grill (reduce primary burner to medium if using gas) and cook, without moving fillets, until flesh side is well marked and releases easily from grill, 4 to 5 minutes.

5 Using fish spatula, gently push each fillet to roll over onto skin side. (If fillets don't lift cleanly off grill, cover and continue to cook 1 minute longer, at which point they should release.) Continue to cook, covered, until centers of fillets are opaque and register 130 degrees, 4 to 5 minutes longer. Using tongs to stabilize fillets, slide spatula under fillets and transfer to platter. (If skin sticks to grill, slide spatula between fillet and skin and lift fillet away from skin.) Tent salmon with aluminum foil.

6 While salmon cooks, place bread on cooler side of grill and cook until golden brown, 4 to 6 minutes, flipping halfway through. Transfer bread to cutting board. Place romaine halves on cooler side of grill and cook until lightly charred on all sides, 3 to 5 minutes, turning as needed. Transfer to cutting board with bread.

7 Using 2 forks, flake salmon into 2-inch pieces. Cut bread into 1-inch cubes and chop romaine hearts into 1-inch pieces. Whisk dressing to recombine. In large bowl, toss lettuce with dressing to coat. Divide salad evenly among 4 plates. Top with salmon and bread cubes. Serve, passing extra Parmesan separately.

Flare Trade

Open Fire Prepare hot half-grill fire in open-fire grill. Set cooking grate at least 6 inches from coals and flames and heat grill until hot, about 5 minutes. Grill salmon on hotter side of grill without moving fish until well marked and releases easily from grill, 3 to 4 minutes. Proceed with step 5.

Grilled Cod and Summer Squash Packets

SERVES 4   **TOTAL TIME** 45 minutes

½ cup extra-virgin olive oil

2 shallots, sliced thin

6 garlic cloves, sliced thin

1½ teaspoons table salt, divided

1¼ teaspoons pepper, divided

1 pound summer squash, sliced ¼ inch thick

12 ounces plum tomatoes, sliced ½ inch thick

¼ cup capers, rinsed

4 (6- to 8-ounce) skinless cod fillets, 1 inch thick

1 lemon, sliced into ¼-inch-thick rounds

2 tablespoons minced fresh parsley

Why This Recipe Works This all-in-one meal of fish and vegetables captures the flavors of summer in a tidy package. Tomatoes and summer squash cook at the same rate as cod fillets, and the foil packet ensures that you don't lose a drop of juices to the flames. Before cooking the vegetables, you'll boost their flavors by tossing them with some potent garlic oil, reserving the rest to drizzle on before serving. Briny capers and lemon slices perk up the packets. Black sea bass, haddock, hake, or pollock may be substituted for the cod. To test for doneness without opening the foil packets, use a permanent marker to mark an "X" on the outside of the foil where the fish fillet is the thickest, then insert an instant-read thermometer through the "X" into the fish to measure its internal temperature.

1 Spray centers of four 18 by 14-inch sheets of aluminum foil with vegetable oil spray. Microwave oil, shallots, garlic, 1 teaspoon salt, and 1 teaspoon pepper in large bowl until garlic begins to brown, about 2 minutes. Add squash, tomatoes, and capers to garlic oil and toss to coat.

2 Pat cod dry with paper towels and sprinkle with remaining ½ teaspoon salt and remaining ¼ teaspoon pepper. Divide vegetable mixture evenly among centers of each piece of foil; reserve garlic oil in bowl. Top each vegetable pile with 1 fillet, then divide lemon slices evenly on top of fillets. Bring short sides of foil together and crimp to seal. Crimp remaining open ends of packets to seal.

3A **For a charcoal grill** Open bottom vent completely. Light large chimney starter filled with charcoal briquettes (6 quarts). When top coals are partially covered with ash, pour evenly over grill. Set cooking grate in place, cover, and open lid vent completely. Heat grill until hot, about 5 minutes.

3B **For a gas grill** Turn all burners to high; cover; and heat grill until hot, about 15 minutes. Leave all burners on high.

4 Place packets on grill, squash side down. Cook until fish registers 135 degrees, about 10 minutes. (To check temperature, poke thermometer through foil of 1 packet and into fish.) Carefully open packets, sprinkle with parsley, and drizzle with reserved garlic oil to taste. Serve.

Flare Trade

Open Fire Prepare hot single-level fire in open-fire grill. Set cooking grate at least 6 inches from coals and flames and heat grill until hot, about 5 minutes. Proceed with step 4.

Grilled Tofu with Charred Broccoli and Peanut Sauce

SERVES 4   **TOTAL TIME** 40 minutes

28 ounces firm tofu

 5 tablespoons warm water

¼ cup creamy peanut butter

 5 teaspoons Thai red curry paste, divided

 3 shallots, sliced thin

½ cup plus 2 tablespoons vegetable oil, plus extra as needed

1½ pounds broccoli crowns, cut into 4 wedges if 3 to 4 inches in diameter or 6 wedges if 4 to 5 inches in diameter

½ teaspoon table salt, divided

¼ teaspoon pepper, divided

Why This Recipe Works Microwave-fried crispy shallots bring savory onion flavor and irresistible texture to grilled tofu and broccoli in this weeknight standout. And instead of discarding the shallot-infused oil, you'll toss it with the broccoli wedges to add extra oomph before grilling them to the perfect level of char and crunch. Red curry paste spices up the slabs of tofu prior to grilling and also helps create a two-ingredient peanut sauce for serving that tastes far more complex than it is. All in all, you get a major flavor reward for a modest assembly of ingredients. Creating nonstick conditions for the grill grate is key here (see page 9).

1   Slice each block of tofu lengthwise into 4 slabs (approximately ¾ inch thick). Spread tofu over paper towel–lined baking sheet, let drain for 20 minutes, then gently press dry with paper towels.

2   Meanwhile, whisk water, peanut butter, and 1 teaspoon curry paste in bowl until smooth; set aside until ready to serve. Microwave shallots and oil in medium bowl for 5 minutes. Stir and continue to microwave in 2-minute increments until beginning to brown (2 to 6 minutes). Repeat stirring and microwaving in 30-second increments until golden brown (30 seconds to 2 minutes). Using slotted spoon, transfer shallots to paper towel–lined plate and season with salt to taste; reserve shallot oil. (You should have about 7 tablespoons reserved oil; if you have less, add vegetable oil to make 7 tablespoons.)

3   Toss broccoli with 5 tablespoons reserved shallot oil, ¼ teaspoon salt, and ⅛ teaspoon pepper in bowl; set aside. Whisk remaining 4 teaspoons curry paste, remaining 2 tablespoons reserved shallot oil, remaining ¼ teaspoon salt, and remaining ⅛ teaspoon pepper together in bowl, then brush tofu all over with curry paste mixture.

4A   For a charcoal grill Open bottom vent completely. Light large chimney starter filled with charcoal briquettes (6 quarts). When top coals are partially covered with ash, pour evenly over grill. Set cooking grate in place, cover, and open lid vent completely. Heat grill until hot, about 5 minutes.

Flare Trade

Open Fire Prepare hot single-level fire in open-fire grill. Set cooking grate at least 6 inches from coals and flames and heat grill until hot, about 5 minutes. Proceed with step 5.

4B For a gas grill Turn all burners to high; cover; and heat grill until hot, about 15 minutes. Leave all burners on high.

5 Clean and oil cooking grate. Grill broccoli and tofu (covered if using gas) until broccoli is charred in spots and tofu is well browned, 6 to 10 minutes, turning broccoli as needed and gently flipping tofu halfway through cooking. Serve tofu and broccoli with reserved peanut sauce and crispy shallots.

Grilled Tofu and Vegetables with Harissa

SERVES 4 to 6   **TOTAL TIME** 45 minutes

28 ounces firm tofu

¼ cup harissa

2 tablespoons water

1 tablespoon honey

1¼ teaspoons table salt, divided

1 teaspoon pepper, divided

½ teaspoon grated lemon zest plus 2 tablespoons juice

1 large red onion, sliced into ½-inch-thick rounds

2 red, yellow, or orange bell peppers, halved lengthwise, stemmed, and seeded

3 tablespoons extra-virgin olive oil, divided

1 head radicchio (10 ounces), quartered

10 ounces grape tomatoes, halved

½ cup fresh mint or parsley leaves, torn

Why This Recipe Works Spicy harissa complements the char of many grilled foods, and tofu slabs make an especially versatile canvas for this aromatic chile paste's complexity. Brushing the tofu with the harissa after grilling preserves the condiment's bright depth. The secret to a satisfying grilled vegetable platter is including a mixture of not just flavors but also textures and temperatures. You'll grill pleasantly bitter radicchio wedges, sweet bell peppers, and zesty red onions alongside the tofu, and top everything off with juicy raw grape tomatoes and fresh mint. Creating nonstick conditions for the grill grate is key here (see page 9).

1   Slice each block of tofu lengthwise into 4 slabs (approximately ¾ inch thick). Spread tofu on paper towel–lined baking sheet, let drain for 20 minutes, then gently press dry with paper towels. Whisk harissa, water, honey, ¼ teaspoon salt, ¼ teaspoon pepper, and lemon zest and juice together in bowl; set aside.

2   Push toothpick horizontally through each onion round to keep rings intact while grilling. Arrange bell peppers skin side up on cutting board and press to flatten with your hand. Brush tofu with 1 tablespoon oil and sprinkle with ½ teaspoon salt and ¼ teaspoon pepper. Brush radicchio, onion, and bell peppers with remaining 2 tablespoons oil and sprinkle with remaining ½ teaspoon salt and remaining ½ teaspoon pepper.

3A   For a charcoal grill Open bottom vent completely. Light large chimney starter filled with charcoal briquettes (6 quarts). When top coals are partially covered with ash, pour evenly over grill. Set cooking grate in place, cover, and open lid vent completely. Heat grill until hot, about 5 minutes.

3B   For a gas grill Turn all burners to high; cover; and heat grill until hot, about 15 minutes. Leave all burners on high.

4   Clean and oil cooking grate. Place tofu and vegetables on grill. Cook (covered if using gas) until radicchio is softened and lightly charred, 5 to 7 minutes, and remaining vegetables and tofu are lightly charred, 10 to 12 minutes, flipping as needed. Transfer items to serving platter as they finish grilling and tent with aluminum foil to keep warm.

5 Remove toothpicks from onion rounds. Brush tofu with half of harissa mixture. Top with tomatoes, sprinkle with mint, and drizzle with remaining harissa mixture. Serve.

Flare Trade

Open Fire Prepare hot single-level fire in open-fire grill. Set cooking grate at least 6 inches from coals and flames and heat grill until hot, about 5 minutes. Proceed with step 4.

Grilled Peach and Tomato Salad with Burrata and Basil

SERVES 4 to 6   **TOTAL TIME** 1¼ hours

Peaches

1½ pounds ripe but slightly firm peaches (4 peaches), halved and pitted

2 tablespoons unsalted butter, melted

Salad

12 ounces ripe tomatoes, cored and cut into ½-inch pieces

¾ teaspoon table salt, divided

5 tablespoons extra-virgin olive oil, divided

1 tablespoon white wine vinegar

8 ounces burrata cheese, room temperature

⅓ cup chopped fresh basil

Flare Trade

Flat-Top Grill Turn all burners to medium-high and heat griddle until hot, about 10 minutes. Turn all burners to medium. Clean griddle. Cook peaches, cut side down, until well browned, 3 to 5 minutes. Flip peaches and cook until tender, 5 to 8 minutes. Let cool, discard skins, then proceed with step 5.

Why This Recipe Works Late summer's juiciest peaches and tomatoes mingle in a dish that's greater than the sum of its already wonderful parts. Grilling peaches enhances their aroma and sweetness; a little butter brushed on the cut halves keeps them from sticking to the grate and speeds browning. You'll grill them over high heat and then move them to a covered baking pan over indirect heat until they're fully softened. After cutting the grilled peaches into wedges, toss them with raw tomato chunks in a simple vinaigrette of white wine vinegar and extra-virgin olive oil. Creamy burrata cheese adds texture and richness to this stunning dish, which is also fabulous made with nectarines or plums. For the best results, use high-quality, ripe, in-season tomatoes and peaches. If burrata is unavailable, sliced fresh mozzarella makes a suitable substitute. Using a metal baking pan on the cooler side of the grill won't harm the pan, but you can use a disposable aluminum pan if preferred; do not use a glass dish.

1   **For the peaches** Brush cut side of peaches with melted butter.

2A   **For a charcoal grill** Open bottom vent completely. Light large chimney starter three-quarters filled with charcoal briquettes (4½ quarts). When top coals are partially covered with ash, pour evenly over half of grill. Set cooking grate in place, cover, and open lid vent completely. Heat grill until hot, about 5 minutes.

2B   **For a gas grill** Turn all burners to high; cover; and heat grill until hot, about 15 minutes. Leave primary burner on high and turn off other burner(s).

3   Clean and oil cooking grate. Arrange peaches cut side down on hotter side of grill and cook (covered if using gas) until grill marks have formed, 5 to 7 minutes, moving peaches as needed to ensure even cooking.

4   Transfer peaches cut side up to 13 by 9-inch baking pan and tent with aluminum foil. Place pan on cooler side of grill. If using gas, turn primary burner to medium. Cover and cook until peaches are very tender and paring knife slips in and out with little resistance, 10 to 15 minutes. When peaches are cool enough to handle, discard skins, then let cool completely.

5 **For the salad** While peaches cool, toss tomatoes with ¼ teaspoon salt and let drain in colander for 30 minutes. Cut each peach half into 4 wedges, then cut each wedge in half crosswise.

6 Whisk ¼ cup oil, vinegar, and remaining ½ teaspoon salt together in large bowl. Add peaches and tomatoes and toss gently to combine; transfer to shallow serving bowl. Place burrata on top of salad and drizzle with remaining 1 tablespoon oil. Season with pepper to taste, then sprinkle with basil. Serve, breaking up burrata with spoon and allowing creamy liquid to meld with dressing.

Grilled Vegetable and Halloumi Salad

SERVES 4 to 6   **TOTAL TIME** 40 minutes

3 tablespoons honey

1 tablespoon minced fresh thyme or rosemary

1 garlic clove, minced

¾ teaspoon table salt, divided

½ teaspoon grated lemon zest plus 3 tablespoons juice

⅛ teaspoon plus ½ teaspoon pepper, divided

1 pound eggplant, sliced into ½-inch-thick rounds

1 head radicchio (10 ounces), quartered

1 zucchini or summer squash, halved lengthwise

1 (8-ounce) block halloumi cheese, sliced into ½-inch-thick slabs

¼ cup extra-virgin olive oil, divided

Why This Recipe Works This warm and hearty salad pairs briny halloumi cheese with nicely charred eggplant, radicchio, and zucchini. Halloumi has a solid consistency and high melting point, making it perfect for grilling; the outside becomes beautifully charred and crisp in contrast to its chewy, warm interior. It takes just 5 to 10 minutes for the slabs of cheese and large pieces of vegetables to become perfectly browned, tender, and redolent with smoky flavor. Then, simply chop all the grilled goodies before tossing everything with a sweet and herbaceous honey and thyme vinaigrette, and dinner is served. If you like, grill some bread to serve alongside. The halloumi may appear to stick to the grill at first, but as it continues to brown it will naturally release and flip easily.

1   Whisk honey, thyme, garlic, ¼ teaspoon salt, lemon zest and juice, and ⅛ teaspoon pepper together in large bowl; set aside. Brush eggplant, radicchio, zucchini, and halloumi with 2 tablespoons oil and sprinkle with remaining ½ teaspoon salt and remaining ½ teaspoon pepper.

2A   For a charcoal grill Open bottom vent completely. Light large chimney starter three-quarter filled with charcoal briquettes (4½ quarts). When top coals are partially covered with ash, pour evenly over grill. Set cooking grate in place, cover, and open lid vent completely. Heat grill until hot, about 5 minutes.

2B   For a gas grill Turn all burners to high; cover; and heat grill until hot, about 15 minutes. Turn all burners to medium-high.

3   Clean and oil cooking grate. Grill vegetables and halloumi (covered if using gas) until radicchio is softened and lightly charred, 3 to 5 minutes, and remaining vegetables and cheese are softened and lightly charred, about 10 minutes, flipping as needed. Transfer vegetables and halloumi to cutting board as they finish cooking. Let cool slightly, then cut into 1-inch pieces.

4   Whisking constantly, slowly drizzle remaining 2 tablespoons oil into honey mixture until emulsified. Add vegetables and halloumi and toss gently to coat. Season with salt and pepper to taste. Serve.

Flare Trade

Flat-Top Grill Turn all burners to medium-high and heat griddle until hot, about 10 minutes. Leave all burners on medium-high. Clean griddle and proceed with step 3.

Open Fire Prepare hot single-level fire in open-fire grill. Set cooking grate at least 6 inches from coals and flames and heat grill until hot, about 5 minutes. Proceed with step 3.

Eggplant

½   cup vegetable oil, divided

15   bird chiles, ground fine
     (1½ tablespoons)

2   garlic cloves, sliced thin

1   (½-inch) piece ginger, peeled
    and sliced thin

1   star anise pod

½   cup fermented black beans

¼   cup hoisin sauce

6   tablespoons Shaoxing wine
    or dry sherry, divided

1   tablespoon sugar

1½ pounds Japanese or Chinese
    eggplant, halved lengthwise
    and cut crosswise into
    1½-inch pieces

1   green bell pepper,
    stemmed, seeded, and
    cut into 1-inch pieces

¼   cup water

6   scallions, green parts cut
    into 1-inch pieces, white
    parts sliced thin

12   sprigs fresh cilantro,
     cut into 2-inch pieces

Why This Recipe Works This stir-fry takes advantage of eggplant's ability to absorb liquid by giving it a seriously tasty Sichuan chili oil to soak up, along with a hint of outdoor smokiness. You'll make the spicy oil inside and then head out to the grill. The corralled-charcoal method makes the wok ripping hot for stir-frying the eggplant until browned; then it almost braises to silky, creamy tenderness once liquid is added. Serve this with rice, if you like (the rice will also help tame the heat). Bird chiles are dried red Thai chiles; use a spice grinder to grind them. Fermented black beans are soybeans that have been packed in salt and fermented; look for them in large supermarkets, in Asian markets, and online. The skin of Japanese eggplant is much thinner than that of globe eggplant, and the flesh contains fewer seeds. If Japanese or Chinese eggplant is unavailable, you can substitute globe eggplant. A 12-inch cast-iron skillet can be used in place of the wok. You will need a 13 by 9-inch disposable aluminum roasting pan.

1   Combine 5 tablespoons oil, bird chiles, garlic, ginger, and star anise in small saucepan and heat over medium-high heat until sizzling. Reduce heat to low and gently simmer until garlic and ginger are soft but not browned, about 5 minutes. Remove from heat and let cool for 5 minutes. Stir in beans, hoisin, 2 tablespoons Shaoxing wine, and sugar until combined; set aside.

2   Using skewer, poke 12 holes in bottom of disposable pan. Open bottom vent of charcoal grill completely and place disposable pan in center. Light large chimney starter three-quarters filled with charcoal briquettes (4½ quarts). When top coals are partially covered with ash, pour into disposable pan. Set cooking grate in place, cover, and open lid vent completely. Heat grill until hot, about 5 minutes.

3   Center 14-inch flat-bottomed carbon-steel wok on cooking grate over coals. Heat 1 tablespoon oil in wok until just smoking. Add half of eggplant and cook, tossing slowly and occasionally, until pieces are browned on most sides and just tender, 6 to 9 minutes. Transfer eggplant to bowl. Repeat with 1 tablespoon oil and remaining eggplant. Add remaining 1 tablespoon oil and bell pepper to wok. Cook, without stirring, until lightly browned, about 3 minutes.

4 Return eggplant to wok and toss to combine. Add water and remaining ¼ cup Shaoxing wine, scraping up any browned bits. Cook until liquid is reduced by half, about 2 minutes. Stir in scallion greens and stir until slightly wilted, about 15 seconds. Remove wok from grill and stir in reserved garlic–black bean sauce until combined. Transfer to serving platter and top with scallion whites and cilantro. Serve immediately.

Flare Trade

Gas Grill Turn all burners to high; cover; and heat grill until hot, about 15 minutes. Leave all burners on high. Center 12-inch cast-iron skillet on cooking grate and proceed with step 3.

Open Fire Prepare hot single-level fire in open-fire grill. Set cooking grate at least 6 inches from coals and flames and heat grill until hot, about 5 minutes. Proceed with step 3.

4 Weekend Gatherings

Diner-Style Breakfast

SERVES 4   **TOTAL TIME** 1 hour

1 pound ground pork

1 tablespoon pure maple syrup

2 garlic cloves, minced

1½ teaspoons dried sage

1 teaspoon pepper, divided

¾ teaspoon table salt, divided

½ teaspoon dried thyme

    Pinch cayenne pepper

1 pound Yukon Gold potatoes, unpeeled, shredded

½ red bell pepper, cut into 1-inch-long matchsticks

3 scallions, sliced thin on bias

4 (½-inch-thick) slices hearty sandwich bread

3 tablespoons extra-virgin olive oil, divided

4 large eggs

Why This Recipe Works This feast will rouse everybody out of bed on a weekend morning. It's supremely satisfying to cook all the components of this classic diner breakfast outdoors: You'll feel like an expert short-order cook while confidently flipping and crisping colorful hash browns, cooking freshly mixed sausage patties, and serving up neatly packaged eggs and toast. It takes just a simple temperature tweak to achieve beautifully browned bread framing sunny-side up eggs. This recipe can be made in strategic batches using a plancha or all at once if you have a flat-top grill. You will need a cast-iron plancha measuring at least 20 by 10 inches. If you don't have a round biscuit or cookie cutter, cut the toast holes with a sturdy drinking glass.

1   Mix pork, maple syrup, garlic, sage, ¾ teaspoon pepper, ½ teaspoon salt, thyme, and cayenne in large bowl until thoroughly combined. Using lightly moistened hands, divide mixture into 8 portions, shape into lightly packed balls, and flatten each ball into ½-inch-thick patty. Press center of each patty with your fingertip to create ¼-inch-deep divot; set aside.

2   Place potatoes in center of clean dish towel. Gather ends of towel and twist tightly to wring out excess moisture from potatoes. Transfer potatoes to large bowl and toss with bell pepper, scallions, remaining ¼ teaspoon pepper, and remaining ¼ teaspoon salt; set aside. Using 2½-inch round cutter, cut out and remove circle from center of each slice of bread. Brush 2 tablespoons oil evenly over both sides of bread.

3A   **For a charcoal grill**   Open bottom vent completely. Light large chimney starter three-quarters filled with charcoal briquettes (4½ quarts). When top coals are partially covered with ash, pour evenly over grill. Set cooking grate in place, center plancha on grill, cover, and open lid vent completely. Heat grill with plancha until hot, about 5 minutes.

3B   **For a gas grill**   Turn all burners to high and heat grill until hot, about 15 minutes. Center plancha on grill, cover, and heat for an additional 5 minutes. Turn all burners to medium-high.

4   Wipe plancha with well-oiled paper towels. Place patties on one half of plancha. Spread potato mixture in even layer on other half of plancha and lightly pack down. Cook until sausage is browned and

registers 160 degrees, 3 to 5 minutes per side. Cook hash until golden brown and crisp on first side, 6 to 8 minutes. Transfer sausage to platter and tent with aluminum foil. Drizzle remaining 1 tablespoon oil over now-empty side of plancha. Flip spatula-sized portions of hash onto oiled side of plancha and cook until golden brown and crisp on second side, 6 to 8 minutes. Transfer hash to platter with sausage and tent with foil.

5   Clean plancha and reduce burners to medium-low (if using gas). Arrange bread on now-empty plancha and cook until golden brown on first side, about 3 minutes. Flip bread and, working quickly, crack 1 egg into each bread hole. Cover and cook until bread is golden brown on second side and egg whites are set, about 4 minutes. Transfer toast to platter with sausage and hash. Serve.

Flare Trade

Flat-Top Grill   Turn all burners to medium-high and heat griddle until hot, about 10 minutes. Turn all burners to medium. Clean griddle and proceed with step 4, cooking sausage, hash, and toast with eggs on griddle at same time. Use 13 by 9-inch disposable aluminum pan to cover toast while eggs cook.

Open Fire   Prepare medium-hot single-level fire in open-fire grill. Set cooking grate at least 6 inches from coals and flames; place plancha on cooking grate; and heat plancha until hot, about 5 minutes. Proceed with step 4, using 13 by 9-inch disposable aluminum pan to cover toast while eggs cook.

Grilled French Toast

SERVES 4   **TOTAL TIME** 30 minutes

2 large eggs

1½ cups whole milk

5 tablespoons unsalted butter, melted

1 teaspoon almond extract or 2 teaspoons vanilla extract

½ teaspoon ground cinnamon

½ teaspoon table salt

8 (¾-inch-thick) slices challah

4 teaspoons sugar

Why This Recipe Works Breakfast outdoors spells adventure, no matter where you're cooking and eating it. This hearty French toast (yes, cook it right on the grill!) will please everybody, and it's actually a cinch to prepare al fresco. Cut thick slices of rich challah, soak them in a simple egg batter enlivened with almond and cinnamon, and then grill them directly on the bars of the grill grate, which gives them irresistibly crispy stripes of caramelization. Serve the French toast with butter, maple syrup, and fresh berries and it's a sure bet that everybody will be talking about this breakfast for the rest of the day. Creating nonstick conditions for the grill grate is key here (see page 9).

1 Lightly beat eggs in shallow dish. Whisk in milk, melted butter, almond extract, cinnamon, and salt (butter will clump slightly).

2A **For a charcoal grill** Open bottom vent completely. Light large chimney starter half filled with charcoal briquettes (3 quarts). When top coals are partially covered with ash, pour evenly over grill. Set cooking grate in place, cover, and open lid vent completely. Heat grill until hot, about 5 minutes.

2B **For a gas grill** Turn all burners to high; cover; and heat grill until hot, about 15 minutes. Turn all burners to medium.

3 Clean and oil cooking grate. Place bread on grill and toast until light golden brown, about 1 minute per side. Working with 1 bread slice at a time, soak in egg mixture until saturated but not falling apart, 10 seconds per side. Using firm slotted spatula, pick up bread slice, allowing excess egg mixture to drip off, and transfer to rimmed baking sheet.

4 Using spatula, transfer soaked bread to grill and cook (covered if using gas) until bread is deep golden brown on first side and releases easily from cooking grate, about 2 minutes. Sprinkle top of each toast with ½ teaspoon sugar, then flip and cook until deep golden brown on second side and sugar begins to caramelize, 1 to 2 minutes. Serve.

Flare Trade

Flat-Top Grill Turn all burners to medium-high and heat griddle until hot, about 10 minutes. Turn all burners to medium. Clean griddle and proceed with step 3.

Open Fire Prepare medium-hot single-level fire in open-fire grill. Set cooking grate at least 6 inches from coals and flames and heat grill until hot, about 5 minutes. Proceed with step 3.

Shakshuka Breakfast Pizza

12 ounces plum tomatoes, cored, halved, and seeded

¼ cup extra-virgin olive oil, divided, plus extra for drizzling

1 teaspoon ground coriander

1 teaspoon smoked paprika

¾ teaspoon table salt

½ teaspoon ground cumin

¼ teaspoon garlic powder

⅛ teaspoon cayenne pepper

1½ cups jarred roasted red peppers, patted dry and chopped, divided

¼ cup panko bread crumbs

⅓ cup water

1 pound pizza dough, room temperature

6 large eggs

½ cup coarsely chopped fresh cilantro

2 ounces feta cheese, crumbled (½ cup)

¼ cup pitted kalamata olives, sliced

Why This Recipe Works Shakshuka—eggs cooked in a simmering sauce of spiced tomatoes—is a breakfast staple across the Maghreb and in Israel. And pizza—well, it's hard to turn down pizza at any time of day. Here the two combine for a fun way to start the day outdoors, with pizza crust standing in for the traditional pita bread wedges that accompany shakshuka. You'll char meaty plum tomatoes on the grill and then stir them into a spicy roasted pepper puree. A two-level fire ensures that the assembled pizza develops a golden bottom crust and tender-yet-set eggs on top. Toss feta cheese, olives, and cilantro onto the finished pizza and then grab a slice to eat in your favorite outdoor spot. We like the convenience of using pizza dough from the pizzeria or supermarket, but if you'd like to make your own, see page 276. Room-temperature dough is much easier to shape than cold, so pull the dough from the fridge about 1 hour before you start cooking.

1A For a charcoal grill Open bottom vent halfway. Light large chimney starter three-quarters filled with charcoal briquettes (4½ quarts). When top coals are partially covered with ash, pour into ring around perimeter of grill, leaving 8-inch clearing in center. Set cooking grate in place, cover, and open lid vent halfway. Heat grill until hot, about 5 minutes.

1B For a gas grill Turn all burners to high; cover; and heat grill until hot, about 15 minutes. Turn all burners to medium-high.

2 Clean and oil cooking grate. Toss tomatoes with 1 tablespoon oil. Grill tomatoes (over coal perimeter if using charcoal; covered if using gas) until lightly charred, 4 to 6 minutes per side.

3 Microwave 2 tablespoons oil, coriander, paprika, salt, cumin, garlic powder, and cayenne in bowl until fragrant, about 30 seconds. Process spice mixture, half of peppers, panko, and water in blender until smooth, about 2 minutes, scraping down sides of blender jar as needed. Add tomatoes and pulse until coarsely chopped, about 5 pulses. Stir in remaining peppers; set aside.

4 Transfer dough to lightly floured counter. Using your hands and rolling pin, press and roll dough into rough 16 by 12-inch rectangle of even thickness. (If dough resists stretching, let it relax for 5 to 10 minutes before trying again.)

5 Brush top of dough rectangle with remaining 1 tablespoon oil. Grill oiled side down (over clearing if using charcoal; covered if using gas) until grill marks form, 2 to 3 minutes, popping any large bubbles that form on top. Using tongs and spatula, carefully peel dough from grate, then rotate dough 90 degrees and continue to cook (covered if using gas) until second set of grill marks appears, 2 to 3 minutes.

6 Reduce burners to medium (if using gas). Working quickly, flip dough and spread sauce evenly over top, leaving 1-inch border around edges. Using back of spoon,

create 6 evenly spaced small wells in sauce, each about 3 inches in diameter. Crack 1 egg into each well. Cover and cook until crust is golden around edges and eggs are just set, 9 to 11 minutes for slightly runny yolks or 11 to 13 minutes for soft-cooked yolks.

7 Transfer pizza to wire rack and let cool for 5 minutes. Transfer pizza to cutting board and sprinkle with cilantro, feta, and olives. Drizzle with extra oil, slice into rectangles, and serve.

Bacon

MAKES about 3½ pounds bacon   **TOTAL TIME** 1¾ hours, plus 7 days curing and 3 hours cooling

1 cup packed light brown sugar

⅓ cup kosher salt

1 tablespoon coarsely cracked pepper

2 teaspoons minced fresh thyme

¾ teaspoon pink curing salt #1

1 bay leaf, crumbled

1 (4-pound) skinless center-cut pork belly, 1½ inches thick

5 (3-inch) wood chunks

Why This Recipe Works The smoky-sweet scent, the crispy bits of fat intertwined with chewy streaks of meat, the irresistible flavor—any way you slice it, bacon is undeniably delicious, but making it from scratch takes it to next-level spectacular. Using the moderate, indirect heat of a charcoal snake setup in a grill, you can achieve truly artisanal results from a slab of pork belly. This bacon makes a killer upgrade to Smoked Turkey Club Panini (page 72), or use it for the best BLTs ever. Look for a flat, rectangular center-cut section of pork belly that's 1½ inches thick, with roughly equal amounts of meat and fat. We used Diamond Crystal kosher salt. If using Morton kosher salt, use only ¼ cup. This recipe uses pink curing salt #1, which includes nitrites, to preserve the pink color of the bacon; it is also called Prague Powder #1, Insta Cure #1, or DQ Curing Salt #1. This recipe was developed for a 22-inch or larger kettle-style charcoal grill. You will need a 13 by 9-inch disposable aluminum roasting pan.

1   Combine sugar, salt, pepper, thyme, pink curing salt, and bay leaf in bowl. Rub pork belly all over with mixture, coating evenly, in 13 by 9-inch glass baking dish. Cover tightly with plastic wrap and refrigerate until pork feels firm yet still pliable, 7 to 10 days, flipping pork every other day.

2   Rinse pork with cold water and pat dry with paper towels (some peppercorns and thyme may remain).

3   Open bottom vent of charcoal grill completely. Arrange 30 briquettes, 2 briquettes wide, around nearly half of perimeter of grill to form C shape, overlapping slightly so briquettes are touching. Place second layer of 30 briquettes, also 2 briquettes wide, on top of first. (Completed arrangement should be 2 briquettes wide by 2 briquettes high.)

4   Evenly space wood chunks along length of charcoal C. Place disposable pan in center of grate, running lengthwise into gap in C. Pour 6 cups water into pan.

5   Light chimney starter filled with 15 briquettes (pile briquettes on 1 side of chimney so they catch). When coals are partially covered with ash, pour them over 1 end of C, making sure lit coals do not touch other end.

Flare Trade

Smoker Heat and maintain smoker temperature of 275 to 300 degrees following manufacturer's guidelines and tips on page 15. Clean and oil smoker grate, then place pork in center of grate. Proceed with step 6.

6   Set cooking grate in place, then clean and oil grate. Place pork belly meat side down over water pan. Cover grill and position lid vent over pork; open vent completely. Cook undisturbed until thickest part of pork registers 150 degrees, 1½ to 2 hours.

7   Transfer bacon to wire rack and let cool for 1 hour. Wrap tightly with plastic wrap and refrigerate until chilled, about 2 hours. (Bacon can be wrapped tightly with plastic and refrigerated for up to 1 month or frozen for up to 2 months.)

8   **To serve**   Using long, sharp knife, slice bacon in half crosswise, then slice halves ⅛ inch thick against grain into strips. Place bacon on preheated plancha over medium-hot fire in charcoal or gas grill in single layer and cook until crispy, 3 to 5 minutes, flipping as needed. Transfer bacon to paper towel–lined plate.

Smoked Chicken Wings

SERVES 4 to 6   **TOTAL TIME** 1½ hours, plus 1 hour brining

Wings

- ¼ cup table salt for brining
- ¼ cup sugar for brining
- 3 pounds chicken wings, cut at joints, wingtips discarded
- 2 teaspoons paprika
- 2 teaspoons chili powder
- 1¼ teaspoons dried oregano
- 1¼ teaspoons pepper
- 1¼ teaspoons garlic powder
- 1 teaspoon sugar
- ¼ teaspoon cayenne pepper
- 2 cups wood chips

Sauce

- 4 tablespoons unsalted butter
- 2 tablespoons cider vinegar
- 2 tablespoons ketchup
- ¼ teaspoon table salt

Flare Trade

Smoker Heat and maintain smoker temperature of 325 to 350 degrees following manufacturer's guidelines and tips on page 15. Clean and oil smoker grate, then arrange wings in center of grate. Proceed with step 5, increasing cooking time to 50 minutes to 1 hour 10 minutes. Omit step 6.

Why This Recipe Works Pronounced smokiness; tender, juicy meat; crisp, fully rendered skin; and a barbecue-inspired spice rub add up to wings with a major "wow" factor. To allow the wings to cook through and smoke for just the right amount of time, build a two-level fire in the grill, start them over indirect heat, and then move them directly over the coals to sear and crisp the skin. An irresistibly savory sauce of melted butter, cider vinegar, and ketchup gives these char-kissed wings a beautiful sheen. We prefer to buy whole wings and butcher them ourselves because they tend to be larger than wings that come split. If you can find only split wings, look for larger ones. Twelve whole wings should equal 3 pounds and yield 24 pieces (12 drumettes and 12 flats). Don't brine the chicken for more than 3 hours in step 1 or it will be too salty. If you'd like to use wood chunks instead of wood chips when using a charcoal grill, substitute two medium wood chunks for the wood chip packet.

1 **For the wings** Dissolve salt and ¼ cup sugar in 2 quarts cold water in large container. Submerge wings in brine, cover, and refrigerate for at least 1 hour or up to 3 hours. Combine paprika, chili powder, oregano, pepper, garlic powder, sugar, and cayenne in large bowl. Measure out 1 tablespoon spice mixture and set aside.

2 **For the sauce** Melt butter in small saucepan over medium-low heat. Add reserved 1 tablespoon spice mixture and cook until fragrant, about 30 seconds. Carefully add vinegar (mixture will bubble up). Bring to simmer, then remove from heat. Whisk in ketchup and salt. Cover and set aside.

3 Using large piece of heavy-duty aluminum foil, wrap chips in 8 by 4½-inch foil packet. (Make sure chips do not poke holes in sides or bottom of packet. If using gas, make sure there are no more than 2 layers of foil on bottom of packet.) Cut 2 evenly spaced 2-inch slits in top of packet. Remove wings from brine and pat dry with paper towels. Toss wings with remaining spice mixture until well coated.

4A **For a charcoal grill** Open bottom vent completely. Light large chimney starter mounded with charcoal briquettes (7 quarts). When top coals are partially covered with ash, pour evenly over half of grill. Place wood chip packet on coals. Set cooking grate in place, cover, and open lid vent completely. Heat grill until hot and wood chips are smoking, about 5 minutes.

4B **For a gas grill** Remove cooking grate and place wood chip packet directly on primary burner. Set grate in place and turn all burners to high. Cover and heat grill until hot and wood chips are smoking, 15 to 25 minutes. Leave primary burner on high and turn off other burner(s). (Adjust primary burner as needed to maintain grill temperature of 400 degrees; if using 3-burner grill, adjust primary burner and second burner.)

5 Clean and oil cooking grate. Place wings, fatty side up, on cooler side of grill (6 to 8 inches from heat source for gas grill), arranging drumettes closest to fire. Cover (position lid vent over chicken if using charcoal) and cook until wings are darkened and register at least 180 degrees, 40 minutes to 1 hour, flipping wings halfway through cooking.

6A **For a charcoal grill** Slide half of wings to hotter side of grill and cook, uncovered, until charred in spots, 1 to 3 minutes per side. Transfer wings to platter and tent with foil. Repeat with remaining wings.

6B **For a gas grill** Turn all burners to high and cook, uncovered, until wings are charred in spots, 5 to 7 minutes per side. Transfer wings to platter and tent with foil.

7 Reheat sauce over medium heat, about 2 minutes. Toss wings and sauce together in bowl. Serve.

Smoked Citrus Chicken

SERVES 4 to 6   **TOTAL TIME** 1¼ hours, plus 1 hour marinating

¼ cup extra-virgin olive oil

4 garlic cloves, minced

1 tablespoon kosher salt

1½ teaspoons ground cumin

1½ teaspoons grated orange zest, plus orange wedges for serving

1 teaspoon grated lemon zest, plus lemon wedges for serving

¾ teaspoon ground cinnamon

½ teaspoon pepper

⅛ teaspoon cayenne pepper

3 pounds bone-in chicken pieces (split breasts cut in half crosswise, drumsticks, and/or thighs), trimmed

1 cup wood chips

Why This Recipe Works This char-grilled chicken infused with citrus and spice is inspired by the chicken made at the restaurant chain El Pollo Loco. Cutting slits into bone-in chicken pieces before marinating gives them more surface area for a bold marinade of orange and lemon zest, cumin, garlic, cinnamon, and cayenne to cling to. Cooking the chicken over indirect heat on a hot grill outfitted with a packet of wood chips infuses the meat with smoky flavor. Charring it on the hotter side of the grill for the last few minutes gives it a deeper color. If you'd like to use wood chunks instead of wood chips when using a charcoal grill, substitute one medium wood chunk for the wood chip packet.

1 Whisk oil, garlic, salt, cumin, orange zest, lemon zest, cinnamon, pepper, and cayenne together in large bowl. Cut two ½-inch-deep slits in skin side of each chicken breast half, two ½-inch-deep slits in skin side of each thigh, and two ½-inch-deep slits in each drumstick. Transfer chicken to bowl with marinade and turn to thoroughly coat. Cover and refrigerate for at least 1 hour or up to 24 hours.

2 Using large piece of heavy-duty aluminum foil, wrap chips in 8 by 4½-inch foil packet. (Make sure chips do not poke holes in sides or bottom of packet. If using gas, make sure there are no more than 2 layers of foil on bottom of packet.) Cut 2 evenly spaced 2-inch slits in top of packet.

3A **For a charcoal grill** Open bottom vent completely. Light large chimney starter mounded with charcoal briquettes (7 quarts). When top coals are partially covered with ash, pour evenly over half of grill. Place wood chip packet on coals. Set cooking grate in place, cover, and open lid vent completely. Heat grill until hot and wood chips are smoking, about 5 minutes.

3B **For a gas grill** Remove cooking grate and place wood chip packet directly on primary burner. Set grate in place and turn all burners to high. Cover and heat grill until hot and wood chips are smoking, 15 to 25 minutes. Leave primary burner on high and turn off other burner(s). (Adjust primary burner as needed to maintain grill temperature between 350 and 400 degrees; if using 3-burner grill, adjust primary burner and second burner.)

Flare Trade

Smoker Heat and maintain smoker temperature of 325 to 350 degrees following manufacturer's guidelines and tips on page 15. Clean and oil smoker grate, then center chicken on grate. Proceed with step 4, increasing cooking time to 40 to 60 minutes. Omit charring in step 5.

4 Clean and oil cooking grate. Place chicken skin side up on cooler side of grill (6 to 8 inches from heat source for gas grill) with breast pieces farthest away from fire. Cover (position lid vent over chicken if using charcoal) and cook until breasts register 160 degrees and drumsticks/thighs register 175 degrees, 22 to 28 minutes, transferring pieces to plate, skin side up, as they come to temperature.

5 Transfer chicken skin side down to hotter side of grill. Cook until skin is well charred, 2 to 5 minutes, moving pieces as needed for even charring. Transfer chicken to platter, tent with foil, and let rest for 10 minutes. Serve with orange and lemon wedges.

Smoked Bourbon Chicken

SERVES 4 to 6   **TOTAL TIME** 2½ hours, plus 1 hour marinating

1¼ cups bourbon

1¼ cups soy sauce

½ cup packed brown sugar

1 shallot, minced

4 garlic cloves, minced

2 teaspoons pepper

2 (3½- to 4-pound) whole
  chickens, giblets discarded

1 cup wood chips

Why This Recipe Works Bourbon and smoke are a flavor match made in heaven. Using a bourbon and soy marinade that doubles as a mopping sauce takes chicken to its flavorful max. Because smoke is attracted to moisture, keeping the skin moist pulls the smoke to the chicken like a magnet. You'll want plenty of surface area to achieve this effect, so you'll split the birds in half and cut slashes into the meat. The chicken halves get a good soak in a portion of the savory-sweet marinade before cooking; once they're on the grill, basting them every 15 minutes or so results in smokin' good bourbon taste. If you'd like to use wood chunks instead of wood chips when using a charcoal grill, substitute one medium wood chunk for the wood chip packet. You will need four 12-inch wooden skewers.

1   Bring bourbon, soy sauce, sugar, shallot, garlic, and pepper to boil in medium saucepan over medium-high heat and cook for 1 minute. Remove from heat and let cool, about 15 minutes. Set aside ¾ cup bourbon mixture for basting chicken. (Bourbon mixture can be refrigerated for up to 3 days.)

2   Place 1 chicken breast side down on cutting board. Using kitchen shears, cut through bones on either side of backbone; discard backbone. Flip chicken and, using chef's knife, split in half lengthwise through center of breastbone. Cut ½-inch-deep slits across breasts, thighs, and legs, about ½ inch apart. Tuck wingtips behind back. Repeat with remaining chicken. Divide chicken halves between two 1-gallon zipper-lock bags and divide remaining bourbon mixture between bags. Seal bags, turn to distribute marinade, and refrigerate for at least 1 hour or up to 24 hours, flipping occasionally.

3   Using large piece of heavy-duty aluminum foil, wrap chips in 8 by 4½-inch foil packet. (Make sure chips do not poke holes in sides or bottom of packet. If using gas, make sure there are no more than 2 layers of foil on bottom of packet.) Cut 2 evenly spaced 2-inch slits in top of packet. Remove chicken halves from marinade and pat dry with paper towels; discard marinade. Insert 1 skewer lengthwise through thickest part of breast down through thigh of each chicken half.

4A   For a charcoal grill Open bottom vent halfway. Light large chimney starter filled with charcoal briquettes (6 quarts). When top coals are partially covered with ash, pour into steeply banked pile against 1 side of grill. Place wood chip packet on coals. Set cooking grate in place, cover, and open lid vent halfway. Heat grill until hot and wood chips are smoking, about 5 minutes.

Flare Trade

Smoker Heat and maintain smoker temperature of 325 to 350 degrees following manufacturer's guidelines and tips on page 15. Clean and oil smoker grate, then place chicken in center of grate. Proceed with step 5, increasing cooking time to 1½ to 1¾ hours.

4B **For a gas grill** Remove cooking grate and place wood chip packet directly on primary burner. Set grate in place and turn all burners to high. Cover and heat grill until hot and wood chips are smoking, 15 to 25 minutes. Leave primary burner on high and turn off other burner(s). (Adjust primary burner as needed to maintain grill temperature between 350 and 375 degrees; if using 3-burner grill, adjust primary burner and second burner.)

5 Clean and oil cooking grate. Place chicken halves skin side up on cooler side of grill (6 to 8 inches from heat source for gas grill) with legs closest to fire. Cover (position lid vent over chicken if using charcoal) and cook, basting every 15 minutes with reserved bourbon mixture, until breasts register 160 degrees and thighs register 175 degrees, 1¼ to 1½ hours, switching placement of chicken halves after 45 minutes. (All of bourbon mixture should be used.) Transfer chicken to carving board, tent with foil, and let rest for 20 minutes. Remove skewers and carve chicken. Serve.

Butterflied Chicken

SERVES 4   **TOTAL TIME** 1¾ hours, plus 1 hour chilling

1 (4-pound) whole chicken, giblets discarded

1 tablespoon packed light brown sugar

2 teaspoons kosher salt

2 teaspoons pepper

Why This Recipe Works Using your grill to roast a whole chicken makes it a meal for all seasons. To make sure the bird cooks evenly, spatchcocking it is the way to go: Cut out the backbone and thread skewers through the breast and drumsticks to help it lie flat and stay intact. To maximize juiciness, you'll build a half-grill fire (with the coals piled on one side of the grill) and cook the chicken on the cooler side, covered, for about an hour. A simple rub of brown sugar, salt, and pepper turns the skin a beautiful bronze. You will need two 12-inch wooden skewers.

1   Place chicken, breast side down, on cutting board. Using kitchen shears, cut through bones on either side of backbone; discard backbone. Flip chicken over and press on breastbone to flatten. Tuck wingtips behind back. Insert 1 skewer down length of chicken through thickest part of breast and into and through drumstick. Repeat with second skewer on other half of chicken.

2   Combine sugar, salt, and pepper in bowl. Rub mixture evenly over skin side of chicken. Transfer chicken skin side up to plate and refrigerate, uncovered, for at least 1 hour or up to 24 hours.

3A   For a charcoal grill Open bottom vent completely. Light large chimney starter mounded with charcoal briquettes (7 quarts). When top coals are partially covered with ash, pour evenly over half of grill. Set cooking grate in place, cover, and open lid vent completely. Heat grill until hot, about 5 minutes.

3B   For a gas grill Turn all burners to high; cover; and heat grill until hot, about 15 minutes. Leave primary burner on high and turn off other burner(s). (Adjust primary burner as needed to maintain grill temperature between 350 and 400 degrees; if using 3-burner grill, adjust primary burner and second burner.)

4   Clean and oil cooking grate. Place chicken skin side up on cooler side of grill (6 to 8 inches from heat source for gas grill) with skewers parallel to fire. Cover (position lid vent over chicken if using charcoal) and cook until breasts register 160 degrees and thighs register 175 degrees, about 1 hour, rotating chicken halfway through cooking.

5   Transfer chicken skin side up to carving board, tent with aluminum foil, and let rest for 15 minutes. Remove skewers and carve chicken. Serve.

Flare Trade

Open Fire Prepare hot half-grill fire in open-fire grill. Set cooking grate at least 6 inches from coals and flames and heat grill until hot, about 5 minutes. Proceed with step 4, placing chicken skin side up on cooler side of grill with skewers parallel to fire. Cook for 40 minutes, rotating chicken halfway through cooking. Flip chicken skin side down and continue to cook until breasts register 160 degrees and thighs register 175 degrees, 20 to 50 minutes, rotating chicken halfway through cooking.

Variations

Grill-Roasted Butterflied Chicken with Barbecue Spice Rub

Increase sugar to 3 tablespoons; in step 2 combine with salt, pepper, 1 tablespoon paprika, 1 tablespoon chili powder, 2 teaspoons garlic powder, and ¼ teaspoon cayenne pepper in bowl. Gently loosen skin covering chicken breast and thighs. Rub one-third of spice mixture underneath skin, then rub remaining spice mixture all over chicken.

Grill-Roasted Butterflied Chicken with Ras el Hanout Spice Rub

Omit pepper. Decrease salt to ¾ teaspoon; in step 2 combine with sugar, 2 tablespoons paprika, 4 teaspoons ground coriander, 4 teaspoons ground cumin, 1 teaspoon ground cardamom, 1 teaspoon ground cinnamon, ½ teaspoon ground cloves, ½ teaspoon ground nutmeg, and ½ teaspoon cayenne pepper in bowl. Gently loosen skin covering chicken breast and thighs. Rub one-third of spice mixture underneath skin, then rub remaining spice mixture all over chicken.

Pollo a La Brasa

SERVES 8   **TOTAL TIME** 2½ hours, plus 24 hours marinating

Sauce

¾   cup mayonnaise

3   tablespoons ají amarillo paste

1½   tablespoons lime juice

1   garlic clove, minced to a paste

1½   teaspoons jarred huacatay paste

Chicken

1   cup cerveza negra or amber ale

¼   cup finely grated garlic

¼   cup lime juice (2 limes)

¼   cup soy sauce

2   tablespoons minced fresh rosemary

4   teaspoons table salt

4   teaspoons yellow mustard

2   teaspoons pepper

2   teaspoons dried oregano

2   teaspoons ground cumin

2   (4- to 4½-pound) whole chickens, giblets discarded

1   cup wood chips

Why This Recipe Works This wildly popular Peruvian dish will convince you that your rotisserie attachment is one of the best grilling investments you've made. Our version calls for soaking two chickens in a beer-based marinade that also includes soy sauce, lime juice, mustard, garlic, and spices. Roasting the birds on the rotisserie over a hot fire produces succulent, smoky meat cloaked in mahogany skin. A serving sauce made with ají amarillo (Peruvian yellow chile pepper) paste and huacatay (black mint) paste amps up the flavors even more. You will need a motorized rotisserie attachment. If using a charcoal grill, you will need a 13 by 9-inch disposable aluminum roasting pan. If you'd like to use wood chunks instead of wood chips when using a charcoal grill, substitute one medium wood chunk for the wood chip packet. Our gas grill instructions are for a three-burner grill. If using a two-burner grill, we recommend halving the recipe and cooking with both burners turned to medium-low (do not halve the wood chip amount). This is traditionally served with french fries and salad.

1   **For the sauce** Whisk all ingredients until smooth. (Sauce can be refrigerated for up to 1 week.)

2   **For the chicken** Whisk beer, garlic, lime juice, soy sauce, rosemary, salt, mustard, pepper, oregano, and cumin together in liquid measuring cup. Using your fingers or handle of wooden spoon, gently loosen skin covering chicken breasts and leg quarters. Using paring knife, poke 10 to 15 holes in fat deposits on skin of backs. Tuck wingtips underneath chickens.

3   Place 1 chicken in bowl with cavity end facing up. Slowly pour half of marinade between skin and meat and rub marinade inside cavity, outside skin, and under skin to distribute. Transfer chicken to 1-gallon zipper-lock bag and add marinade left in bowl to bag; seal bag. Repeat with remaining chicken and remaining half of marinade. Refrigerate for 24 hours, flipping bags halfway through marinating.

4   Transfer chickens to rimmed baking sheet. Tie knot around each chicken tail with 12-inch piece of kitchen twine, then tie legs together and secure to tail using ends of twine. Tuck wingtips behind back. Turn chickens breast side up and line them up so breast ends touch. Thread rotisserie skewer lengthwise through chickens. Center chickens on skewer, leaving 1-inch gap between chickens. Attach rotisserie forks to skewer and insert tines into chicken thighs; secure forks by tightening screws.

5 Using large piece of heavy-duty aluminum foil, wrap chips in 8 by 4 ½-inch foil packet. (Make sure chips do not poke holes in sides or bottom of packet. If using gas, make sure there are no more than 2 layers of foil on bottom of packet.) Cut 2 evenly spaced 2-inch slits in top of packet.

6A **For a charcoal grill** Open bottom vent halfway and place disposable pan in center of grill. Light large chimney starter filled with charcoal briquettes (6 quarts). When top coals are partially covered with ash, pour into 2 even piles flush against long sides of disposable pan. Place wood chip packet on 1 pile of coals. Position rotisserie motor attachment on grill so that skewer runs parallel to coals. Cover and open lid vent halfway. Heat grill until hot and wood chips are smoking, about 5 minutes.

6B **For a gas grill** Remove cooking grate and place wood chip packet directly on primary burner. Position rotisserie motor attachment on grill and turn all burners to high. Cover and heat grill until hot and wood chips are smoking, 15 to 25 minutes. Turn 2 outside burners to medium and turn off center burner. (Adjust outside burners as needed to maintain grill temperature between 350 and 375 degrees.)

7 Attach rotisserie skewer to motor and start motor. Cover and cook until breasts register 160 degrees and thighs registers 175 degrees, 1¼ hours to 1½ hours.

8 Transfer chickens, still on skewer, to carving board and let rest for 15 minutes. Using large wad of paper towels in each hand, carefully remove rotisserie forks and skewer from chickens. Carve chickens, transfer to platter, and serve with sauce.

Thai Cornish Game Hens with Chili Dipping Sauce

SERVES 4   **TOTAL TIME** 1½ hours, plus 6 hours marinating

Game Hens

- 1 cup coarsely chopped fresh cilantro leaves and stems
- 12 garlic cloves, peeled
- ¼ cup packed light brown sugar
- 2 teaspoons ground white pepper
- 2 teaspoons ground coriander
- 2 teaspoons table salt
- ¼ cup fish sauce
- 4 (1¼- to 1½-pound) Cornish game hens, giblets discarded

Chili Dipping Sauce

- ½ cup distilled white vinegar
- ½ cup granulated sugar
- 1 tablespoon minced Thai chiles
- 3 garlic cloves, minced
- ¼ teaspoon table salt

Why This Recipe Works For the fantastic Thai street food called gai yang, food vendors butterfly and flatten small chickens and then marinate them in a garlic-herb paste before grilling them over a low charcoal fire until the meat is juicy and the skin is crisp. By using Cornish hens, you can enjoy a smoky, sweet, and savory meal from your grill that's close to the real thing. Flattening the hens allows them to cook quickly and evenly, and a garlicky paste-like marinade clings nicely to them. Cooking the hens skin side up over the cooler side of a half-grill fire gives their fatty skin time to render while the meat cooks; finishing them over the hotter side crisps the skin. A spicy vinegar-and-sugar-based dipping sauce adds a final punch of flavor. If your hens weigh 1½ to 2 pounds, grill three hens instead of four and extend the initial cooking time in step 6 by 5 minutes. If you can't find Thai chiles, substitute Fresno or red jalapeño chiles.

1 **For the game hens** Pulse cilantro leaves and stems, garlic, sugar, white pepper, coriander, and salt in food processor until finely chopped, 10 to 15 pulses; transfer to small bowl. Add fish sauce and stir until marinade has consistency of loose paste.

2 Place 1 hen breast side down on cutting board. Using kitchen shears, cut through bones on either side of backbone; discard backbone. Flip hen and press on breastbone to flatten. Trim any excess fat and skin. Repeat with remaining 3 hens.

3 Rub hens all over with marinade. Transfer hens and any excess marinade to 1-gallon zipper-lock bag and refrigerate for at least 6 hours or up to 24 hours, flipping bag halfway through marinating.

4 **For the chili dipping sauce** Bring vinegar to boil in small saucepan over high heat. Add sugar and stir to dissolve. Reduce heat to medium-low and simmer until vinegar mixture is slightly thickened, 5 minutes. Remove from heat and let vinegar mixture cool completely. Add Thai chiles, garlic, and salt and stir until combined. Transfer sauce to airtight container and refrigerate until ready to use. (Sauce can be refrigerated for up to 2 weeks. Bring to room temperature before serving.)

5A   For a charcoal grill Open bottom vent completely. Light large chimney starter filled with charcoal briquettes (6 quarts). When top coals are partially covered with ash, pour evenly over half of grill. Set cooking grate in place, cover, and open lid vent completely. Heat grill until hot, about 5 minutes.

5B   For a gas grill Turn all burners to high; cover; and heat grill until hot, about 15 minutes. Leave primary burner on high and turn off other burner(s). (Adjust primary burner as needed to maintain grill temperature between 350 and 400 degrees; if using 3-burner grill, adjust primary burner and second burner.)

6   Clean and oil cooking grate. Remove hens from bag, leaving any marinade that sticks to hens in place. Tuck wingtips behind backs and turn legs so drumsticks face inward toward breasts. Place hens skin side up on cooler side of grill (6 to 8 inches from heat source for gas grill) with legs and thighs facing fire. Cover (position lid vent over hens if using charcoal) and cook until skin is browned and breasts register 145 to 150 degrees, 30 to 35 minutes, rotating hens halfway through cooking.

7   Using tongs, carefully flip hens skin side down and move to hotter side of grill. Cover and cook until skin is crisp, deeply browned, and charred in spots and breasts register 160 degrees and thighs register 175 degrees, 3 to 5 minutes, being careful to avoid burning.

8   Transfer hens skin side up to cutting board; tent with aluminum foil and let rest for 10 minutes. Slice each hen in half or into 4 pieces and serve, passing chili dipping sauce separately.

Flare Trade

Open Fire Prepare hot half-grill fire in open-fire grill. Set cooking grate at least 6 inches from coals and flames and heat grill until hot, about 5 minutes. Proceed with step 6, placing hens skin side up on cooler side of grill. Cook for 20 minutes, rotating hens halfway through cooking. Flip hens skin side down and continue to cook until breasts register 160 degrees and thighs register 175 degrees, 20 to 25 minutes, rotating hens halfway through cooking. Omit step 7.

Smoked Turkey

SERVES 10 to 12   **TOTAL TIME** 3¾ hours, plus 1½ hours salting and resting

2 tablespoons kosher salt

2 tablespoons packed light brown sugar

1 (12- to 14-pound) turkey, neck and giblets discarded

4 (3-inch) wood chunks

Why This Recipe Works Deep-fried turkey has its fans, but when we're cooking turkey outdoors, we smoke it. It's a showstopper anytime, but it also frees up your oven for other dishes at holiday meals. To get the long, low burn needed for grill-smoking a big bird in your charcoal grill, you'll arrange the coals in a C shape around the perimeter of the grill bottom. Lighting both ends of the C allows the coals to slowly ignite in succession. Wood chunks on top of the charcoal provide bursts of smoke throughout cooking. Removing the turkey when the breast registers 160 degrees ensures moist meat and beautifully bronzed skin. If you're using a self-basting or kosher turkey, omit the salt. This recipe was developed for a 22-inch or larger kettle-style charcoal grill. You will need a 13 by 9-inch disposable aluminum roasting pan.

1   Combine salt and sugar in bowl. Place turkey breast side down on cutting board with cavity facing counter edge. Using kitchen shears, cut through bones on either side of backbone, staying as close as possible to backbone. Discard backbone. Flip turkey and press down firmly on breast with heels of your hands to flatten breastbone. Using your fingers or handle of wooden spoon, carefully separate skin from thighs and breast. Using skewer, poke 15 to 20 holes in fat deposits on breast halves and thighs.

2   Rub bone side of turkey evenly with 1 tablespoon salt mixture. Flip turkey skin side up and rub 2 tablespoons salt mixture evenly under skin. Tuck wing-tips under turkey. Pat skin side of turkey dry with paper towels. Sprinkle surface of turkey with remaining 1 tablespoon salt mixture and rub in mixture with your hands, coating skin evenly. Transfer turkey to rimmed baking sheet and let sit at room temperature for 1 hour. (Turkey can be refrigerated, uncovered, for up to 24 hours; let sit at room temperature for 1 hour before proceeding.)

3   Open bottom vent of charcoal grill completely. Arrange 50 briquettes, 2 briquettes wide, around perimeter of grill to form C shape, overlapping slightly so briquettes are touching and leaving 10-inch gap between ends of C. Place second layer of 50 briquettes, also 2 briquettes wide, on top of first. (Completed arrangement should be 2 briquettes wide by 2 briquettes high.)

4   Evenly space wood chunks along length of charcoal C. Set disposable pan in center of grate, running lengthwise into gap in C. Pour 6 cups water into pan.

Flare Trade

Smoker Heat and maintain smoker temperature of 325 to 350 degrees following manufacturer's guidelines and tips on page 15. Clean and oil smoker grate, then place turkey skin side up in center of grate. Proceed with step 6. Rotate turkey 180 degrees in step 7 (do not flip) and insert temperature probe into thickest part of breast. Cover and continue to cook until breast registers 160 degrees and thighs register 175 degrees, 1 to 1½ hours.

5   Light chimney starter filled with 20 briquettes (pile briquettes on 1 side of chimney so they catch). When coals are partially covered with ash, use tongs to pile 10 coals on each end of charcoal C, where briquettes meet water pan, so both ends of C ignite.

6   Set cooking grate in place, then clean and oil grate. Position turkey skin side down over water pan, with drumsticks pointing toward arc of charcoal C. Cover grill, position lid vent over turkey, and open vent completely. Cook turkey undisturbed for 2 hours.

7   Using grill gloves, flip turkey skin side up, again positioning it over water pan with drumsticks pointing toward arc of charcoal C. Insert temperature probe into thickest part of breast. Cover and cook, undisturbed, until breast registers 160 degrees (check temperature of both sides of breast) and thighs register 175 degrees, about 1 hour.

8   Transfer turkey to carving board and let rest for 30 minutes. Carve turkey and serve.

Grilled Pork Loin with Apple-Cranberry Filling

SERVES 6   **TOTAL TIME** 2½ hours

Filling

1½	cups (4 ounces) dried apples
1	cup apple cider
¾	cup packed light brown sugar
½	cup cider vinegar
½	cup dried cranberries
1	large shallot, halved and sliced thin
1	tablespoon grated fresh ginger
1	tablespoon yellow mustard seeds
½	teaspoon ground allspice
⅛-¼	teaspoon cayenne pepper

Pork

1	(2½- to 3-pound) boneless pork loin roast, trimmed
1	teaspoon table salt, divided
½	teaspoon pepper, divided
2	cups wood chips

Why This Recipe Works Pork loin has a subtle sweetness that benefits from the smoky heat of the grill, and stuffing it is a clever way to keep this lean cut juicy. If you start with a short, wide roast, just a few strategic cuts will give you a long, flat sheet that's easy to fill and roll up. Poaching apples and cranberries in a blend of apple cider, cider vinegar, and spices develops a pleasantly dense, chewy filling. As a bonus, the leftover poaching liquid gets reduced to a glaze that beautifully burnishes the roast. This recipe is best prepared with a loin that is 7 to 8 inches long and 4 to 5 inches wide. For a spicier stuffing, use the larger amount of cayenne. If you'd like to use wood chunks instead of wood chips when using a charcoal grill, substitute two medium wood chunks for the wood chip packet.

1   **For the filling** Bring all ingredients to simmer in medium saucepan over medium-high heat. Cover, reduce heat to low, and cook until apples are very soft, about 20 minutes. Transfer mixture to fine-mesh strainer set over bowl and press with back of spoon to extract as much liquid as possible. Return liquid to saucepan and simmer over medium-high heat until reduced to ⅓ cup, about 5 minutes; set aside for glazing. Pulse apple mixture in food processor until coarsely chopped, about 15 pulses. Transfer filling to bowl and refrigerate until needed.

2   **For the pork** Position roast fat side up. Insert knife on long side of roast ½ inch from bottom and cut horizontally, stopping ½ inch before edge. Open up flap. Cut through thicker half of roast about ½ inch from bottom, stopping about ½ inch before edge. Open up flap. Repeat until pork is even ½-inch thickness throughout. If uneven, cover with plastic wrap and use meat pounder to even out. Sprinkle interior with ½ teaspoon salt and ¼ teaspoon pepper and spread filling in even layer over pork, leaving ½-inch border. Roll roast tightly and tie crosswise with kitchen twine at 1-inch intervals. (Stuffed roast can be covered and refrigerated for up to 24 hours; let sit at room temperature for 1 hour before proceeding.)

3   Pat roast dry with paper towels and sprinkle with remaining ½ teaspoon salt and remaining ¼ teaspoon pepper. Using large piece of heavy-duty aluminum foil, wrap chips in 8 by 4½-inch foil packet. (Make sure chips do not poke holes in sides or bottom of packet. If using gas, make sure there are no more than 2 layers of foil on bottom of packet.) Cut 2 evenly spaced 2-inch slits in top of packet.

4A **For a charcoal grill** Open bottom vent halfway. Light large chimney starter three-quarters filled with charcoal briquettes (4½ quarts). When top coals are partially covered with ash, pour evenly over half of grill. Place wood chip packet on coals. Set cooking grate in place, cover, and open lid vent halfway. Heat grill until hot and wood chips are smoking, about 5 minutes.

4B **For a gas grill** Remove cooking grate and place wood chip packet directly on primary burner. Set cooking grate in place; turn all burners to high; cover; and heat grill until hot and wood chips are smoking, 15 to 25 minutes. Leave primary burner on medium-high and turn off other burner(s). (Adjust primary burner as needed to maintain grill temperature between 300 and 325 degrees; if using 3-burner grill, adjust primary burner and second burner.)

5 Clean and oil cooking grate. Place roast fat side up on cooler side of grill (6 to 8 inches from heat source for gas grill), cover (position lid vent over roast if using charcoal), and cook until meat registers 130 to 135 degrees, 55 minutes to 1 hour 10 minutes, flipping roast halfway through cooking.

6 Brush roast evenly with reserved glaze. (Reheat glaze, if necessary, to make it spreadable.) Continue to cook until glaze is glossy and meat registers 140 degrees, 5 to 10 minutes. Transfer roast to carving board, tent with foil, and let rest for 15 minutes. Remove twine and slice roast ½ inch thick. Serve.

Variation

Grilled Pork Loin with Apple, Cherry, and Caraway Filling

Substitute dried cherries for cranberries and 1 teaspoon caraway seeds for ginger, mustard seeds, and allspice. Stir 2 teaspoons minced fresh thyme into filling after processing.

Memphis-Style Wet Ribs

SERVES 6 to 8   **TOTAL TIME** 5 hours, plus 30 minutes resting

Spice Rub

- 2 tablespoons paprika
- 1 tablespoon packed brown sugar
- 1 tablespoon table salt
- 1 teaspoon pepper
- 1 teaspoon onion powder
- 1 teaspoon garlic powder

Barbecue Sauce

- ¾ cup ketchup
- ⅓ cup apple juice
- 2 tablespoons molasses
- 2 tablespoons cider vinegar
- 2 tablespoons Worcestershire sauce
- 1 tablespoon yellow mustard
- 1 teaspoon pepper

Mop

- ¼ cup apple juice
- ¼ cup cider vinegar
- 1½ teaspoons yellow mustard

Ribs

- 2 (2½- to 3-pound) racks St. Louis-style spareribs, trimmed
- 5 (3-inch) wood chunks

Why This Recipe Works Meaty, tender-chewy racks of ribs are one of the pinnacles of outdoor cooking—and they're totally achievable on your backyard grill (or smoker). A clever grill setup called a charcoal C keeps the heat going low and slow for the duration. A potent spice rub seasons the ribs and also creates the backbone for a tangy barbecue sauce that's brushed on toward the end of their grill time. (In Memphis lingo, that's what makes them "wet.") In between, you'll apply a traditional mop of apple juice and cider vinegar to keep the ribs moist on the grill. This recipe was developed for a 22-inch or larger kettle-style charcoal grill. You will need a 13 by 9-inch disposable aluminum roasting pan.

1   **For the spice rub** Combine all ingredients in bowl.

2   **For the barbecue sauce** Combine ketchup, apple juice, molasses, vinegar, Worcestershire, mustard, and 2 tablespoons prepared spice rub in medium saucepan and bring to boil over medium heat. Reduce heat to medium-low and simmer until thickened and reduced to 1 cup, about 10 minutes. Off heat, stir in pepper; set aside.

3   **For the mop** Whisk apple juice, vinegar, mustard, and ¼ cup prepared barbecue sauce together in bowl; set aside.

4   **For the ribs** Place ribs on rimmed baking sheet and pat dry with paper towels. Flip ribs meaty side down. Sprinkle bone side of ribs with about one-third of remaining spice mixture. Flip ribs and sprinkle meaty side with remaining spice mixture.

5   Open bottom vent of charcoal grill completely. Arrange 40 briquettes, 2 briquettes wide, around half of perimeter of grill to form C shape, overlapping slightly so briquettes are touching. Place second layer of 40 briquettes, also 2 briquettes wide, on top of first. (Completed arrangement should be 2 briquettes wide by 2 briquettes high.)

6   Evenly space wood chunks along length of charcoal C. Place disposable pan in center of grate, running lengthwise into gap of C. Pour 6 cups water into pan.

7   Light chimney starter filled with 15 briquettes (pile briquettes on 1 side of chimney so they catch). When coals are partially covered with ash, pour them over 1 end of C, making sure lit coals do not touch other end.

8   Set cooking grate in place, then clean and oil grate. Place ribs side by side on grill, meaty side up, lengthwise over water pan. Cover grill, position lid vent over ribs, and open lid vent completely. Cook for 2 hours, basting meaty side of ribs with mop halfway through cooking.

9   Rotate ribs 180 degrees. Brush meaty side of ribs with remaining mop. Cover grill and continue to cook, undisturbed, for 1 hour. Brush meaty side of ribs with half of barbecue sauce and continue to cook, opening lid as little as possible, until tender and fork inserted between ribs meets little resistance, 1 to 2 hours.

10   Transfer ribs meaty side up to clean rimmed baking sheet. Brush meaty side of ribs with remaining sauce. Cover sheet tightly with aluminum foil and let ribs rest for 30 minutes. Cut ribs between bones. Serve.

Flare Trade

Smoker Heat and maintain smoker temperature of 275 to 300 degrees following manufacturer's guidelines and tips on page 15. Clean and oil smoker grate, then place ribs in center of grate. Proceed with step 8, increasing cooking time to 2½ hours.

Ribs

- 1 tablespoon table salt
- 2 tablespoons pepper
- 1 tablespoon garlic powder
- 2 (2½- to 3-pound) racks St. Louis-style spareribs, trimmed
- 5 (3-inch) wood chunks

Sauce

- ¼ cup ketchup
- ¼ cup packed brown sugar
- 2 tablespoons cider vinegar
- 2 tablespoons light corn syrup
- 1 teaspoon Worcestershire sauce
- 1 teaspoon pepper
- ½ teaspoon table salt
- ½ teaspoon garlic powder
- ¼ teaspoon ground cumin

Flare Trade

Smoker Heat and maintain smoker temperature of 275 to 300 degrees following manufacturer's guidelines and tips on page 15. Clean and oil smoker grate, then place ribs in center of grate. Proceed with step 5, increasing cooking time to 2½ hours.

Why This Recipe Works With their sweet, peppery, sticky sauce, Kansas City ribs have legions of fans just as Memphis-style ribs do. No matter which style your crowd is clamoring for, you'll use the same grill setup: a charcoal C that burns slowly for hours without interruption. The simple dry rub of salt, pepper, and garlic powder promotes ample bark while the ribs smoke. The sauce—a blend of ketchup, brown sugar, spices, and a touch of corn syrup—is applied at the halfway point so it can tighten into a nice glaze as the ribs cook and then brushed on again when the ribs come off the grill for an extra-sticky flavor boost. This recipe was developed for a 22-inch or larger kettle-style charcoal grill. You will need a 13 by 9-inch disposable aluminum roasting pan.

1   **For the ribs** Combine salt, pepper, and garlic powder in bowl. Place ribs on rimmed baking sheet and pat dry with paper towels. Flip ribs meaty side down. Sprinkle bone side of ribs with about one-third of spice mixture. Flip ribs and sprinkle meaty side with remaining spice mixture.

2   Open bottom vent of charcoal grill completely. Arrange 40 briquettes, 2 briquettes wide, around half of perimeter of grill to form C shape, overlapping slightly so briquettes are touching. Place second layer of 40 briquettes, also 2 briquettes wide, on top of first. (Completed arrangement should be 2 briquettes wide by 2 briquettes high.)

3   Evenly space wood chunks along length of charcoal C. Place disposable pan in center of grate, running lengthwise into gap in C. Pour 6 cups water into pan.

4   Light chimney starter filled with 15 briquettes (pile briquettes on 1 side of chimney so they catch). When coals are partially covered with ash, pour them over 1 end of C, making sure lit coals do not touch other end.

5   Set cooking grate in place, then clean and oil grate. Place ribs side by side on grill, meaty side up, lengthwise over water pan. Cover grill, position lid vent over ribs, and open vent completely. Cook, undisturbed, for 2 hours.

6   **For the sauce** Meanwhile, whisk all ingredients together in small saucepan and cook over medium heat until sugar has dissolved; set aside. (Sauce does not need to come to boil.)

7 Rotate ribs 180 degrees. Brush meaty side of ribs with half of sauce. Cover grill and continue to cook, opening lid as little as possible, until tender and fork inserted between ribs meets little resistance, 2 to 3 hours.

8 Transfer ribs to clean rimmed baking sheet, meaty side up. Brush meaty side of ribs with remaining sauce. Cover sheet tightly with aluminum foil and let ribs rest for 30 minutes. Cut ribs between bones. Serve.

Barbecue Pork

SERVES 8 to 10   **TOTAL TIME** 5¼ hours, plus 19½ hours salting and resting

3 tablespoons kosher salt

1½ tablespoons pepper

1 (6-pound) bone-in pork butt roast, with ¼-inch fat cap

4 (3-inch) wood chunks

1 recipe Lexington-Style Barbecue Sauce or Eastern North Carolina–Style Barbecue Sauce

Why This Recipe Works When you're talking barbecue in North Carolina, you're talking pork, and a pork butt roast feeds a hungry crowd in style. The charcoal C grill setup provides low, slow, indirect heat, so you'll need to refuel only once during the long cooking time. Wrapping the bone-in pork butt in foil when it reaches 170 degrees gives the meat plenty of time to absorb smoke flavor and develop a crusty bark without its exterior getting too bitter. There are two distinct styles of barbecue pork in North Carolina; we've got chopping and saucing options for both, so you can choose. Or do half and half and earn even more applause. This recipe was developed for a 22-inch or larger kettle-style charcoal grill. You will need a 13 by 9-inch disposable aluminum roasting pan.

1 Combine salt and pepper in bowl. Place pork on large sheet of plastic wrap and sprinkle all over with salt mixture. Wrap tightly with plastic and refrigerate for at least 18 hours or up to 24 hours.

2 Open bottom vent of charcoal grill completely. Arrange 60 briquettes, 2 briquettes wide, around perimeter of grill to make C shape, overlapping slightly so briquettes are touching and leaving 8-inch gap between ends of C. Place second layer of 60 briquettes, also 2 briquettes wide, on top of first. (Completed arrangement should be 2 briquettes wide by 2 briquettes high.)

3 Evenly space wood chunks along length of charcoal C. Place disposable pan in center of grate, running lengthwise into gap in C. Pour 6 cups water into pan.

4 Light chimney starter filled with 15 briquettes (pile briquettes on 1 side of chimney so they catch). When coals are partially covered with ash, pour them over 1 end of C, making sure lit coals do not touch other end.

5 Set cooking grate in place, then clean and oil grate. Unwrap pork and position fat side down over water pan. Insert temperature probe into thickest part of pork. Cover grill, position lid vent over gap in C, and open vent completely. Cook, undisturbed, until pork registers 170 degrees, 4 to 5 hours.

Flare Trade

Smoker Heat and maintain smoker temperature of 275 to 300 degrees following manufacturer's guidelines and tips on page 15. Clean and oil smoker grate, then place pork in center of grate. Proceed with step 5, increasing cooking time to 4½ to 5½ hours and rotating pork halfway through cooking. Wrap pork in foil as directed, then proceed with step 8, increasing cooking time to 1½ to 2½ hours.

6 Place 2 large sheets of aluminum foil on rimmed baking sheet. Remove probe from pork. Using grill gloves, lift pork and transfer to center of 1 sheet of foil, fat side down. Wrap tightly with first sheet of foil, minimizing air pockets between foil and pork. Wrap with second sheet of foil. (Use additional foil, if necessary, to completely wrap pork; foil wrap should be airtight.) Make small mark on foil with marker to keep track of fat side.

7 Remove cooking grate. Starting at still-unlit end of snake, pour 2 quarts unlit briquettes about one-third of way around perimeter of grill over gap in C and spent coals. Replace cooking grate.

8 Return wrapped pork to grill over water pan, fat side down. Reinsert probe into thickest part of pork. Cover grill and continue to cook until pork registers 200 degrees, 1 to 2 hours.

9 Remove probe. Transfer pork to carving board, fat side up, and let rest in foil for 1½ hours. Remove bone from pork. For Lexington style, chop pork with cleaver into 1-inch pieces. For eastern North Carolina style, chop pork into ¼-inch pieces. Toss with ⅔ cup sauce. Serve, passing remaining sauce separately.

Lexington-Style Barbecue Sauce

Bring 2 cups cider vinegar, 1 cup ketchup, 2 teaspoons granulated garlic, 2 teaspoons pepper, 1½ teaspoons kosher salt, and 1 teaspoon red pepper flakes to boil in small saucepan over medium-high heat. Reduce heat to medium-low and simmer for 5 minutes. Transfer sauce to bowl and let cool completely.

Eastern North Carolina-Style Barbecue Sauce

Whisk 1½ cups cider vinegar, 1 cup Texas Pete Original Hot Sauce, ¼ cup packed light brown sugar, 2 teaspoons kosher salt, 1 teaspoon, pepper, and 1 teaspoon red pepper flakes together in bowl.

Cuban-Style Pork with Mojo

SERVES 6 to 8   **TOTAL TIME** 5½ hours, plus 13½ hours salting and resting

Pork

- ⅓ cup kosher salt
- ⅓ cup packed light brown sugar
- 1 tablespoon lime zest (2 limes)
- 1 tablespoon orange zest
- 3 garlic cloves, minced
- 2 teaspoons ground cumin
- 2 teaspoons dried oregano
- ½ teaspoon red pepper flakes
- 1 (5-pound) boneless pork butt roast, fat cap trimmed to ¼ inch

Mojo

- ⅓ cup extra-virgin olive oil
- 6 garlic cloves, minced
- ⅓ cup pineapple juice
- ⅓ cup orange juice
- ⅓ cup lime juice (3 limes)
- 1 tablespoon yellow mustard
- 1¼ teaspoons ground cumin
- 1 teaspoon kosher salt
- ¾ teaspoon pepper
- ¾ teaspoon dried oregano
- ¼ teaspoon red pepper flakes
  Thinly sliced onion rounds

Why This Recipe Works Roast pork in Cuba means pernil: crackling-crisp skin and tender meat infused with flavor. We take it outdoors, seasoning boneless pork butt for a good stretch of time and then cooking it slowly over indirect fire in two stages, first unwrapped and then wrapped in aluminum foil. For supreme tenderness, let it rest for a full 90 minutes before slicing. The traditional tangy, garlicky, fruity sauce gives this dish its mojo. Avoid buying a boneless pork butt wrapped in netting; it will contain smaller, separate lobes of meat rather than one whole roast. We used Diamond Crystal kosher salt here. If using Morton kosher salt, which is denser, use ¼ cup. This recipe was developed for a 22-inch or larger kettle-style charcoal grill. You will need a 13 by 9-inch disposable aluminum roasting pan. Pernil is traditionally served with black beans, rice, and fried plantains.

1 **For the pork** Combine salt, sugar, lime zest, orange zest, garlic, cumin, oregano, and pepper flakes in bowl. Using sharp knife, cut 1-inch crosshatch pattern in fat cap, making sure not to cut into meat.

2 Place pork on large double layer of plastic wrap. Sprinkle pork all over with spice mixture. Wrap pork tightly in plastic, place on plate, and refrigerate for at least 12 hours or up to 24 hours.

3 **For the mojo** While pork is resting, heat oil and garlic in small saucepan over low heat, stirring often, until tiny bubbles appear and garlic is fragrant and straw-colored, 3 to 5 minutes. Let cool for at least 5 minutes. Whisk pineapple juice, orange juice, lime juice, mustard, cumin, salt, pepper, oregano, and pepper flakes into cooled garlic oil. Set aside.

4 Open bottom vent of charcoal grill completely. Arrange 60 briquettes, 2 briquettes wide, around perimeter of grill to form C shape, overlapping slightly so briquettes are touching and leaving 8-inch gap between ends of C. Place second layer of 60 briquettes, also 2 briquettes wide, on top of first. (Completed arrangement should be 2 briquettes wide by 2 briquettes high.) Place disposable pan in center of grate, running lengthwise into gap in C. Pour 6 cups water into pan.

5 Light chimney starter filled with 15 briquettes (pile briquettes on 1 side of chimney so they catch). When coals are partially covered with ash, pour them over 1 end of C, making sure lit coals do not touch other end.

6 Set cooking grate in place, then clean and oil grate. Unwrap pork and position fat side down over water pan. Insert temperature probe into thickest part of pork. Cover grill, position lid vent over gap in C, and open vent completely. Cook, undisturbed, until pork registers 170 degrees, 4 to 5 hours.

7 Place 2 large sheets of aluminum foil on rimmed baking sheet. Remove probe from pork. Using grill gloves, lift pork and transfer to center of 1 sheet of foil, fat side down. Wrap tightly with first sheet of foil, minimizing air pockets between foil and pork. Wrap with second sheet of foil. (Use additional foil, if necessary, to completely wrap pork; foil wrap should be airtight.) Make small mark on foil with marker to keep track of fat side.

8 Remove cooking grate. Starting at still-unlit end of C, pour 2 quarts unlit briquettes about one-third of way around perimeter of grill over gap in C and spent coals. Replace cooking grate.

9 Return wrapped pork to grill over water pan, fat side down. Reinsert probe into thickest part of pork. Cover grill and continue to cook until pork registers 195 degrees, 1 to 2 hours longer.

10 Remove probe. Transfer pork to carving board, fat side up, and let rest in foil for 1½ hours. Scrape off and discard fat from top of roast. Slice ¼ inch thick (some meat may shred; this is OK) and transfer to serving platter. Serve with onion and mojo.

Flare Trade

Gas Grill Turn all burners to high, cover, and heat grill until hot; about 15 minutes. Turn primary burner to medium-high and turn off other burner(s). (Adjust primary burner as needed to maintain grill temperature of 275 to 300 degrees; if using 3-burner grill, adjust primary burner and second burner). Clean and oil cooking grate, then place roast on cooler side of grill (6 to 8 inches from heat source). Proceed with step 6, rotating pork halfway through cooking. Wrap pork in foil as directed, then return to cooler side of grill and proceed with step 9.

Smoked Prime Rib

SERVES 8 to 10   **TOTAL TIME** 3¼ hours, plus 24¾ hours salting and resting

Prime Rib

- 1 (6- to 7-pound) first-cut beef standing rib roast (3 bones), fat cap trimmed to ¼ inch
- 2 tablespoons kosher salt
- 1 tablespoon pepper
- 3 (3-inch) wood chunks

Horseradish Sauce

- ½ cup mayonnaise
- ⅓ cup prepared horseradish
- 2 tablespoons lemon juice
- 1 garlic clove, minced
- 1 teaspoon Worcestershire sauce
- 1 teaspoon pepper
- ¾ teaspoon kosher salt
  Pinch cayenne pepper

Flare Trade

Smoker Heat and maintain smoker temperature of 275 to 300 degrees following manufacturer's guidelines and tips on page 15. Clean and oil smoker grate, then place roast in center of grate. Proceed with step 5, rotating roast halfway through cooking.

Why This Recipe Works The contrast of cooking and serving an elegant roast in a rustic outdoor setting makes it even more special. Smoking a prime rib elevates this already grand cut of meat to an entirely new level of flavor. A charcoal C grill setup supplies sufficient heat to cook the roast through without recharging, so you can relax with your guests. You'll want a temperature probe so you can tell when the beef is cooked properly. This recipe was developed for a 22-inch or larger kettle-style charcoal grill. You will need a 13 by 9-inch disposable aluminum roasting pan.

1 **For the prime rib** Using sharp knife, cut 1-inch crosshatch pattern in fat cap of roast, being careful not to cut into meat. Rub salt and pepper over entire roast and into crosshatch. Transfer to large plate and refrigerate, uncovered, for at least 24 hours or up to 4 days.

2 Open bottom vent of charcoal grill completely. Arrange 40 briquettes, 2 briquettes wide, around half of perimeter of grill to form C shape, overlapping slightly so briquettes are touching. Place second layer of 40 briquettes, also 2 briquettes wide, on top of first. (Completed arrangement should be 2 briquettes wide by 2 briquettes high.)

3 Evenly space wood chunks along length of charcoal C. Place disposable pan in center of grate, running lengthwise into gap in C. Pour 6 cups water into pan.

4 Light chimney starter filled with 15 briquettes (pile briquettes on 1 side of chimney so they catch). When coals are partially covered with ash, pour them over 1 end of C, making sure lit coals do not touch other end.

5 Set cooking grate in place, then clean and oil grate. Place roast over water pan, fat side up, with bones facing gap in C. Insert temperature probe into center of roast. Cover grill, position lid vent over roast, and open vent completely. Cook, undisturbed, until meat registers 115 degrees (for medium-rare), 2½ to 3¼ hours.

6 **For the horseradish sauce** Meanwhile, combine all ingredients in bowl. Cover and refrigerate for at least 30 minutes to allow flavors to meld.

7 Transfer roast to carving board, tent with aluminum foil, and let rest for 45 minutes. Carve meat from bones and slice ¾ inch thick. Serve with sauce.

Texas-Style Barbecue Brisket

SERVES 12 to 15   **TOTAL TIME** 6¼ to 8¼ hours, plus 14 hours salting and resting

1 (10- to 12-pound) whole beef brisket, fat cap trimmed to ¼ to ½ inch

¼ cup kosher salt

¼ cup pepper

5 (3-inch) wood chunks

Why This Recipe Works A whole Texas-style brisket, complete with dark, peppery bark, smoked on your charcoal grill? Totally doable. Arranging a long line of briquettes in a C formation gives you enough low, slow, indirect heat to require refueling only once during the largely hands-off cooking time. Overnight seasoning enhances the brisket's flavor. Cooking the brisket fat side down provides a protective barrier against the direct heat of the fire, as does wrapping it in foil toward the end of cooking. Letting the brisket rest for 2 hours before serving ensures it's ultramoist by allowing the juices time to redistribute evenly—and also gives you plenty of time to get the party started. We call for a whole beef brisket here, with the flat and point cuts intact; you may need to special-order this cut. This recipe was developed for a 22-inch or larger kettle-style charcoal grill. You will need a 13 by 9-inch disposable aluminum roasting pan and a cooler.

1   With brisket positioned point side up, use sharp knife to remove excess fat from deep pocket where flat and point are attached. Trim and discard short edge of flat if less than 1 inch thick. Flip brisket and remove any large deposits of fat from underside.

2   Combine salt and pepper in bowl. Place brisket on rimmed baking sheet and sprinkle all over with salt mixture. Cover with plastic wrap and refrigerate for at least 12 hours or up to 24 hours.

3   Open bottom vent of charcoal grill completely. Arrange 60 briquettes, 2 briquettes wide, around perimeter of grill to form C shape, overlapping slightly so briquettes are touching and leaving 8-inch gap between ends of C. Place second layer of 60 briquettes, also 2 briquettes wide, on top of first. (Completed arrangement should be 2 briquettes wide by 2 briquettes high.)

4   Evenly space wood chunks along length of charcoal C. Place disposable pan in center of grate, running lengthwise into gap of C. Pour 6 cups water into pan.

5   Light chimney starter filled with 15 briquettes (pile briquettes on 1 side of chimney so they catch). When coals are partially covered with ash, pour them over 1 end of C, making sure lit coals do not touch other end.

Flare Trade

Smoker Heat and maintain smoker temperature of 275 to 300 degrees following manufacturer's guidelines and tips on page 15. Clean and oil smoker grate, then place brisket in center of grate. Proceed with step 6, increasing cooking time to 4½ to 5½ hours and rotating brisket halfway through cooking. Wrap brisket in foil as directed, then return to smoker grate. Proceed with step 9.

6 Set cooking grate in place, then clean and oil grate. Place brisket, fat side down, directly over water pan, with point end facing gap in C. Insert temperature probe into side of upper third of point. Cover grill, position lid vent over gap in C, and open vent completely. Cook, undisturbed, until meat registers 170 degrees, 4 to 5 hours.

7 Place 2 large sheets of aluminum foil on rimmed baking sheet. Remove temperature probe from brisket. Using grill gloves, lift brisket and transfer to center of foil, fat side down. Wrap brisket tightly with first layer of foil, minimizing air pockets between foil and brisket. Rotate brisket 90 degrees and wrap with second layer of foil. (Use additional foil, if necessary, to completely wrap brisket; foil wrap should be airtight.) Make small mark on foil with marker to keep track of fat/point side.

8 Remove cooking grate. Starting at still-unlit end of C, pour 3 quarts unlit briquettes about halfway around perimeter of grill over gap in C and spent coals. Replace cooking grate.

9 Return foil-wrapped brisket to grill over water pan, fat side down, with point end facing where gap in C used to be. Reinsert temperature probe into point. Cover grill and continue to cook until meat registers 205 degrees, 1 to 2 hours.

10 Remove temperature probe. Transfer foil-wrapped brisket to cooler, point side up. Close cooler and let rest for at least 2 hours or up to 3 hours. Transfer brisket to carving board, unwrap, and position fat side up. Slice flat against grain ¼ inch thick, stopping once you reach base of point. Rotate point 90 degrees and slice point against grain (perpendicular to first cut) ¼ inch thick. Serve.

Texas-Style Smoked Beef Ribs

SERVES 6 to 8   **TOTAL TIME** 6½ hours, plus 30 minutes resting

3 tablespoons kosher salt

3 tablespoons pepper

2 (4- to 5-pound) racks beef plate ribs, 1 to 1½ inches of meat on top of bone, trimmed

5 (3-inch) wood chunks

Why This Recipe Works Tap into your inner Fred Flintstone with these massive ribs wrapped in a pink smoke ring and a bit of honest Texas chew from the gloriously dark crust. They start with racks of beef plate ribs, each with 1 to 1½ inches of meat on top of the bone to ensure they don't shrivel down during cooking. Arranging five wood chunks on top of the charcoal C grill setup provides steady smoke to infuse the meat with big, big flavor. Cooking them to 210 degrees ensures that the collagen melts properly, resulting in ultratender meat. Beef plate ribs are substantially larger than short ribs; you may need to special-order these. This recipe was developed for a 22-inch or larger kettle-style charcoal grill. You will need a 13 by 9-inch disposable aluminum roasting pan.

1   Combine salt and pepper in bowl, then sprinkle ribs all over with mixture.

2   Open bottom vent of charcoal grill completely. Arrange 60 briquettes, 2 briquettes wide, around perimeter of grill to form C shape, overlapping slightly so briquettes are touching and leaving 8-inch gap between ends of C. Place second layer of 60 briquettes, also 2 briquettes wide, on top of first. (Completed arrangement should be 2 briquettes wide by 2 briquettes high.)

3   Evenly space wood chunks along length of C. Place disposable pan in center of grate, running lengthwise into gap of C. Pour 6 cups water into pan.

4   Light chimney starter filled with 15 briquettes (pile briquettes on 1 side of chimney so they catch). When coals are partially covered with ash, use tongs to place them at 1 end of C, making sure lit coals do not touch other end.

5   Set cooking grate in place, then clean and oil grate. Position ribs next to each other on cooking grate, bone side down, crosswise over water pan and gap in C (they will be off-center; this is OK). Cover grill, positioning lid vent over gap in C, and open vent completely. Cook, undisturbed, until rack of ribs overhanging gap in C registers 210 degrees in meatiest portion, 5½ to 6¼ hours.

6   Transfer ribs to carving board, tent with aluminum foil, and let rest for 30 minutes. Cut ribs between bones and serve.

Flare Trade

Smoker Heat and maintain smoker temperature of 275 to 300 degrees following manufacturer's guidelines and tips on page 15. Clean and oil smoker grate, then place ribs in center of grate. Proceed with step 5, increasing cooking time to 6 to 6¾ hours and rotating ribs halfway through cooking.

Rotisserie Leg of Lamb with Cauliflower, Grape, and Arugula Salad

SERVES 8 to 10   **TOTAL TIME** 2½ hours, plus 12½ hours chilling and resting

Lamb and Salad

- ½ cup plus 2 tablespoons extra-virgin olive oil, divided
- 12 garlic cloves (6 halved, 6 minced)
- 4 sprigs fresh rosemary, cut into thirds, plus 2 teaspoons minced fresh rosemary
- 8 anchovy fillets (4 cut into thirds, 4 minced)
- 4¾ teaspoons kosher salt, divided
- 1 tablespoon Dijon mustard, divided
- 2 teaspoons grated lemon zest
- 1 teaspoon pepper
- 1 (6- to 8-pound) bone-in leg of lamb, fat trimmed to ¼ inch
- 1 large head cauliflower (3 pounds), cored and cut into 1-inch florets
- 1 red onion, halved and sliced thin
- 9 ounces seedless red grapes
- 3 tablespoons balsamic vinegar
- 10 ounces (10 cups) baby arugula
- 1 fennel bulb, ¼ cup fronds chopped coarse, stalks discarded, bulb halved, cored, and sliced thin

Sour Cream Sauce

- 1 cup sour cream
- ½ cup minced fresh parsley
- ¼ cup Dijon mustard

Why This Recipe Works A leg of lamb on the rotisserie produces a culinary work of art, as visually stunning as it is outstandingly delicious. The key to making such a large cut taste great and remain juicy is a good, long salting period in a potent rub of garlic, anchovies, mustard, and rosemary. As the lamb turns on its spit, its flavorful juices and rendered fat drip onto a pan of cauliflower, onion, and grapes, which form the base of an elegant, indulgent salad. Bone-in leg of lamb is sometimes labeled "semi-boneless." This can be confusing but it's what you want; it means that the hipbone and aitchbone are removed, which is helpful when it comes time to carve. If you happen to find a leg with the whole bone, ask the butcher to remove these parts for proper cooking. This recipe was developed for a 22-inch or larger kettle-style charcoal grill. You will need a motorized rotisserie attachment and two 13 by 9-inch disposable aluminum roasting pans.

1 **For the lamb and salad** Combine 2 tablespoons oil, minced garlic, minced rosemary, minced anchovies, 4 teaspoons salt, 2 teaspoons mustard, lemon zest, and pepper in bowl. Place lamb leg on rimmed baking sheet. Using paring knife, make twelve 1-inch-deep incisions into fat side of lamb. Stuff each opening with 1 garlic clove half, 1 piece rosemary sprig, and 1 piece anchovy. Tie lamb with kitchen twine at 1½-inch intervals and rub with garlic paste. Cover and refrigerate for at least 12 hours or up to 24 hours.

2 Thread rotisserie skewer lengthwise through center of lamb leg; center leg on skewer. Attach rotisserie forks to skewer and insert tines into lamb; secure forks by tightening screws. Toss cauliflower and onion with 2 tablespoons oil and ¼ teaspoon salt in disposable pan. Scatter grapes over top.

3 Open bottom vent of charcoal grill halfway and place second disposable pan in center of grill. Light large chimney starter filled with charcoal briquettes (6 quarts). When top coals are partially covered with ash, pour into 2 even piles on either side of disposable pan. Position rotisserie motor attachment on grill so that skewer runs parallel to coals. Cover, open lid vent halfway, and heat grill until hot, about 5 minutes.

4 Set pan with vegetables into pan in grill. Attach rotisserie skewer to motor and start motor. Cover and cook until thickest part of leg, ½ inch from bone, registers 120 to 125 degrees (for medium-rare), 1¼ hours to 1¾ hours.

5 Transfer lamb, still on skewer, to carving board. Transfer pan with vegetables to wire rack. Tent lamb with aluminum foil and let rest for 30 minutes.

6 **For the sour cream sauce** Combine all ingredients in bowl; set aside for serving. (Sauce can be refrigerated for up to 2 days.)

7 Whisk vinegar, remaining ½ teaspoon salt, and remaining 1 teaspoon mustard together in large bowl. Whisking constantly, drizzle in remaining 6 tablespoons oil. Add grill-roasted vegetables, arugula, and sliced fennel and toss to combine. Season with salt and pepper to taste and sprinkle with fennel fronds. Using large wad of paper towels in each hand, carefully remove rotisserie forks and skewer from lamb. Carve lamb from bone and slice thin. Serve with salad and sauce.

Flare Trade

Gas Grill Cut onion into ½-inch thick rounds, cut cauliflower into 2-inch pieces, and halve grapes. Brush onion and cauliflower with 2 tablespoons oil and sprinkle with ¼ teaspoon salt; set aside vegetables and grapes while cooking lamb. Remove cooking grate. Position rotisserie motor attachment on grill. Turn all burners to high; cover; and heat grill until hot, about 15 minutes. Turn outside burners to medium and center burner off (if using 2-burner grill, turn both burners to medium) and cook lamb as directed in step 4. (Adjust burners as needed to maintain grill temperature between 350 and 375 degrees.) While lamb rests, set cooking grate in place; turn all burners to medium-high; and heat grill until hot, about 5 minutes. Grill onion and cauliflower, covered, until lightly browned and tender, 10 to 15 minutes, turning as needed. Chop vegetables before tossing with arugula and fennel in step 7. Sprinkle salad with grapes before serving.

Hot-Smoked Whole Side of Salmon

SERVES 16   **TOTAL TIME** 1½ hours, plus 8 hours curing and drying

½ cup sugar for curing

½ cup kosher salt for curing

1 (4-pound) skin-on side of salmon, thin end of tail removed and reserved for another use, pin bones removed, and belly fat trimmed

1–1½ cups wood chips

Why This Recipe Works If you love the sweet, salty flavor and silky texture of hot-smoked salmon, but not its $40 per pound price tag, this is the recipe for you—and it's quite simple: Cover a whole side of salmon with a blanket of sugar and salt, chill for a few hours, rinse the salmon, and let it dry in the refrigerator until a tacky film forms on the surface. Cook the seasoned fish over indirect heat with plenty of hardwood smoke until moist and succulent, ready to be eaten right away as an entrée (try it with one of the sauces), flaked over a salad, or whatever strikes your fancy. Cut into portions and wrapped tightly, this salmon freezes well. We used Diamond Crystal kosher salt. If using Morton kosher salt, which is denser, use only 6 tablespoons. We developed this recipe with farmed salmon. If you would like to use wild fish, we recommend king salmon. The recipe can be halved, using a 2-pound center-cut fillet and half as much sugar and salt in the cure; the cooking time will be about the same. We prefer hickory chips here, but any kind of hardwood chips will work. If you'd like to use wood chunks instead of wood chips when using a charcoal grill, substitute one medium wood chunk for the wood chip packet.

1 Combine sugar and salt in small bowl. Place salmon on wire rack set in rimmed baking sheet. Spread sugar mixture evenly over surface of flesh, pressing gently to adhere. Refrigerate, uncovered, for 4 hours.

2 Rinse salmon under cold water and return to rack. Pat dry with paper towels. Refrigerate, uncovered, until surface of fillet is tacky and matte, at least 4 hours or up to 20 hours.

3 Using large piece of heavy-duty aluminum foil, wrap chips (1 cup if using charcoal; 1½ cups if using gas) in 8 by 4½-inch foil packet. (Make sure chips do not poke holes in sides or bottom of packet. If using gas, make sure there are no more than 2 layers of foil on bottom of packet.) Cut 3 evenly spaced 2-inch slits in top of packet.

4A **For a charcoal grill** Open bottom vent halfway. Light large chimney starter half filled with charcoal briquettes (3 quarts). Place 6 unlit briquettes on 1 side of grill. When top coals are partially covered with ash, pour into steeply banked pile over unlit briquettes. Place wood chip packet on coals. Set cooking grate in place, cover, and open lid vent halfway. Heat grill until hot and wood chips are smoking, about 5 minutes.

Flare Trade

Smoker Heat and maintain smoker temperature of 275 to 300 degrees following manufacturer's guidelines and tips on page 15. Clean and oil smoker grate, then arrange prepared foil rectangle and salmon in center of grate. Proceed with step 5, increasing cooking time to 60 to 80 minutes and rotating salmon halfway through cooking.

4B   For a gas grill Remove cooking grate and place wood chip packet directly on primary burner. Set grate in place. Turn primary burner to high (leave other burners off); cover; and heat grill until hot and wood chips are smoking, 15 to 25 minutes. Turn primary burner to medium. (Adjust primary burner as needed to maintain grill temperature between 275 and 300 degrees.)

5   Clean and oil cooking grate. Fold large piece of heavy-duty foil into 18 by 6-inch rectangle. Spray lightly with vegetable oil spray. Place foil rectangle on cooler side of grill (on gas grill arrange foil parallel to primary burner, spaced 8 to 10 inches from heat source) and place salmon on foil. Cover grill (positioning lid vent over salmon if using charcoal) and cook until center of thickest part is still translucent when checked with tip of paring knife and registers 125 degrees (for farmed salmon) or 120 degrees (for wild salmon), 50 minutes to 1 hour 10 minutes.

6   Using foil as sling, transfer salmon to platter. Carefully slide foil out from beneath salmon. Serve.

"Smoked Salmon Platter" Sauce

Whisk 1 large egg yolk, 2 teaspoons Dijon mustard, and 2 teaspoons sherry vinegar together in medium bowl. Whisking constantly, slowly drizzle in ½ cup vegetable oil until emulsified, about 1 minute. Gently fold in 2 tablespoons rinsed capers plus 1 teaspoon caper brine, 1 chopped large hard-cooked egg, 2 tablespoons minced shallot, and 2 tablespoons minced fresh dill. Serve with smoked salmon.

Apple-Mustard Sauce

Whisk ¼ cup whole-grain mustard, 3 tablespoons unsweetened applesauce, 2 tablespoons Dijon mustard, 4 teaspoons cider vinegar, 1 tablespoon honey, 1 tablespoon minced fresh chives, and ¼ teaspoon table salt in bowl until combined. Serve with smoked salmon.

New England Clambake

SERVES 4   **TOTAL TIME** 1 hour, plus 30 minutes soaking

½ cup table salt for brining

4 ears corn, husks and silk removed

½ teaspoon plus ⅛ teaspoon pepper, divided

1½ pounds small red or yellow potatoes, unpeeled, halved

4 tablespoons unsalted butter, melted, divided, plus extra for serving

¾ teaspoon table salt, divided

2 (1¼- to 1½-pound) live lobsters

1 pound kielbasa

2 pounds littleneck clams, scrubbed

Lemon wedges

Why This Recipe Works Clambakes on the beach are a beloved rite of summer all along the East Coast. But if you can't get to the shore, this grilled clambake captures all the smoky flavor and party vibes of the traditional version—with no shovel required. Because you're working with a limited-size cooking surface, cooking in two stages is key. The brined ears of corn, garlicky kielbasa, and parcooked skewered potatoes go over a hot fire first and then wait patiently while the split, buttered lobsters and the clams cook over more moderate heat. Use potatoes measuring 1 to 2 inches in diameter; if your potatoes are larger, quarter them and increase the microwaving time as needed in step 2. You will need four 12-inch metal skewers.

1 Dissolve ½ cup salt in 4 quarts cold water in large pot. Add corn and soak for at least 30 minutes or up to 8 hours. Before grilling, remove corn from water, pat dry with paper towels, and sprinkle with ¼ teaspoon pepper.

2 Toss potatoes with 1 tablespoon melted butter, ¼ teaspoon salt, and ⅛ teaspoon pepper in bowl. Microwave, covered, until potatoes offer slight resistance when pierced with tip of paring knife, about 6 minutes, stirring halfway through. Drain, then toss with additional 1 tablespoon melted butter. Thread potatoes cut side out onto four 12-inch metal skewers.

3 Split lobsters in half lengthwise, removing internal organs. Using back of chef's knife, whack 1 side of each claw to crack shell. Brush tail meat with 1 tablespoon melted butter and sprinkle with remaining ½ teaspoon salt and remaining ¼ teaspoon pepper.

4A For a charcoal grill Open bottom vent completely. Light large chimney starter filled with charcoal briquettes (6 quarts). When top coals are partially covered with ash, pour evenly over grill. Set cooking grate in place, cover, and open lid vent completely. Heat grill until hot, about 5 minutes.

4B For a gas grill Turn all burners to high; cover; and heat grill until hot, about 15 minutes. Leave all burners on high. (Adjust primary burner as needed to maintain grill temperature of 325 to 350 degrees; if using 3-burner grill, adjust primary burner and second burner.)

5 Clean and oil cooking grate. Grill kielbasa, corn, and potatoes until kielbasa is seared and hot throughout, corn is lightly charred, and potatoes are brown and tender, 10 to 16 minutes, flipping and turning as needed.

Flare Trade

Open Fire Prepare hot single-level fire in open-fire grill. Set cooking grate at least 6 inches from coals and flames and heat grill until hot, about 5 minutes. Proceed with step 5.

Transfer kielbasa to cutting board and vegetables to serving platter as they finish cooking and tent with aluminum foil.

6   Lay lobsters, flesh side down, and clams on grill. Cook until clams have opened and lobsters are cooked through, 8 to 14 minutes, flipping lobsters and brushing tail meat with remaining 1 tablespoon melted butter halfway through grilling. As lobsters and clams finish cooking, transfer to serving platter with vegetables, preserving any juices that have accumulated inside their shells. Discard any clams that refuse to open.

7   Slice kielbasa into 1-inch pieces and transfer to serving platter with lobsters. Remove skewers from potatoes. Serve with lemon wedges and extra melted butter.

Grill-Roasted Whole Cauliflower with Tahini-Yogurt Sauce

SERVES 4 to 6   **TOTAL TIME** 1¼ hours

Tahini-Yogurt Sauce

- ½ cup tahini
- ¼ cup plain Greek yogurt
- ¼ cup water, plus extra as needed
- 3 tablespoons lemon juice
- 1 garlic clove, minced

Cauliflower

- 1 head cauliflower (2 pounds)
- ¼ cup table salt for brining
- ½ cup sugar for brining
- ¼ cup extra-virgin olive oil
- 1½ teaspoons ground turmeric
- ¼ teaspoon pepper
- 2 tablespoons chopped toasted pistachios
- 2 tablespoons chopped fresh parsley

Why This Recipe Works You don't need to cook a large cut of meat to present an entrée off the grill that will impress your guests: This whole head of cauliflower, brined for optimum seasoning and caramelization and gorgeously golden from turmeric, is both dramatic and delicious. Parcooking the cauliflower in the microwave ensures that it's tender throughout by the time the exterior is deeply charred. Creamy tahini-yogurt sauce underscores the smoky element and pistachios add crunch. Choose a cauliflower head with plenty of leaves, if you like; cauliflower leaves are edible and become delightfully crispy on the grill. Look for a head of cauliflower with densely packed florets that feels heavy for its size. This recipe can be doubled—make one batch of brine and soak the heads in it one at a time, then microwave them one at a time.

1   For the tahini-yogurt sauce Whisk all ingredients in bowl until combined. Adjust consistency with extra water as needed and season with salt and pepper to taste. (Sauce can be refrigerated for up to 2 days.)

2   For the cauliflower Trim stem of cauliflower, keeping leaves intact, so it sits flat. Dissolve salt and sugar in 2 quarts cold water in large bowl. Holding cauliflower upside down by stem, gently dunk in brine and let sit for 5 minutes. Flip and continue to submerge for 1 minute until evenly moistened (do not pat dry). Transfer cauliflower stem down to large plate and cover with inverted large bowl. Microwave until cauliflower is translucent and tender and paring knife inserted in thickest stem of florets (not into core) meets no resistance, 8 to 14 minutes.

3   Carefully transfer cauliflower to paper towel–lined plate and pat dry. Whisk oil, turmeric, and pepper together in small bowl, then brush cauliflower with oil mixture.

4A   For a charcoal grill Open bottom vent completely. Light large chimney starter filled with charcoal briquettes (6 quarts). When top coals are partially covered with ash, pour evenly over half of grill. Set cooking grate in place, cover, and open lid vent completely. Heat grill until hot, about 5 minutes.

4B **For a gas grill** Turn all burners to high; cover; and heat grill until hot, about 15 minutes. Leave primary burner on high and turn off other burner(s). (Adjust primary burner as needed to maintain grill temperature of 350 to 400 degrees; if using 3-burner grill, adjust primary burner and second burner.)

5 Place cauliflower stem side down on cooler side of grill (6 to 8 inches from heat source for gas grill). Cover and cook until cauliflower is deeply browned and leaves are charred and crisp, 35 to 55 minutes, rotating cauliflower halfway through cooking. Using spatula and tongs, transfer cauliflower to plate.

6 Spread two-thirds of tahini-yogurt sauce over serving platter. Center cauliflower stem side down on sauce and sprinkle with pistachios and parsley. Cut into wedges and serve, passing remaining sauce separately.

Grilled Vegetable Platter

SERVES 4 to 6   **TOTAL TIME** 1 hour

Lemon–Basil Vinaigrette

2 tablespoons lemon juice

4 teaspoons Dijon mustard

2 garlic cloves, minced

½ teaspoon table salt

¼ teaspoon pepper

6 tablespoons extra-virgin olive oil

¼ cup chopped fresh basil, plus basil leaves for garnish

Grilled Vegetable Platter

2 red bell peppers

1 red onion, cut into ½-inch-thick rounds

4 plum tomatoes, cored and halved lengthwise

2 zucchini, ends trimmed, sliced lengthwise into ¾-inch-thick planks

1 eggplant, ends trimmed, cut crosswise into ½-inch-thick rounds

3 tablespoons extra-virgin olive oil

½ teaspoon table salt

½ teaspoon pepper

8 ounces burrata cheese, room temperature

Why This Recipe Works A bounteous assortment of grilled vegetables served with a citrus-kissed vinaigrette makes for a casual and fabulously charry spread. The vegetables are even better at room temperature than they are hot, so you can easily make this ahead, if you like. It makes an excellent starter to keep everybody happy at the outdoor table while you continue to grill up more goodies, or you can easily customize the platter with add-ons to make this the centerpiece of your meal. The burrata is a great start; its creamy insides will mingle with the vegetables on guests' plates. Also consider additions such as crusty bread slices toasted on the grill, marinated olives, marinated white beans, high-quality tuna packed in oil, and/or grilled lemon halves to squeeze over whatever you please. If burrata is unavailable, sliced fresh mozzarella makes a suitable substitute.

1   **For the lemon-basil vinaigrette** Whisk lemon juice, mustard, garlic, salt, and pepper together in bowl. Whisking constantly, slowly drizzle in oil. Stir in basil and season with salt and pepper to taste. (Vinaigrette can be refrigerated for up to 2 days. Bring to room temperature and whisk to recombine before serving.)

2   **For the grilled vegetable platter** Slice ¼ inch off tops and bottoms of bell peppers and remove cores. Make slit down 1 side of each bell pepper, then press flat into 1 long strip, removing ribs and remaining seeds with knife as needed. Cut strips in half crosswise (you should have 4 bell pepper pieces).

3   Push toothpick horizontally through each onion round to keep rings intact while grilling. Brush onion, bell peppers, tomatoes, and zucchini all over with oil, then brush eggplant with remaining oil (it will absorb more oil than other vegetables). Sprinkle vegetables with salt and pepper.

4A   **For a charcoal grill** Open bottom vent completely. Light large chimney starter filled with charcoal briquettes (6 quarts). When top coals are partially covered with ash, pour evenly over grill. Set cooking grate in place, cover, and open lid vent completely. Heat grill until hot, about 5 minutes.

4B   **For a gas grill** Turn all burners to high; cover; and heat grill until hot, about 15 minutes. Turn all burners to medium-high.

5 Clean and oil cooking grate. Grill vegetables until skins of bell peppers and tomatoes are well browned and onions, eggplant, and zucchini are tender, 10 to 16 minutes, flipping and moving vegetables as necessary to ensure even cooking and transferring vegetables to baking sheet as they finish cooking. Place bell peppers in bowl, cover with plastic wrap, and let steam to loosen skins, about 5 minutes.

6 Remove toothpicks from onion and separate rings. When cool enough to handle, peel bell peppers, discarding skins; slice into 1-inch-thick strips.

Arrange vegetables and burrata attractively on serving platter with lemon-basil vinaigrette. Garnish platter with basil leaves. Serve warm or at room temperature.

Flare Trade

Open Fire Prepare hot single-level fire in open-fire grill. Set cooking grate at least 6 inches from coals and flames and heat grill until hot, about 5 minutes. Proceed with step 5.

Smoky Tomato and Eggplant Phyllo Pie

SERVES 4 to 6   **TOTAL TIME** 1½ hours, plus 45 minutes resting and cooling

1   pound ripe tomatoes, cored and sliced ½ inch thick

1¼   teaspoons table salt, divided

9   tablespoons extra-virgin olive oil, divided

1   pound eggplant, sliced into ¼-inch-thick rounds

¼   teaspoon pepper, divided

3   garlic cloves, minced

2   teaspoons minced fresh oregano or ¾ teaspoon dried

2   cups wood chips

12   (14 by 9-inch) phyllo sheets, thawed

6   ounces mozzarella cheese, shredded (1½ cups)

2   tablespoons grated Parmesan cheese

1   tablespoon chopped fresh basil

Why This Recipe Works This visually stunning tart is an unexpected outdoor pleasure that would be equally welcome as part of a brunch spread as it would be at dinnertime. Paper-thin phyllo layers grill-bake to a beautiful golden color and shatteringly crisp texture. Tucked inside is a filling of eggplant and tomatoes layered between mozzarella and Parmesan. Grilling the eggplant and tomatoes before assembling the tart gives them deeper flavor and delightful char. Layering 12 sheets of phyllo creates a crust sturdy enough to stand up to the abundance of vegetables, and the mozzarella melts into the crust, insulating it from becoming soggy. Either fresh or block mozzarella works well here. Phyllo dough is also available in larger 18 by 14-inch sheets; if using, cut them in half to make 14 by 9-inch sheets. Don't thaw the phyllo in the microwave; let it sit in the refrigerator overnight or on the counter for 4 to 5 hours. If you'd like to use wood chunks instead of wood chips when using a charcoal grill, substitute two medium wood chunks for the wood chip packet. You will need a 10-inch cast-iron skillet.

1   Place tomato slices in single layer on double layer of paper towels and sprinkle with ½ teaspoon salt; let sit for 30 minutes. Place second double layer paper towels on top of tomatoes and press to dry tomatoes. Brush tomatoes with 1 tablespoon oil. Brush eggplant with 2 tablespoons oil and sprinkle with ¼ teaspoon salt and ⅛ teaspoon pepper; set aside.

2   Combine garlic, oregano, 1 tablespoon oil, remaining ½ teaspoon salt, and remaining ⅛ teaspoon pepper in bowl; set aside. Using large piece of heavy-duty aluminum foil, wrap chips in 8 by 4 ½-inch foil packet. (Make sure chips do not poke holes in sides or bottom of packet. If using gas, make sure there are no more than 2 layers of foil on bottom of packet.) Cut 2 evenly spaced 2-inch slits in top of packet.

3A   **For a charcoal grill** Open bottom vent halfway. Light large chimney starter mounded with charcoal briquettes (7 quarts). When top coals are partially covered with ash, pour two-thirds evenly over half of grill, then pour remaining coals over other half of grill. Place wood chip packet along one side of grill near border between hotter and cooler coals. Set cooking grate in place, cover, and open lid vent halfway. Heat grill until hot and wood chips are smoking, about 5 minutes.

3B **For a gas grill** Remove cooking grate and place wood chip packet directly on primary burner. Set grate in place and turn all burners to high. Cover and heat grill until hot and wood chips are smoking, 15 to 25 minutes. Leave primary burner on high and turn other burner(s) to medium. (Adjust primary burner as needed to maintain grill temperature of 425 to 450 degrees; if using 3-burner grill, adjust primary burner and second burner.)

4 Clean and oil cooking grate. Grill tomatoes on hotter side of grill (covered if using gas) until charred and starting to soften, about 4 minutes, do not flip. Transfer to platter. Grill eggplant on hotter side of grill (covered, if using gas) until browned and tender, 8 to 10 minutes, flipping as needed. Transfer to platter with tomatoes.

5 Brush 10-inch cast iron skillet with 1 tablespoon oil. Place 1 phyllo sheet into prepared skillet, then lightly brush phyllo with oil. Turn skillet 30 degrees and place

second phyllo sheet on first phyllo sheet, leaving any overhanging phyllo in place. Brush second phyllo sheet with oil. Repeat turning skillet and layering remaining 10 phyllo sheets in pinwheel pattern, brushing each with oil (you should have 12 total layers of phyllo).

6 Sprinkle mozzarella evenly in center of phyllo in 9-inch circle. Shingle tomatoes and eggplant on top of mozzarella in concentric circles, alternating tomatoes and eggplant as you go. Brush reserved garlic oil over vegetables and sprinkle with Parmesan.

7 Gently fold edges of phyllo over vegetable mixture, pleating every 2 to 3 inches as needed, and lightly brush edges with remaining oil. Place skillet on cooler side of grill and cook, covered, until phyllo is crisp and golden brown, 30 to 35 minutes. Let cool for 15 minutes. Sprinkle with basil. Cut into wedges and serve.

5 Over an Open Fire

Smoky Potato Salad

SERVES 4   **TOTAL TIME** 1¼ hours

5 tablespoons extra-virgin olive oil, divided

2 tablespoons white wine vinegar

1 teaspoon whole-grain mustard, plus extra for serving

1 garlic clove, minced

¾ teaspoon table salt, divided

½ teaspoon sugar

½ teaspoon celery seeds

¼ teaspoon pepper

1½ pounds Yukon Gold potatoes, unpeeled, sliced ¾ inch thick

1 red bell pepper, quartered, stemmed, and seeded

1 pickling cucumber (12 ounces), quartered lengthwise

¼ cup chopped fresh parsley, basil, and/or tarragon

8 hot dogs

8 hot dog buns, split lengthwise

Why This Recipe Works Along with s'mores, hot dogs are the first food that many of us learn how to cook over an open fire: Just spear 'em with a stick and dance them over the flames. This recipe dresses up these icons of campfire cooking with charred cucumbers (trust us) and a vibrant smoky potato salad. The cucumber spears are grilled until they develop a caramelized crust; the resulting crisp-tender texture is reminiscent of grilled zucchini. Yukon Golds make a rich base for the potato salad. In order to cook them outdoors from start to finish, you'll slice them into thick rounds and cook them over indirect heat to ensure that they turn tender while developing light char. Leaving the potato peels on helps the slices hold together. Grilled red bell pepper adds sweetness to the salad, and a simple vinaigrette with a touch of mustard ties it together. If a pickling cucumber is unavailable, substitute two Persian cucumbers, halved lengthwise.

1   Whisk ¼ cup oil, vinegar, mustard, garlic, ½ teaspoon salt, sugar, celery seeds, and pepper together in large bowl; set aside. Toss potatoes, bell pepper, and cucumber with remaining 1 tablespoon oil and remaining ¼ teaspoon salt.

2   Light 3-layer log cabin fire in open-fire grill (see page 13). When most logs have carbonized and broken down into large coals, spread evenly into 2-inch-thick layer over half of grill. Arrange any logs that have not broken down on perimeter of fire, away from cooler side of grill, and top with fresh logs. (Moderate flames will remain as larger coals and logs burn. Continue to maintain hot half-grill fire by pulling fresh coals created by burning logs onto spent coals and adding fresh logs in their place.) Set cooking grate at least 6 inches from coals and flames and heat grate until hot, about 5 minutes.

3   Clean and oil cooking grate. Grill cucumber, cut side down, on hotter side of grill, turning as needed, until lightly charred on cut sides, 8 to 10 minutes. Grill potatoes and bell pepper on cooler side of grill, turning occasionally, until tender and lightly charred on all sides, 15 to 20 minutes. Transfer vegetables to cutting board as they finish cooking. Cut cucumber quarters in half lengthwise. Cut potatoes and bell pepper into rough 1-inch pieces. Add potatoes, bell pepper, and parsley to dressing and gently toss to coat. Season with salt and pepper to taste. Set cucumber and potato salad aside for serving.

4 Grill hot dogs and buns on hotter side of grill until hot dogs are well browned and buns are lightly toasted, 1 to 2 minutes per side. Transfer hot dogs and buns to platter as they finish cooking. Arrange hot dogs in buns and top with cucumber. Serve with potato salad, passing extra mustard separately.

Flare Trade

Charcoal Grill Prepare hot half-grill fire using 6 quarts charcoal. Proceed with step 3.

Gas Grill Turn all burners to high; cover; and heat grill until hot, about 15 minutes. Leave primary burner on high and turn other burner(s) to low. Proceed with step 3, placing vegetables on cooler side of grill and cooking covered.

Chicken Souvlaki

SERVES 4   **TOTAL TIME** 1¾ hours, plus 30 minutes brining

Tzatziki Sauce

- 1 tablespoon lemon juice
- 1 small garlic clove, minced to paste
- ¾ cup plain Greek yogurt
- ½ cucumber, peeled, halved lengthwise, seeded, and chopped fine (½ cup)
- 3 tablespoons minced fresh mint
- 1 tablespoon minced fresh parsley
- ¼ teaspoon table salt

Chicken

- 2 tablespoons table salt for brining
- 1½ pounds boneless, skinless chicken breasts, trimmed and cut into 1-inch pieces
- ⅓ cup extra-virgin olive oil
- 2 tablespoons minced fresh parsley
- 1 teaspoon finely grated lemon zest plus ¼ cup juice (2 lemons)
- 1 teaspoon honey
- 1 teaspoon dried oregano
- ½ teaspoon pepper
- 1 green bell pepper, quartered, stemmed, and seeded, each quarter cut into 4 chunks
- 1 small red onion, halved lengthwise, each half cut into 4 chunks
- 4 (8-inch) pitas

Why This Recipe Works At least as appealing as souvlaki's tangy, smoky flavor is how easily you can make it over an open fire (the traditional cooking method). Just toss pieces of brined boneless chicken with olive oil, lemon juice, oregano, parsley, pepper, and honey and skewer them. Bell peppers and onions at the ends of each skewer make edible shields to protect the chicken while it cooks. This tzatziki is fairly mild; double the garlic for a more assertive flavor. A rasp-style grater quickly turns the garlic into a paste. Serving the souvlaki wrapped in warm pitas keeps the meal prep entirely outdoors; if you like, you can serve the chicken, vegetables, and tzatziki with rice instead. You will need four 12-inch metal skewers.

1 **For the tzatziki sauce** Whisk lemon juice and garlic together in small bowl. Let sit for 10 minutes. Stir in yogurt, cucumber, mint, parsley, and salt. Cover and refrigerate until needed.

2 **For the chicken** Dissolve 2 tablespoons salt in 1 quart cold water. Submerge chicken in brine, cover, and refrigerate for 30 minutes. While chicken is brining, combine oil, parsley, lemon zest and juice, honey, oregano, and pepper in medium bowl. Transfer ¼ cup oil mixture to large bowl and set aside to toss with cooked chicken.

3 Remove chicken from brine and pat dry with paper towels. Toss chicken with remaining oil mixture. Thread 4 pieces of bell pepper, concave side up, onto one 12-inch metal skewer. Thread one-quarter of chicken onto skewer. Thread 2 chunks of onion onto skewer and place skewer on plate. Repeat skewering remaining chicken and vegetables on 3 more skewers. Lightly moisten 2 pita breads with water. Sandwich 2 unmoistened pita breads between moistened pita breads and wrap stack tightly in lightly greased heavy-duty aluminum foil.

4 Light 3-layer log cabin fire in open-fire grill (see page 13). When most logs have carbonized and broken down into large coals, spread evenly into 2-inch-thick layer over half of grill. Arrange any logs that have not broken down on perimeter of fire, away from cooler side of grill, and top with fresh logs. (Moderate flames will remain as larger coals and logs burn. Continue to maintain hot half-grill fire by pulling fresh coals created by burning logs onto spent coals and adding fresh logs in their place.) Set cooking grate at least 6 inches from coals and flames and heat grate until hot, about 5 minutes.

5 Clean and oil cooking grate. Grill skewers on hotter side of grill, turning occasionally, until chicken and vegetables are well browned on all sides and chicken registers 160 degrees, 20 to 30 minutes. Using fork, push chicken and vegetables off skewers into bowl of reserved oil mixture. Stir gently, breaking up onion chunks; cover with foil and let sit for 5 minutes.

6 Meanwhile, place packet of pitas on cooler side of grill. Flip occasionally to heat, about 5 minutes.

7 Lay each warm pita on 12-inch square of foil. Spread each pita with 2 tablespoons tzatziki. Place one-quarter of chicken and vegetables in middle of each pita. Roll into cylindrical shape and serve with remaining tzatziki.

Flare Trade

Charcoal Grill Prepare hot single-level fire using 7 quarts charcoal. Proceed with step 5, heating pitas for 2 to 3 minutes in step 6.

Gas Grill Turn all burners to high; cover; and heat grill until hot, about 15 minutes. Leave all burners on high. Proceed with step 5, cooking skewers covered. Heat pitas for 2 to 3 minutes in step 6.

Grilled Jerk Chicken

SERVES 4   **TOTAL TIME** 1½ hours, plus 1 hour marinating

4 scallions

¼ cup vegetable oil

¼ cup soy sauce

2 tablespoons cider vinegar

1 tablespoon packed brown sugar

1-2 habanero chiles, stemmed

10 sprigs fresh thyme

5 garlic cloves, peeled

2½ teaspoons ground allspice

1½ teaspoons table salt

½ teaspoon ground cinnamon

½ teaspoon ground ginger

3 pounds bone-in chicken pieces (split breasts cut in half crosswise, drumsticks, and/or thighs), trimmed

Lime wedges

Why This Recipe Works For that wood-smoke char that's authentic to jerk chicken, cooking it over an open fire is the way to go. You also need a marinade that's fiery, fresh, and just a bit sweet: Habaneros, scallions, garlic, thyme sprigs, and warm spices headline a list of ingredients that come together in less than a minute in a blender. Once marinated, the bone-in chicken pieces cook over indirect heat; then, for a pure burst of flavor, you'll brush another layer of marinade all over the pieces and sear them over direct heat. Use more or fewer habaneros depending on your desired level of spiciness. You can also remove the seeds and ribs from the habaneros or substitute jalapeños for less heat. We recommend wearing food-handling gloves or plastic bags on your hands when handling the chiles. Use thyme sprigs with a generous amount of leaves; there's no need to separate the leaves from the stems.

1 Process scallions, oil, soy sauce, vinegar, sugar, habanero(s), thyme sprigs, garlic, allspice, salt, cinnamon, and ginger in blender until smooth, about 30 seconds, scraping down sides of blender jar as needed. Measure out ¼ cup marinade and refrigerate until ready to use.

2 Place chicken and remaining marinade in 1-gallon zipper-lock bag. Press out air, seal bag, and turn to coat chicken in marinade. Refrigerate for at least 1 hour or up to 24 hours, turning occasionally.

3 Light 3-layer log cabin fire in open-fire grill (see page 13). When most logs have carbonized and broken down into large coals, spread evenly into 2-inch-thick layer over half of grill. Arrange any logs that have not broken down on perimeter of fire, away from cooler side of grill, and top with fresh logs. (Moderate flames will remain as larger coals and logs burn. Continue to maintain hot half-grill fire by pulling fresh coals created by burning logs onto spent coals and adding fresh logs in their place.) Set cooking grate at least 6 inches from coals and flames and heat grate until hot, about 5 minutes.

4 Clean and oil cooking grate. Grill chicken on cooler side of grill, turning and moving pieces as needed to ensure even browning, until breasts register 160 degrees and drumsticks/thighs register 175 degrees, 30 to 45 minutes. Transfer pieces skin side up to plate as they finish cooking.

5   Brush skin side of chicken with half of reserved marinade. Place chicken skin side down on hotter side of grill. Brush with remaining reserved marinade and cook until lightly charred, 1 to 3 minutes per side. Check browning often and move pieces as needed for even char. Transfer chicken to platter, tent with aluminum foil, and let rest for 5 minutes. Serve with lime wedges.

Flare Trade

Charcoal Grill Prepare hot half-grill fire using 6 quarts charcoal. Proceed with step 4; place chicken on cooler side of grill, 6 to 8 inches from heat source, and cook covered for 22 to 30 minutes.

Gas Grill Turn all burners to high; cover; and heat grill until hot, about 15 minutes. Leave primary burner on high and turn off other burner(s). Proceed with step 4; place chicken on cooler side of grill and cook covered for 22 to 30 minutes.

Kalbi

¾ cup packed dark brown sugar

⅔ cup soy sauce

1 cup coarsely chopped onion

½ cup canned pineapple chunks, plus 3 tablespoons juice

½ green kiwi, peeled

6 garlic cloves, smashed and peeled

¼ cup rice wine, such as michiu, cheongju, or mirin

2 tablespoons toasted sesame oil

3 pounds flanken-style beef short ribs, ¼ inch thick, trimmed

Why This Recipe Works Sweet and savory Korean charred ribs are irresistible. This preparation is typically cooked over wood and made with beef short ribs cut thin flanken-style, across the bones. (You can find this cut at Asian markets, especially ones that specialize in Korean ingredients.) Kalbi marinade usually gets its fruity sweetness from ripe Asian pear; canned pineapple is a reliable year-round stand-in. Green kiwi adds more sweetness plus enzymes that tenderize the meat. Aside from making sure to marinate the ribs for at least 24 hours, the biggest tip for success is to cook the kalbi for longer than you might think. While their thinness certainly speeds things up, you still need to allow the fat to render and the connective tissues to break down. You'll know when the kalbi are done because the bones will pull away cleanly from the meat with just a little resistance. An 8-ounce can of pineapple chunks will yield enough for this recipe. We prefer green kiwi (not yellow) for this marinade. Rinsing the meat is necessary to remove any bone fragments that may be stuck to the ribs as a result of how they're cut. Garnish the kalbi with sliced scallions, if desired.

1 Whisk sugar and soy sauce in bowl until sugar has dissolved. Process sugar mixture, onion, pineapple and juice, kiwi, garlic, wine, and oil in blender until smooth, about 30 seconds. Transfer marinade to 13 by 9-inch baking dish.

2 Line rimmed baking sheet with triple layer of paper towels. Rinse ribs under cold running water to remove any bone fragments, then transfer to prepared sheet. Pat tops of ribs dry with additional paper towels.

3 Working with a few ribs at a time, transfer to marinade, turn gently to coat, and submerge in marinade. Cover dish with plastic wrap and refrigerate for at least 24 hours or up to 2 days.

4 Light 3-layer log cabin fire in open-fire grill (see page 13). When most logs have carbonized and broken down into large coals, spread evenly into 1-inch-thick layer over grill. Arrange any logs that have not broken down on perimeter of fire and top with fresh logs. (Moderate flames will remain as larger coals and logs burn. Continue to maintain hot single-level fire by pulling fresh coals created by burning logs onto spent coals and adding fresh logs in their place.) Set cooking grate at least 6 inches from coals and flames and heat grate until hot, about 5 minutes.

5 Clean and oil cooking grate. Grill ribs until evenly browned, about 6 minutes per side, moving ribs as needed for even cooking and to prevent flare-ups. Transfer ribs to platter, tent with aluminum foil, and let rest for 5 minutes. Serve.

Flare Trade

Charcoal Grill Prepare medium-hot single-level fire using 4½ quarts charcoal. Proceed with step 5.

Gas Grill Turn all burners to high; cover; and heat grill until hot, about 15 minutes. Turn all burners to medium-high. Proceed with step 5.

Thick-Cut Rib Steaks with Ember-Baked Potatoes

SERVES 4 to 6   **TOTAL TIME** 1¾ hours, plus 1¼ hours resting

2 (1½- to 2-pound) double-cut bone-in rib steaks, 1¾ to 2 inches thick, trimmed

4 teaspoons kosher salt

2 teaspoons pepper

4 russet potatoes (12 ounces each), unpeeled, each lightly pricked with fork in 6 places

1 whole head garlic, outer papery skin removed and top quarter of head cut off and discarded

1 teaspoon extra-virgin olive oil

8 tablespoons unsalted butter, softened

1 tablespoon minced fresh chives

1 teaspoon grated lemon zest

Why This Recipe Works Generous cowboy-cut rib steaks and baked potatoes satisfy the heartiest of appetites—and baking the potatoes right in the embers of the fire while the steaks grill above lets you work up that appetite outdoors while your meal cooks. Getting these double-thick bone-in steaks to medium-rare while achieving a flavorful seared crust demands a low-and-slow approach, so you'll slow-roast the steaks on the cooler side before giving them a sear over the hot coals. Wrapping the potatoes in aluminum foil helps trap steam and keep the skins from becoming leathery (as well as keep the ashes off your plate). For just-right baked potato texture, start them about half an hour before the steaks hit the grill. An ember-roasted head of garlic makes for a fabulous flavored butter. It's important to let the steaks come to 55 degrees before grilling; otherwise, the times and temperatures will be inaccurate. Use heavy-duty aluminum foil here; regular foil will not withstand the heat from the coals.

1 Set wire rack in rimmed baking sheet. Pat steaks dry with paper towels and sprinkle with salt. Place steaks on prepared rack and let sit at room temperature until meat registers 55 degrees, about 1 hour. Sprinkle steaks with pepper.

2 Wrap potatoes individually in double layer of heavy-duty aluminum foil. Stack two 12-inch sheets of foil, place garlic head cut side up in center of sheets, and drizzle with oil. Tightly crimp foil around garlic to seal.

3 Light 3-layer log cabin fire in open-fire grill (see page 13). When most logs have carbonized and broken down into large coals, spread evenly into 2-inch-thick layer over half of grill. Arrange any logs that have not broken down on perimeter of fire, away from cooler side of grill, and top with fresh logs. (Moderate flames will remain as larger coals and logs burn. Continue to maintain hot half-grill fire by pulling fresh coals created by burning logs onto spent coals and adding fresh logs in their place.)

4 Nestle potatoes into coals and place garlic along perimeter of coals. Cook for 30 minutes. Flip potatoes and rotate garlic, then set cooking grate at least 6 inches from coals and flames and heat grate until hot, about 5 minutes.

5 Clean and oil cooking grate. Place steaks on cooler side of grill with bones facing fire. Cook, turning occasionally and keeping bones facing fire, until steaks register 95 degrees, 20 to 40 minutes.

6   Slide steaks to hotter side of grill and cook until well browned and meat registers 120 to 125 degrees (for medium-rare), about 4 minutes per side. Continue to cook potatoes and garlic until center of largest potato registers at least 205 degrees, about 10 minutes. Transfer steaks to clean wire rack set in rimmed baking sheet, tent with foil, and let rest for 15 minutes. Transfer potatoes and garlic to plate and let cool slightly.

7   Remove garlic from foil. Squeeze head from root end to extrude garlic into bowl; discard skins. Mash garlic, butter, chives, and lemon zest together and season with salt and pepper to taste. Remove potatoes from foil. Using paring knife, make 2 slits, forming X, in each potato. Using clean dish towel, hold ends and squeeze slightly to push flesh up and out. Season with salt and pepper to taste. Transfer steaks to cutting board and cut meat from bone. Slice steaks against grain ½ inch thick. Serve steaks and potatoes with garlic butter.

Flare Trade

Charcoal Grill Open bottom vent halfway. Arrange 4 quarts unlit charcoal briquettes in even layer over half of grill. Light large chimney starter filled with 15 briquettes (pile briquettes on 1 side of chimney so they catch). When coals are partially covered with ash, pour evenly over unlit coals. Nestle potatoes into coals and place garlic along perimeter of coals. Cover, open lid vent halfway, and cook for 30 minutes. Fifteen minutes before grilling steaks, light chimney starter filled halfway with charcoal briquettes (3 quarts). Remove potatoes and garlic from coals and pour lit coals directly over spent coals. Flip and rotate potatoes and garlic and return to coals. Set cooking grate in place; cover; and heat grill until hot, about 5 minutes. Proceed with step 5.

Grilled Flank Steak and Vegetables with Chimichurri

SERVES 6   **TOTAL TIME** 2 hours, plus 1 hour resting

Chimichurri

- ¼ cup hot water
- 2 teaspoons dried oregano
- 1 teaspoon table salt
- 1⅓ cups fresh parsley leaves
- ⅔ cup fresh cilantro leaves
- 6 garlic cloves, minced
- ½ teaspoon red pepper flakes
- ¼ cup red wine vinegar
- ½ cup extra-virgin olive oil

Steak and Vegetables

- 1 red onion, cut into ¾-inch-thick rounds
- 2 zucchini, halved lengthwise
- 2 tablespoons extra-virgin olive oil
- 1 eggplant, cut into ½-inch-thick rounds
- 1 teaspoon table salt, divided
- ½ teaspoon pepper, divided
- 1 (2- to 2½-pound) flank steak, trimmed

Why This Recipe Works Simply seasoned beef cooked over an open wood fire is arguably Argentina's greatest cooking tradition. This homage takes advantage of the magic that flames can work with a good steak. Beefy, moist flank steak cooks relatively quickly over a very hot fire; cooking just to medium-rare keeps it tender. A boldly flavored, spicy sauce made with parsley, cilantro, and garlic based on the Argentine staple, chimichurri, is a natural match. The steak and abundant vegetables need minimal prep and, once the fire is ready, both cook in about half an hour, leaving you plenty of time for a relaxing meal around the fire pit.

1 **For the chimichurri** Combine hot water, oregano, and salt in small bowl and let sit until oregano is softened, about 15 minutes. Pulse parsley, cilantro, garlic, and pepper flakes in food processor until coarsely chopped, about 10 pulses. Add water mixture and vinegar and pulse to combine, about 5 pulses. Transfer mixture to bowl and slowly whisk in oil until combined. Cover and let sit at room temperature for 1 hour. (Chimichurri can be refrigerated for up to 3 days; bring to room temperature before serving.)

2 **For the steak and vegetables** Push toothpick horizontally through each onion round to keep rings intact while grilling. Brush onion and zucchini with oil, then brush eggplant with remaining oil (it will absorb more oil than other vegetables). Sprinkle vegetables with ½ teaspoon salt and ¼ teaspoon pepper.

3 Light 3-layer log cabin fire in open-fire grill (see page 13). When most logs have carbonized and broken down into large coals, spread evenly into 1-inch-thick layer over grill. Arrange any logs that have not broken down on perimeter of fire and top with fresh logs. (Moderate flames will remain as larger coals and logs burn. Continue to maintain hot single-level fire by pulling fresh coals created by burning logs onto spent coals and adding fresh logs in their place.) Set cooking grate at least 6 inches from coals and flames and heat grate until hot, about 5 minutes.

4 Clean and oil cooking grate. Pat steak dry with paper towels and sprinkle with remaining ½ teaspoon salt and remaining ¼ teaspoon pepper. Grill steak and vegetables until meat registers 120 to 125 degrees (for medium-rare), 10 to 14 minutes, and vegetables are well browned and tender, 10 to 20 minutes, flipping steak every 2 minutes and flipping vegetables as needed to ensure even char. Transfer steak to cutting board, tent with aluminum foil, and let rest while vegetables finish. Transfer vegetables to platter as they finish cooking.

5 Remove toothpicks from onion and separate rings. Cut steak in half lengthwise with grain to create 2 narrow steaks. Slice each steak thin on bias against grain. Serve steak with vegetables, passing chimichurri separately.

Fireside Chili

1 (4-pound) boneless beef chuck-eye roast, trimmed and cut into 1-inch-thick steaks

1 teaspoon table salt

1 teaspoon pepper

1 onion, cut into 1-inch-thick rounds

¼ cup vegetable oil

3 tablespoons ancho chile powder

2 tablespoons paprika

2 tablespoons ground cumin

1 tablespoon ground coriander

1 tablespoon garlic powder

2 teaspoons dried oregano

1 (28-ounce) can crushed tomatoes

2 (15-ounce) cans pinto beans, undrained

1 cup water

2 teaspoons sugar

2 tablespoons cider vinegar

Why This Recipe Works Chuck roast steaks, quickly seared over an open fire for smoky goodness and then cut into hearty chunks, are the foundation of this rich, meaty chili that you'll want to dig into while sitting around the campfire. A combination of ancho chile powder, paprika, herbs, and spices builds layers of potent flavor. Adding fresh logs at the fire's edge keeps the heat going through the long, leisurely cooking session. Pinto beans up the stick-to-your-ribs factor; plus, their canning liquid gives the sauce a velvety consistency that wonderfully cloaks the chunks of meat. If you have a hanging Dutch oven and swivel arm attachment for your open-fire grill, you can remove the grate after step 3 and hang the Dutch oven 6 inches from the coals in step 4. Serve with your favorite chili toppings.

1 Light 3-layer log cabin fire in open-fire grill (see page 13). When most logs have carbonized and broken down into large coals, spread evenly into 1-inch-thick layer over grill. Arrange any logs that have not broken down on perimeter of fire and top with fresh logs. (Moderate flames will remain as larger coals and logs burn. Continue to maintain hot single-level fire by pulling fresh coals created by burning logs onto spent coals and adding fresh logs in their place.) Set cooking grate at least 6 inches from coals and flames and heat grate until hot, about 5 minutes.

2 Pat steaks dry with paper towels and sprinkle with salt and pepper. Push toothpick horizontally through each onion round to keep rings intact while grilling.

3 Clean and oil cooking grate. Grill steaks and onion until well browned on both sides, 6 to 10 minutes total. Transfer steaks and onion to cutting board as they finish cooking and let cool slightly. Cut steaks into 1-inch pieces, discarding any excess fat. Discard toothpicks and chop onion coarse.

4 Consolidate coals into 2-inch-thick layer over half of grill, keeping new and spent logs away from cooler side. Set Dutch oven over cooler side of grill, at least 6 inches from coals and flames, and heat oil until shimmering. Add chile powder, paprika, cumin, coriander, garlic powder, and oregano and cook until fragrant, about 1 minute. Stir in tomatoes, beans and their canning liquid, water, sugar, beef and any accumulated juices, and onion. Bring to simmer; cover Dutch oven; and cook until meat is tender, 2½ to 3 hours, stirring occasionally to prevent sticking. (Continue to maintain hot half-grill fire by pulling fresh coals created by burning logs onto spent coals and adding fresh logs in their place.)

Flare Trade

Charcoal Grill Prepare hot single-level fire using 7 quarts charcoal. Proceed with step 2, cooking steaks and onion covered in step 3. Consolidate coals to half of grill in step 4 and place Dutch oven on cooler side of grill. Proceed with recipe, covering Dutch oven to cook chili and adding hot coals to grill as needed to maintain hot half-grill fire.

Gas Grill Turn all burners to high; cover; and heat grill until hot, about 15 minutes. Keep all burners on high. Proceed with step 2, cooking steaks and onion covered in step 3. Turn primary burner to medium and turn off other burner(s) in step 4. Place Dutch oven on hotter side of grill and proceed with recipe, covering Dutch oven to cook chili and adjusting burner as needed to maintain gentle simmer.

5 Remove chili from grill and let sit, uncovered, for 10 minutes. Stir in any fat that has risen to top of chili, then stir in vinegar and season with salt to taste. Serve.

Grilled Harissa–Rubbed Rack of Lamb with Ember–Baked Carrots

SERVES 4 to 6   TOTAL TIME 1¾ hours

- 1½ pounds carrots, trimmed
- ½ cup extra-virgin olive oil, divided
- 1½ teaspoons table salt, divided
- ½ teaspoon pepper, divided
- 6 garlic cloves, minced
- 2 tablespoons paprika
- 1 tablespoon ground coriander
- 1 tablespoon ground dried Aleppo pepper
- 1 teaspoon ground cumin
- ¾ teaspoon caraway seeds
- 2 (1½- to 2-pound) racks of lamb (8 ribs each), fat trimmed to ⅛ to ¼ inch and rib bones frenched
- 2 tablespoons chopped toasted almonds
- 2 tablespoons minced fresh cilantro

Flare Trade

Charcoal Grill Prepare hot half-grill fire using 7 quarts charcoal. Proceed with step 4.

Gas Grill Turn all burners to high; cover; and heat grill until hot, about 15 minutes. Leave primary burner on high and turn off other burner(s). Clean and oil cooking grate, then place carrot packet on hotter side of grill and proceed with step 4.

Why This Recipe Works With its juicy pink meat, rich crust, and impressive presentation, rack of lamb is a bona fide showstopper. If you grill this piece of meat improperly, you've made a costly mistake, but fear not with this open-fire technique, which delivers consistent perfection. Trimming excess fat from the racks avoids flare-ups, as does starting the lamb over indirect heat. For flavorful meat and a crust that's nicely charred, not scorched, you'll apply a paste of flavorful homemade harissa during the last minutes of grilling. Whole carrots, lightly seasoned and cooked in foil right in the embers, are a fuss-free and delicious side. We developed this recipe with domestic lamb, but you may substitute lamb imported from New Zealand or Australia. Since imported racks of lamb are generally smaller, begin checking for doneness sooner in step 6. Choose carrots that are 1 to 1½ inches in diameter. Be sure to use heavy-duty aluminum foil; regular foil will not withstand the heat from the coals.

1   Toss carrots with 1 tablespoon oil, ½ teaspoon salt, and ¼ teaspoon pepper. Stack two 12 by 8-inch sheets of heavy-duty aluminum foil. Center carrots on prepared sheets, top with second double layer of foil, and crimp edges to create tightly sealed packet; set aside.

2   Combine remaining 7 tablespoons oil, garlic, paprika, coriander, Aleppo pepper, cumin, caraway seeds, and ½ teaspoon salt in bowl. Microwave until bubbling and very fragrant, about 1 minute, stirring halfway through microwaving. Let harissa cool to room temperature. Pat lamb dry with paper towels, sprinkle with remaining ½ teaspoon salt and remaining ¼ teaspoon pepper, and rub with 2 tablespoons harissa.

3   Light 3-layer log cabin fire in open-fire grill (see page 13). When most logs have carbonized and broken down into large coals, spread evenly into 2-inch-thick layer over half of grill. Arrange any logs that have not broken down on perimeter of fire, away from cooler side of grill, and top with fresh logs. (Moderate flames will remain as larger coals and logs burn. Continue to maintain hot half-grill fire by pulling fresh coals created by burning logs onto spent coals and adding fresh logs in their place.)

4 Nestle carrot packet on border of coals, away from flames. Cook for 10 minutes. Flip and rotate packet and continue to cook carrots until tender (pierce foil with paring knife to check), about 20 minutes.

5 Meanwhile, after flipping carrot packet, set cooking grate at least 6 inches from coals and flames and heat grate until hot, about 5 minutes.

6 Clean and oil cooking grate. Place racks bone side up on cooler side of grill with meaty side facing fire. Cook until meat is lightly browned, faint grill marks appear, and fat begins to render, 8 to 12 minutes. Flip racks bone side down and slide to hotter side of grill. Cook until well

browned on bone side, 3 to 4 minutes. Brush racks with 1 tablespoon harissa, flip bone side up, and cook until well browned on meaty side, 3 to 4 minutes.

7 Stand up racks, leaning them against each other for support, and cook until bottoms are well browned and meat registers 120 to 125 degrees (for medium-rare), 3 to 8 minutes.

8 Transfer racks to carving board and transfer carrot packet to platter. Tent lamb with foil and let rest for 15 minutes. Cut between ribs to separate chops. Remove carrots from foil packet and sprinkle with almonds and cilantro. Serve, passing remaining harissa separately.

Grilled Halibut with Spicy Orange and Fennel Salad

SERVES 4 **TOTAL TIME** 1½ hours

- ½ cup extra-virgin olive oil, divided
- 3 tablespoons white wine vinegar
- 1–2 teaspoons Calabrian chili paste
- 1 teaspoon table salt, divided
- 2 oranges, plus ½ teaspoon grated orange zest
- 1 large shallot, sliced thin
- 2 fennel bulbs, bases lightly trimmed, ¼ cup fronds torn, stalks discarded
- 4 (6- to 8-ounce) skin-on halibut fillets, 1 to 1½ inches thick
- ¼ cup fresh mint leaves

Why This Recipe Works The open fire isn't just for cuts of meat: You can also grill elegant fish fillets like this halibut, with firm flesh that resists flaking apart while picking up plenty of smoky flavor and appealing char marks. A spicy orange and fennel salad provides a wonderful contrast to the rich fish. Grilling the orange slices and fennel wedges caramelizes some of their natural sugars and deepens their flavor. For a spicier dish, use the larger amount of chili paste. Jarred crushed red peppers or sambal oelek are good substitutes for the chili paste. Look for fennel bulbs that measure 3½ to 4 inches in diameter and weigh about 1 pound with the stalks (12 to 14 ounces without); trim the bases sparingly so that the bulbs remain intact. If your fennel doesn't have fronds, substitute basil or parsley leaves or use more mint. If halibut isn't available, you can substitute four skin-on swordfish or mahi mahi steaks, 1 to 1½ inches thick. If you can find a 2-pound skin-on full halibut steak (1½ to 2 inches thick and 10 to 12 inches long), grill that for 20 to 30 minutes. Creating nonstick conditions for the grill grate is key here (see page 9).

1 Whisk ¼ cup oil, vinegar, chili paste, ¼ teaspoon salt, and orange zest together in medium bowl. Stir in shallot and set aside.

2 Cut each fennel bulb lengthwise through core into 8 wedges (do not remove core). Cut away peel and pith from oranges, then slice crosswise into 1-inch-thick rounds. Brush fennel and oranges with 2 tablespoons oil and sprinkle with ¼ teaspoon salt. Pat halibut dry with paper towels, brush with remaining 2 tablespoons oil, and sprinkle with remaining ½ teaspoon salt.

3 Light 3-layer log cabin fire in open-fire grill (see page 13). When most logs have carbonized and broken down into large coals, spread evenly into 1-inch-thick layer over grill. Arrange any logs that have not broken down on perimeter of fire and top with fresh logs. (Moderate flames will remain as larger coals and logs burn. Continue to maintain hot single-level fire by pulling fresh coals created by burning logs onto spent coals and adding fresh logs in their place.) Set cooking grate at least 6 inches from coals and flames and heat grate until hot, about 5 minutes.

Flare Trade

Charcoal Grill Prepare hot single-level fire using 7 quarts charcoal. Proceed with step 4.

Gas Grill Turn all burners to high; cover; and heat grill until hot, about 15 minutes. Keep all burners on high. Proceed with step 4.

4 Clean and oil cooking grate. Grill fennel and oranges, turning as needed, until lightly charred on all sides, 8 to 10 minutes; transfer to plate. Clean and oil cooking grate again. Grill halibut, turning once during cooking (using metal spatula), until fish flakes when gently prodded with paring knife and registers 130 degrees, 10 to 15 minutes. Carefully transfer halibut to cutting board, tent with aluminum foil, and let rest while assembling salad.

5 Arrange fennel and oranges attractively on platter, top with fennel fronds and mint, and drizzle with shallot mixture. Remove skin from fillets by slipping knife or spatula between them. Serve halibut with salad.

Over an Open Fire   **259**

Grilled Whole Trout with Wilted Swiss Chard and Apple–Cherry Relish

SERVES 4   **TOTAL TIME** 1½ hours

¼ cup extra-virgin olive oil, divided

1 teaspoon grated lemon zest plus 2 tablespoons juice, plus lemon wedges for serving

1 tablespoon pure maple syrup

1 tablespoon Dijon mustard

1 small shallot, minced

1 small Fuji, Gala, or Pink Lady apple, cored and cut into ¼-inch pieces (½ cup)

⅓ cup dried cherries

2 teaspoons minced fresh oregano

1½ teaspoons table salt, divided

½ teaspoon pepper, divided

4 (10- to 12-ounce) butterflied whole trout, scaled, gutted, and fins snipped off with scissors

2 tablespoons mayonnaise

1 teaspoon honey

1½ pounds Swiss chard, trimmed

Flare Trade

Charcoal Grill Prepare hot single-level fire using 7 quarts charcoal. Proceed with step 4.

Gas Grill Turn all burners to high; cover; and heat grill until hot, about 15 minutes. Keep all burners on high. Proceed with step 4.

Why This Recipe Works Whole trout, whether from a lake, stream, or supermarket, taste and look amazing when you cook them outdoors gathered around an open fire. Sized just right to feed one person each, the trout cook quickly; a light coat of mayonnaise and honey keeps the skin from sticking to the grate and turns it bronzed and crisp. The chard leaves are also cooked whole, producing a range of textures and flavors from the charred, paper-thin edges to the tender, meaty stems. Served with a tart-sweet and crunchy fruit relish, this meal celebrates rustic freshness. To take the temperature of the fish, insert the thermometer into the fillets through the opening by the gills. Do not flip the fish over in one motion. Instead, use two thin metal spatulas to gently lift the fish from the grate and then slide it from the spatula back onto the grate. Creating nonstick conditions for the grill grate is key here (see page 9).

1   Whisk 2 tablespoons oil, lemon juice, maple syrup, mustard, and shallot in bowl until well combined. Stir in apple and cherries; set aside for serving.

2   Combine lemon zest, oregano, 1 teaspoon salt, and ¼ teaspoon pepper in separate bowl. Pat trout dry with paper towels inside and out. Open up each fish and sprinkle zest mixture evenly over flesh. Close up fish and let sit for 10 minutes. Stir mayonnaise and honey together. Brush mayonnaise mixture evenly over entire exterior of each fish.

3   Light 3-layer log cabin fire in open-fire grill (see page 13). When most logs have carbonized and broken down into large coals, spread evenly into 1-inch-thick layer over grill. Arrange any logs that have not broken down on perimeter of fire and top with fresh logs. (Moderate flames will remain as larger coals and logs burn. Continue to maintain hot single-level fire by pulling fresh coals created by burning logs onto spent coals and adding fresh logs in their place.) Set cooking grate at least 6 inches from coals and flames and heat grate until hot, about 5 minutes.

4   Clean and oil cooking grate. Grill fish until skin is browned and beginning to blister, 2 to 4 minutes. Using thin metal spatula, lift bottom of thick backbone edge of fish from cooking grate just enough to slide second thin metal spatula under fish. Remove first spatula, then use it

to support raw side of fish while using second spatula to flip fish over. Grill until second side is browned and beginning to blister and thickest part of fish registers 130 to 135 degrees, 2 to 4 minutes. Transfer fish to serving platter, tent with aluminum foil, and let rest while cooking Swiss chard.

5 Toss Swiss chard with remaining 2 tablespoons oil, remaining ½ teaspoon salt, and remaining ¼ teaspoon pepper. Grill Swiss chard in even layer, turning frequently, until leaves are wilted and lightly charred and stems are crisp-tender, 6 to 9 minutes. Transfer Swiss chard to serving platter with fish. Serve with apple-cherry relish.

Paella for a Crowd

SERVES 8   **TOTAL TIME** 2 hours

1½ pounds boneless, skinless chicken thighs, trimmed and halved crosswise

1¾ teaspoons table salt, divided

1 teaspoon pepper

12 ounces jumbo shrimp (16 to 20 per pound), peeled and deveined

5 tablespoons extra-virgin olive oil, divided

6 garlic cloves, minced, divided

1¾ teaspoons hot smoked paprika, divided

3 tablespoons tomato paste

4 cups chicken broth

⅔ cup dry sherry

1 (8-ounce) bottle clam juice

Pinch saffron threads, crumbled (optional)

1 onion, chopped fine

½ cup jarred roasted red peppers, rinsed, patted dry, and chopped fine

3 cups arborio rice

1 pound littleneck or cherrystone clams, scrubbed

8 ounces Spanish-style chorizo sausage, cut into ½-inch pieces

1 cup frozen peas, thawed

Lemon wedges

Why This Recipe Works Knock your guests' socks off with paella cooked over a live fire. Strategically adding fresh wood ensures consistent heat output. Using roasted red peppers and tomato paste (instead of fresh peppers and tomatoes) streamlines the process, and browning the chicken thighs on the grate, rather than in the pan, adds grilled flavor. To make sure everything reaches the finish line at once, timing and placement are key: The chicken goes in first, arranged around the perimeter of the pan, followed by the chorizo and seafood in the center. The rice absorbs the liquid, and the grains in contact with the pan form the caramelized crust known as soccarat that will have everyone reaching for more. We developed this recipe for a 15- to 17-inch paella pan; however, a heavy roasting pan measuring at least 14 by 11 inches also works. If littlenecks are unavailable, use 1½ pounds shrimp in step 1; season them with ½ teaspoon salt.

1 Pat chicken dry with paper towels and sprinkle with 1 teaspoon salt and pepper. Toss shrimp with 1½ teaspoons oil, ½ teaspoon garlic, ¼ teaspoon paprika, and ¼ teaspoon salt in bowl until evenly coated; set aside.

2 Heat 1½ teaspoons oil in medium saucepan over medium heat until shimmering. Add remaining garlic and cook, stirring constantly, until garlic sticks to bottom of saucepan and begins to brown, about 1 minute. Add tomato paste and remaining 1½ teaspoons paprika and continue to cook, stirring constantly, until dark brown bits form on bottom of saucepan, about 1 minute. Stir in broth; sherry; clam juice; and saffron, if using. Increase heat to high and bring to boil. Remove saucepan from heat and set aside.

3 Light 3-layer log cabin fire in open-fire grill (see page 13). When most logs have carbonized and broken down into large coals, spread evenly into 1-inch-thick layer over grill. Arrange any logs that have not broken down on perimeter of fire and top with fresh logs. (Moderate flames will remain as larger coals and logs burn. Continue to maintain hot single-level fire by pulling fresh coals created by burning logs onto spent coals and adding fresh logs in their place.) Set cooking grate at least 6 inches from coals and flames and heat grate until hot, about 5 minutes.

4 Clean and oil cooking grate. Place chicken on grill and cook until both sides are lightly browned, 5 to 7 minutes; transfer chicken to plate and clean cooking grate.

5 Place paella pan on grill and add remaining ¼ cup oil. When oil begins to shimmer, add onion, red peppers, and remaining ½ teaspoon salt. Cook, stirring frequently, until onion begins to brown, 4 to 7 minutes. Stir in rice until grains are well coated with oil.

6 Arrange chicken around perimeter of pan. Pour chicken broth mixture and any accumulated chicken juices over rice. Smooth rice into even layer, making sure no rice sticks to sides of pan or rests atop chicken. When liquid reaches gentle simmer, place shrimp in center of pan in single layer. Arrange clams in center of pan, evenly dispersing with shrimp and pushing hinge side of clams into rice slightly so they stand up. Distribute chorizo evenly over surface of rice. Cook, moving and rotating pan to maintain gentle simmer across entire surface of pan, until rice is almost cooked through, 12 to 18 minutes.

7 Sprinkle peas over paella and cook until liquid is absorbed and rice on bottom of pan sizzles and forms uniform golden-brown crust, 10 to 15 minutes. (Slide pan around grill as needed for even crust formation.) Remove from grill, cover, and let sit for 10 minutes. Serve with lemon wedges.

Flare Trade

Charcoal Grill Open bottom vent completely. Light large chimney starter mounded with charcoal briquettes (7 quarts). When top coals are partially covered with ash, pour evenly over grill. Using tongs, arrange 20 unlit briquettes evenly over coals. Set cooking grate in place, cover, and open lid vent completely. Heat grill until hot, about 5 minutes. Proceed with step 4.

Gas Grill Turn all burners to high; cover; and heat grill until hot, about 15 minutes. Keep all burners on high. Proceed with step 4. Reduce burners to medium and proceed with step 5. In step 6, cover and adjust burners as needed to maintain simmer.

Ember-Roasted Beet Salad with Spiced Yogurt and Watercress

SERVES 4 to 6   **TOTAL TIME** 1¼ hours

2 pounds beets, trimmed,

1¼ cups plain Greek yogurt

¼ cup minced fresh cilantro, divided

3 tablespoons extra-virgin olive oil, divided

1 teaspoon plus 2 pinches table salt, divided

1 teaspoon grated fresh ginger

¾ teaspoon grated lime zest plus 2 tablespoons juice, divided, plus extra juice for seasoning (2 limes)

1 garlic clove, minced

½ teaspoon ground cumin

½ teaspoon ground coriander

¼ teaspoon pepper

3 tablespoons water, plus extra as needed

5 ounces (5 cups) watercress, torn into bite-size pieces

¼ cup shelled pistachios, toasted and chopped, divided

Why This Recipe Works Cooking beets on an open fire is not only fun, it's also an easy process that yields fantastic results. When you roast them directly in glowing coals, whole beets develop a crusty, charred shell that peels off readily to reveal a tender, pleasantly earthy, and beguilingly smoky interior. Arranged on a bed of tangy Greek yogurt dressing along with a layer of fresh, peppery greens and crunchy pistachios, these jewels are more than worth starting a fire for. But if you like, set a grate over the coals and make Grilled Flatbreads (page 270) or even burgers to serve alongside. Be sure to wear food-handling gloves when peeling and cutting the beets to prevent your hands from becoming stained. The moisture content of Greek yogurt varies, so add the water slowly in step 3. Look for beets that are 2 to 3 inches in diameter. We like to make this salad with watercress, but you could also use thinly sliced beet greens or baby arugula.

1   Light 3-layer log cabin fire in open-fire grill (see page 13). When most logs have carbonized and broken down into large coals, spread evenly into 1-inch-thick layer over grill. Arrange any logs that have not broken down on perimeter of fire and top with fresh logs. (Moderate flames will remain as larger coals and logs burn. Continue to maintain hot single-level fire by pulling fresh coals created by burning logs onto spent coals and adding fresh logs in their place.)

2   Set beets directly into coals, at least 6 inches from flames, and cook, rotating and flipping every 5 minutes, until beets are well charred and can be easily pierced with paring knife, 20 to 40 minutes. Transfer beets to large bowl as they finish cooking, cover tightly with plastic wrap, and let cool slightly. Once beets are cool enough to handle, rub off charred skins with paper towels, then cut into ¾-inch wedges.

3   Whisk yogurt, 3 tablespoons cilantro, 2 tablespoons oil, ½ teaspoon salt, ginger, lime zest and 1 tablespoon juice, garlic, cumin, coriander, and pepper together in bowl. Slowly whisk in water until mixture has consistency of regular yogurt; whisk in additional water 1 tablespoon at a time, as needed. Season with salt, pepper, and extra lime juice to taste. Spread yogurt mixture over serving platter.

4 Toss watercress with 2 tablespoons pistachios, 2 teaspoons oil, 1 teaspoon lime juice, and pinch salt in bowl and toss to coat. Arrange watercress mixture on top of yogurt mixture, leaving 1-inch border of yogurt mixture. Add beets to now-empty bowl and toss with remaining 1 teaspoon oil, remaining 2 teaspoons lime juice, and remaining pinch salt. Place beet mixture on top of watercress mixture. Sprinkle salad with remaining 2 tablespoons pistachios and remaining 1 tablespoon cilantro. Serve.

Flare Trade

Charcoal Grill Open bottom vent halfway. Arrange 4 quarts unlit charcoal briquettes in even layer over half of grill. Light large chimney starter filled with 15 briquettes (pile briquettes on 1 side of chimney so they catch). When coals are partially covered with ash, pour evenly over unlit coals. Set beets directly into coals. Cover, open lid vent halfway, and cook as directed in step 2.

6 Grilled Breads

Grilled Flour Tortillas

MAKES twelve 6-inch tortillas   **TOTAL TIME** 1 hour, plus 30 minutes chilling

2¾ cups (13¾ ounces) all-purpose flour

1½ teaspoons table salt

6 tablespoons (2½ ounces) vegetable shortening, cut into 6 pieces

¾ cup plus 2 tablespoons (7 ounces) warm tap water

Why This Recipe Works Take Smoked Salmon Tacos (page 114) or Grilled Steak Fajitas (page 134) to the next level by grilling some home-made flour tortillas (or sub these for the corn tortillas in the taco recipes in chapter 2). With an easy-to-roll dough and a superfast cooking time, flour tortillas are a natural for outdoor cooking, and the results are miles above store-bought. They are also very forgiving. These tortillas cook over a medium fire, but if yours is a little hotter or a little cooler because of what else you are grilling, you can adjust the time up or down by a minute or two. Just pay attention to the visual cues. If you like, you can make six 12-inch tortillas to use in Grilled Chicken and Vegetable Quesadillas (page 56); divide the dough in half in step 1 and cut each half into three equal pieces. You may need the help of the rolling pin to flip them onto the grill, and the grilling time will be about 2 minutes per side.

1   Whisk flour and salt together in large bowl. Using your hands, rub shortening into flour mixture until mixture resembles coarse meal. Stir warm water into flour mixture with wooden spoon until incorporated and dough comes together. Transfer dough to clean counter and knead by hand to form smooth, cohesive ball, about 30 seconds. Divide dough into quarters and cut each quarter into 3 equal pieces (about 2 ounces each). Roll each piece into ball and transfer to plate. Cover with plastic wrap and refrigerate for at least 30 minutes or up to 3 days.

2   Line rimmed baking sheet with parchment paper and sprinkle generously with flour. Roll 1 piece of dough into 6-inch-round tortilla on lightly floured counter (keep remaining pieces covered). Transfer tortilla to prepared sheet. Repeat with remaining dough balls, stacking tortillas between pieces of floured parchment on sheet.

Flare Trade

Flat-Top Grill Turn all burners to medium-high and heat griddle until hot, about 10 minutes. Turn all burners to medium. Clean griddle and proceed with step 4.

Open Fire Prepare medium-hot single-level fire in open-fire grill. Set cooking grate at least 6 inches from coals and flames and heat grill until hot, about 5 minutes. Proceed with step 4.

3A   For a charcoal grill Open bottom vent completely. Light large chimney starter two-thirds filled with charcoal briquettes (4 quarts). When top coals are partially covered with ash, pour evenly over grill. Set cooking grate in place, cover, and open lid vent completely. Heat grill until hot, about 5 minutes.

3B   For a gas grill Turn all burners to high; cover; and heat grill and until hot, about 15 minutes. Turn all burners to medium.

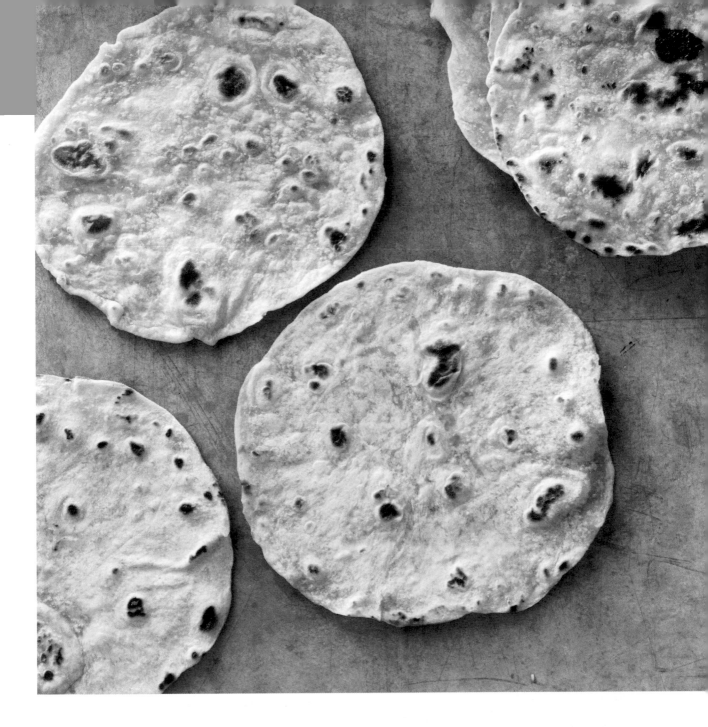

4 Clean and oil cooking grate. Working quickly, transfer 6 tortillas to grill. Cook until surface begins to bubble and bottoms are lightly charred, about 1 minute. Flip tortillas and cook until puffed and bottom is lightly charred, about 1 minute. Transfer to plate and cover with dish towel. Clean and oil cooking grate. Repeat with remaining tortillas. Serve.

Grilled Flatbreads

MAKES 4 flatbreads   **TOTAL TIME** 1 hour, plus 1¾ hours rising

½ cup (4 ounces) ice water

⅓ cup plain whole-milk yogurt

3 tablespoons vegetable oil

1 large egg yolk

2 cups (10 ounces) all-purpose flour

1¾ teaspoons sugar

½ teaspoon instant or rapid-rise yeast

1¾ teaspoons table salt

2 tablespoons unsalted butter, melted

Why This Recipe Works The beautifully blistered naan that are produced by tandoor ovens were our inspiration for these flatbreads. Yogurt, oil, and an egg yolk make these soft, rich, and pleasingly chewy. If garlic is your thing, check out the variation; it's used in four different ways for big allium flavor. Eat these alongside a yogurt-based dip, make them a meal with the Grilled Vegetable Platter (page 234), or sub them for store-bought naan in Grilled Garam Masala Chicken, Tomatoes, and Naan with Chutney (page 122). This recipe works best with a high-protein all-purpose flour such as King Arthur. Do not use nonfat yogurt. It's important to use ice water to prevent the dough from overheating in the food processor.

1 In measuring cup or small bowl, combine water, yogurt, oil, and egg yolk. Process flour, sugar, yeast, and salt in food processor until combined, about 3 seconds. With processor running, slowly add water mixture and process until dough forms sticky ball that clears sides of bowl, 30 to 60 seconds.

2 Transfer dough to lightly floured counter and knead until smooth, about 1 minute. Shape dough into tight ball and place in large, lightly oiled bowl. Cover with plastic wrap and let rise at room temperature for 30 minutes. Fold partially risen dough over itself 8 times by gently lifting and folding edge of dough toward middle, turning bowl 90 degrees after each fold. Cover with plastic and let rise for 30 minutes. Repeat folding, turning, and rising 1 more time, for total of three 30-minute rises.

3 Transfer dough to lightly floured counter and divide into 4 equal pieces. Shape each piece into smooth, tight ball. Place dough balls on lightly oiled rimmed baking sheet, at least 2 inches apart; cover loosely with greased plastic. Let stand for 15 to 20 minutes.

4A For a charcoal grill Open bottom vent completely. Light large chimney starter filled with charcoal briquettes (6 quarts). When top coals are partially covered with ash, pour into ring around perimeter of grill, leaving 8-inch clearing in center. Set cooking grate in place, cover, and open lid vent completely. Heat grill until hot, about 5 minutes.

4B For a gas grill Turn all burners to high; cover; and heat grill until hot, about 15 minutes. Turn all burners to medium-high.

Flare Trade

Flat-Top Grill Turn all burners to medium-high and heat griddle until hot, about 10 minutes. Leave all burners on medium-high. Clean griddle and proceed with step 5, cooking flatbreads all at once.

Open Fire Prepare medium-hot single-level fire in open-fire grill. Set cooking grate at least 6 inches from coals and flames and heat grill until hot, about 5 minutes. Proceed with step 5.

5 Line rimmed baking sheet with floured parchment paper. Transfer 1 dough ball to lightly floured counter and sprinkle with flour. Using your hands and rolling pin, press and roll ball into 9-inch round of even thickness, sprinkling dough and counter with flour as needed to prevent sticking. Using fork, poke entire surface of round 20 to 25 times. Repeat with remaining dough, stacking rounds between pieces of floured parchment on prepared sheet.

6 Clean and oil cooking grate. Grill 2 flatbreads (over clearing if using charcoal), until bottoms are lightly charred, about 90 seconds. Flip flatbreads and grill until lightly charred on second side and cooked through, 1 to 2 minutes. (If flatbread puffs up, gently poke with fork to deflate.) Transfer flatbreads to platter, brush tops with half of melted butter, and cover loosely with aluminum foil. Repeat with remaining flatbreads and remaining butter. Serve immediately.

Variations

Hand-Mixed Grilled Flatbreads

Whisk flour, sugar, yeast, and salt together in large bowl. Using rubber spatula, fold water mixture into flour mixture, scraping up dry flour from bottom of bowl and pressing dough until cohesive and shaggy and all flour is incorporated. Proceed with step 2, increasing kneading time to 5 to 7 minutes. (Coat your hands with flour if dough begins to stick.)

Grilled Garlic Flatbreads

Microwave 3 thinly sliced garlic cloves with oil until garlic is golden and crisp, 2 to 3 minutes, stirring halfway through microwaving. Using fork, remove garlic and reserve. Add garlic oil to yogurt and egg mixture and crispy garlic to food processor with flour. Add 2 minced garlic cloves and ½ teaspoon garlic powder to butter before melting.

Mana'eesh Za'atar

MAKES 3 flatbreads   **TOTAL TIME** 1 hour, plus 2¾ hours rising

¾ cup plus 2 tablespoons (7 ounces) ice water

5 tablespoons extra-virgin olive oil, divided

2½ cups (12½ ounces) all-purpose flour

1½ teaspoons instant or rapid-rise yeast

1½ teaspoons table salt, divided

3 tablespoons za'atar

Why This Recipe Works Mana'eesh, a beloved street food in Lebanon, are typically baked in a very hot oven—a factor that makes these flatbreads a great candidate for grilling over fire. This version, topped with olive oil and the tangy, herbal spice blend za'atar, is a favorite. Poking the dough all over with a fork before baking helps prevent uneven puffing and promotes a chewy yet tender crust. Grilling these flatbreads over medium-high heat encourages them to cook through inside while delicate, charry bubbles form on top of the bread and the bottom turns an even golden brown. It's important to use ice water to prevent the dough from overheating in the food processor. Try these with Baba Ghanoush (page 34) or Grilled Lamb Kofte (page 60).

1   In measuring cup or small bowl, combine ice water and 2 tablespoons oil. Process flour, yeast, and 1 teaspoon salt in food processor until combined, about 3 seconds. With processor running, slowly add water mixture and process until dough forms sticky ball that clears sides of bowl, 30 to 60 seconds.

2   Transfer dough to lightly floured counter and knead until smooth, about 1 minute. Shape dough into tight ball and place in large, lightly oiled bowl. Cover with plastic wrap and let dough rise at room temperature until almost doubled in size, 2 to 2½ hours.

3   Combine za'atar, remaining 3 tablespoons oil, and remaining ½ teaspoon salt in bowl; set aside. On clean counter, divide dough into 3 equal pieces (about 7 ounces each). Shape each piece of dough into smooth, tight ball; cover loosely with plastic and let rest for 15 minutes.

4A   For a charcoal grill Open bottom vent completely. Light large chimney starter three-quarters filled with charcoal briquettes (4½ quarts). When top coals are partially covered with ash, pour into ring around perimeter of grill, leaving 8-inch clearing in center. Set cooking grate in place, cover, and open lid vent completely. Heat grill until hot, about 5 minutes.

4B   For a gas grill Turn all burners to high; cover; and heat grill until hot, about 15 minutes. Turn all burners to medium-high.

Flare Trade

Flat-Top Grill Turn all burners to medium-high and heat griddle until hot, about 10 minutes. Turn all burners to medium. Clean griddle and proceed with step 5, cooking all flatbreads at once.

Open Fire Prepare medium-hot single-level fire in open-fire grill. Set cooking grate at least 6 inches from coals and flames and heat grill until hot, about 5 minutes. Proceed with step 5.

5   Line rimmed baking sheet with floured parchment paper. Transfer 1 ball to lightly floured counter and sprinkle with flour. Using your hands and rolling pin, press and roll into 9-inch round of even thickness, sprinkling dough and counter with flour as needed to prevent sticking. Using fork, poke entire surface of round 20 to 25 times. Repeat with remaining dough, stacking rounds between pieces of floured parchment on sheet.

6   Clean and oil cooking grate. Grill 2 flatbreads (over clearing if using charcoal), covered, until bottoms are lightly charred, about 90 seconds. Flip flatbreads and spread one-third of za'atar mixture (about 1½ tablespoons) over surface of each flatbread with back of dinner spoon, stopping ½ inch from edge. Firmly tap dough all over with your fingertips about 6 times. Grill, covered, until lightly charred on second side and cooked through, 1 to 2 minutes. (If flatbread puffs up, gently poke with fork to deflate.) Transfer flatbreads to platter and tent with aluminum foil. Repeat with remaining flatbread and za'atar mixture. Slice or tear and serve.

Variation
Hand-Mixed Mana'eesh Za'atar
Whisk flour, yeast, and 1 teaspoon salt together in large bowl. Using rubber spatula, fold water mixture into flour mixture, scraping up dry flour from bottom of bowl and pressing dough until cohesive and shaggy and all flour is incorporated. Proceed with step 2, increasing kneading time to 5 to 7 minutes. (Coat your hands with flour if dough begins to stick.)

Grilled Pizza

SERVES 4 to 6   **TOTAL TIME** 2 hours, plus 24 hours resting

Dough

- 3 cups (16½ ounces) bread flour
- 1 tablespoon sugar
- ¼ teaspoon instant or rapid-rise yeast
- 1¼ cups plus 2 tablespoons (11 ounces) ice water
- 1 tablespoon extra-virgin oil
- 1½ teaspoons table salt

Sauce

- 1 (14-ounce) can whole peeled tomatoes, drained with juice reserved
- 2 tablespoons extra-virgin olive oil
- 2 teaspoons minced fresh oregano
- ½ teaspoon sugar, plus extra for seasoning
- ½ teaspoon table salt
- ¼ teaspoon red pepper flakes

Pizza

- ½ cup plus 1 tablespoon extra-virgin olive oil, divided, plus extra for drizzling
- 3 ounces Parmesan cheese, grated (1½ cups)
- 8 ounces fresh whole-milk mozzarella cheese, torn into bite-size pieces (2 cups)
- 3 tablespoons shredded fresh basil
- Coarse sea salt

Why This Recipe Works Taking your pizza party outside is a winning move. The intense heat of a grill is significantly closer to commercial pizza oven temperatures than what your indoor oven can achieve, producing a golden-brown pizza crust with flavorful grill marks in a matter of minutes. Our pizza dough uses a tiny amount of yeast, a lot of water, and a long, 24-hour proof, which makes for an easy-to-stretch dough that bakes up thin, with small air bubbles. Stretching the dough on a generously oiled baking sheet makes it less sticky and helps it crisp up over the flames. To make sure the toppings cook as quickly as the crust, you'll prewarm the sauce and use a combo of fast-melting fresh mozzarella and finely grated Parmesan. It's important to use ice water to prevent the dough from overheating in the food processor. This recipe works best with a high-protein bread flour such as King Arthur.

1 **For the dough** Process flour, sugar, and yeast in food processor until combined, about 3 seconds. With processor running, slowly add ice water and process until dough is just combined and no dry flour remains, about 10 seconds. Let dough stand for 10 minutes.

2 Add oil and salt to dough and process until dough forms satiny, sticky ball that clears sides of bowl, 30 to 60 seconds. Transfer dough to lightly oiled counter and knead until smooth, about 1 minute. Divide dough into 3 equal pieces (about 9⅓ ounces each). Shape each piece into tight ball, transfer to well-oiled rimmed baking sheet (alternatively, place dough balls in individual well-oiled bowls), and coat top of each ball lightly with oil. Cover tightly with plastic wrap (taking care not to compress dough) and refrigerate for at least 24 hours or up to 3 days.

3 **For the sauce** Pulse tomatoes in food processor until finely chopped, 12 to 15 pulses. Transfer to medium bowl and stir in reserved juice, oil, oregano, sugar, salt, and pepper flakes. Season with extra sugar and salt to taste, cover, and refrigerate until ready to use. (Sauce can be refrigerated for up to 3 days.)

4 One hour before cooking pizza, remove dough from refrigerator and let stand at room temperature.

Recipe continues on page 278

5A **For a charcoal grill** Open bottom vent halfway. Light large chimney starter three-quarters filled with charcoal briquettes (4½ quarts). When top coals are partially covered with ash, pour into ring around perimeter of grill, leaving 8-inch clearing in center. Set cooking grate in place, cover, and open lid vent halfway. Heat grill until hot, about 5 minutes.

5B **For a gas grill** Turn all burners to high; cover; and heat grill until hot, about 15 minutes. Turn all burners to medium-high.

6 While grill is heating, transfer sauce to small saucepan and bring to simmer over medium heat. Cover and keep warm.

7 **For the pizza** Clean and oil cooking grate. Pour ¼ cup oil onto center of rimmed baking sheet. Transfer 1 dough round to sheet and coat both sides of dough with oil. Using your fingertips and palms, gently press and stretch dough to form rough 12 by 8-inch oval of even thickness. Using both hands, gently grab corners of dough on long side of oval. Using fluid motion, lift dough, allowing it to stretch further into rough 16 by 12-inch oval, and carefully transfer to grill. (Dough oval will droop slightly to form half-moon or snowshoe shape.) Cook (over clearing if using charcoal; covered if using gas) until grill marks form on first side, 1 to 6 minutes. Using tongs and spatula, carefully peel dough from grate, then rotate dough 90 degrees and continue to cook (covered if using gas) until second set of grill marks appears, 1 to 6 minutes. Flip dough and cook (covered if using gas) until second side of dough is lightly charred in spots, 2 to 6 minutes. Using tongs or pizza peel, transfer crust to cutting board so side that was grilled first is facing down. Repeat with remaining 2 dough rounds, adding 1 tablespoon oil to sheet for each round and keeping grill cover closed when not in use to retain heat.

8 Drizzle top of 1 crust with 1 tablespoon oil. Sprinkle one-third of Parmesan evenly over surface. Arrange one-third of mozzarella pieces, evenly spaced, on surface of pizza. Dollop one-third of sauce in evenly spaced 1-tablespoon mounds over surface of pizza. Using pizza peel or over-turned rimmed baking sheet, transfer pizza to grill; cover and cook (over medium-low heat for gas) until bottom is well browned and mozzarella is melted, 3 to 5 minutes, checking bottom and rotating frequently to prevent burning. Transfer pizza to cutting board, sprinkle with 1 tablespoon basil, drizzle lightly with extra oil, and season with salt to taste. Cut into wedges and serve. Repeat with remaining 2 crusts and remaining oil, cheese, sauce, and basil.

Variations

Grilled Pizza with Corn, Cherry Tomatoes, Pesto, and Ricotta

Omit tomato sauce and fresh mozzarella. While grill is heating, toss 1 cup quartered cherry tomatoes with 1 teaspoon oil, 1 minced garlic clove, and ¼ teaspoon salt in bowl. Combine 1 cup whole-milk ricotta cheese, 1 teaspoon grated lemon zest, and ½ teaspoon salt in second bowl. After adding Parmesan, dollop one-third of ricotta mixture and ¼ cup pesto in evenly spaced 1-tablespoon mounds over surface of each pizza. Scatter one-third of prepared tomatoes and ¼ cup fresh corn kernels over each pizza. Continue with step 8, cooking pizza until well browned and toppings are warmed through, 3 to 5 minutes.

Grilled Pizza with Soppressata, Banana Peppers, and Hot Honey

In step 8, after topping each pizza with mozzarella, scatter with 4 thin slices soppressata, cut into quarters, and 2 tablespoons sliced banana pepper rings. Drizzle with hot honey before serving.

PORTABLE OUTDOOR PIZZA OVEN

A portable pizza oven is a pizza lover's dream come true. Fueled by propane and/or wood or charcoal, these outdoor appliances reach temperatures similar to those of professional pizza ovens—meaning you can turn out pro-quality pizza right in your own backyard. For information on which models we like, see page 23. Here are some tips and recipes to get you started on your way to being an expert pizza chef.

Use the Right Tools for Success

- An **infrared thermometer** is important to verify the correct pizza oven temperature. Check the temperature in the center of the oven, as there will be hot spots depending on the proximity of the cooking surface to the flame.

- A **thin metal pizza peel** is a must for safely getting your pizza into and out of the oven.

- For ease of use and fire safety, you'll want to set up your pizza oven on a **sturdy, heatproof table**.

Start with Good Dough

- We adjusted our regular thin-crust pizza dough recipe for optimum performance in an outdoor pizza oven, adjusting the hydration level slightly and omitting the sugar to cut the risk of burning.

- As with our regular pizza dough, a one- to three-day proof in the fridge minimizes air bubbles and develops flavor in the crust.

Shape a Pie Like a Pro

- Smaller pizzas are easier to maneuver, so consider starting with those before trying larger pies.

- Dust the pizza peel liberally with bread flour or semolina.

- Once the shaped dough is transferred to the peel, gently shake the peel and dust it with more flour as needed before topping the dough to ensure there's no sticking when you slide it into the oven.

- Don't top your pizza until it's on the peel, right before baking.

- Make sure to center the pie in the pizza oven to promote even baking.

- Expect a learning curve; your first couple of pizzas may burn, stick, or cook unevenly. Enjoy the process!

Develop Those Spots: The Leopard Effect

"Leoparding" is the coveted pattern of deep brown spots on pizza crust that occurs as small blisters in the dough char. You'll find it on pizzas baked in high-heat wood-fired ovens, particularly Neapolitan-style pizzas, and it adds an extra dimension of flavor to the pie. Here's how to get it in your portable pizza oven.

- Start high and go low: Preheating the oven on high to reach 800 to 850 degrees is crucial. Drop the temperature to low once the pizza is in the oven to ensure that the dough bakes through at the same rate as the cheese melts, and the blisters on the dough's surface become charred.

- The pizza should take between 2 and 3 minutes to cook. If it takes longer, increase the oven temperature slightly while cooking.

- Between pizzas, allow the oven to fully reheat to 800 to 850 degrees, 3 to 5 minutes.

- For the first 30 seconds of baking, don't move the pizza. This allows the bottom crust to firm up so that the peel can easily slide underneath for easy rotating.

- Thereafter, rotating the pizza every 20 to 30 seconds is crucial for even cooking. (If you have a single back-burner oven, rotate it a quarter-turn. If you have an L-shaped burner oven, rotate it a one-third turn.)

Don't Neglect Cleanup

- To clean, let the pizza oven cool fully and then flip the pizza stone. The residue left on the bottom will carbonize during your next pizza cooking session. Once the oven is cooled, you can flip the stone again and brush off the carbonized residue using a stiff-bristled brush. Continue this process after every use.

Pizza Dough for the Outdoor Pizza Oven

MAKES two 13-inch or four 9½-inch pizzas
TOTAL TIME 20 minutes, plus 24 hours resting

- 3 cups (16½ ounces) bread flour
- ½ teaspoon instant or rapid-rise yeast
- 1⅓ cups (10⅝ ounces) ice water
- 1 tablespoon extra-virgin olive oil
- 1½ teaspoons table salt

1 Pulse flour and yeast in food processor until combined, about 5 pulses. With processor running, slowly add ice water and process until dough is just combined and no dry flour remains, about 10 seconds. Let dough rest for 10 minutes.

2 Add oil and salt to dough and process until dough forms satiny, sticky ball that clears sides of bowl, 30 to 60 seconds. Transfer dough to lightly oiled surface and knead to form smooth, tight ball, about 30 seconds. Place seam side down in lightly greased large bowl, cover tightly with plastic wrap, and refrigerate for at least 24 hours or up to 3 days.

Whole-Wheat Pizza Dough for the Outdoor Pizza Oven

MAKES two 13-inch or four 9½-inch pizzas
TOTAL TIME 20 minutes, plus 24 hours resting

- 1½ cups (8¼ ounces) whole-wheat flour
- 1 cup (5½ ounces) bread flour
- ¾ teaspoon instant or rapid-rise yeast
- 1¼ cups (10 ounces) ice water
- 2 tablespoons extra-virgin olive oil
- 1½ teaspoons table salt

1 Pulse flours and yeast in food processor until combined, about 5 pulses. With processor running, slowly add ice water and process until dough is just combined and no dry flour remains, about 10 seconds. Let dough rest for 10 minutes.

2 Add oil and salt to dough and process until dough forms satiny, sticky ball that clears sides of bowl, 30 to 60 seconds. Transfer dough to lightly oiled surface and knead to form smooth, tight ball, about 30 seconds. Place seam side down in lightly greased large bowl, cover tightly with plastic wrap, and refrigerate for at least 24 hours or up to 3 days.

Thin-Crust Pizza for the Outdoor Pizza Oven

MAKES two 13-inch pizzas or four 9½-inch pizzas
TOTAL TIME 1¼ hours, plus 1 hour resting

Why This Recipe Works You'll love the simplicity of a Neapolitan-inspired tomato-and-cheese pizza in the outdoor oven. The sauce will yield more than needed for the recipe; extra sauce can be refrigerated for up to one week or frozen for up to one month.

- 1 (28-ounce) can whole peeled tomatoes, drained
- 1 tablespoon extra-virgin olive oil
- 1 teaspoon red wine vinegar
- 2 garlic cloves, minced
- 1 teaspoon table salt
- 1 teaspoon dried oregano
- ¼ teaspoon pepper
- 1 recipe Pizza Dough for the Outdoor Pizza Oven or Whole-Wheat Pizza Dough for the Outdoor Pizza Oven (page 282)
- 1 ounce Parmesan cheese, grated (½ cup)
- 8 ounces fresh whole milk-mozzarella cheese, torn into bite-size pieces (2 cups)

1 Process tomatoes, oil, vinegar, garlic, salt, oregano, and pepper in food processor until smooth, about 30 seconds. Transfer sauce to medium bowl and refrigerate.

2 Remove dough from refrigerator and divide in half (for two 13-inch pies) or quarters (for four 9½-inch pies). Shape each dough piece into smooth, tight ball. Place on lightly oiled rimmed baking sheet, spacing them at least 3 inches apart. Cover loosely with greased plastic wrap and let rest for 1 hour.

3 Preheat portable outdoor pizza oven on high to 800 to 850 degrees, 20 to 30 minutes. Coat 1 ball of dough generously with flour and place on well-floured counter. Using your fingertips, gently flatten into 8-inch disk, leaving 1 inch of outer edge slightly thicker than center.

Topping Tips

You can dress up your pizzas with additional toppings, as long as they're prepared correctly and added judiciously to avoid sogginess. Here are a few guidelines.

Delicate vegetables and herbs: Leafy greens such as baby spinach and herbs like basil are best placed either beneath the cheese to shield them from the intense heat or added raw atop the fully cooked hot pizza.

Hardy vegetables: Aim for a maximum of 6 ounces per 13-inch pie or 3 ounces per 9½-inch pie, spread out in a single layer. Thinly slice and lightly sauté (or microwave for a minute or two along with a little olive oil) sturdy vegetables such as onions, peppers, and mushrooms.

Meats: Plan for 4 ounces per 13-inch pie or 2 ounces per 9½-inch pie. We prefer to poach meats such as sausage (broken up into ½-inch chunks), pepperoni, or ground beef for 4 to 5 minutes in a wide skillet along with ¼ cup of water, which helps render the fat while keeping the meat moist. Or you could simply drape paper-thin slices of prosciutto over the top of the finished pizza.

4A For two 13-inch pizzas Using your hands, gently stretch disk into 12-inch round, working along edges and giving disk quarter turns as you stretch. Transfer dough to well-floured peel and stretch into 13-inch round. Using back of spoon or ladle, spread ⅓ cup tomato sauce in thin layer over surface of dough, leaving ½-inch border around edge. Sprinkle ¼ cup Parmesan evenly over sauce, followed by 1 cup mozzarella.

4B For four 9½-inch pizzas Using your hands, gently stretch disk into 9-inch round, working along edges and giving disk quarter turns as you stretch. Transfer dough to well-floured peel and stretch into 9½-inch round. Using back of spoon or ladle, spread 2 tablespoons tomato sauce in thin layer over surface of dough, leaving ¼-inch border around edge. Sprinkle 2 tablespoons Parmesan evenly over sauce, followed by ½ cup mozzarella.

5 Slide pizza carefully onto stone, reduce oven temperature to low, and bake until crust is spotty brown and cheese is bubbly and beginning to brown, 2 to 3 minutes, rotating pizza every 20 to 30 seconds. Remove pizza and place on wire rack for 5 minutes before slicing and serving. Repeat from step 3 to shape, top, and bake remaining pizza(s).

Big and Fluffy Biscuits

MAKES 8 biscuits   **TOTAL TIME** 1 hour

3 cups (15 ounces) all-purpose flour

1 tablespoon baking powder

½ teaspoon baking soda

1 teaspoon table salt

8 tablespoons unsalted butter, cut into ½-inch pieces and softened, plus 1 tablespoon melted

4 tablespoons vegetable shortening, cut into ½-inch pieces

1¾ cups buttermilk

Why This Recipe Works Treat yourself to tender, fluffy biscuits for breakfast—hot off the grill! Dare we say that they're easy enough to throw together even before you've had your morning coffee? The one-bowl dough is portioned right into a cast-iron skillet, which means there's no fussy rolling or cutting required. The heavy skillet distributes the heat of the grill evenly to ensure crisp bottoms and nicely browned crusts. A little butter brushed on the tops of the biscuits before grill-baking enhances their rich flavor and promotes browning. Choose between the classic version or either of the citrus-herb variations—or try all three. You will need a 12-inch cast-iron skillet.

1A For a charcoal grill Open bottom vent completely. Light large chimney starter filled with charcoal briquettes (6 quarts). When top coals are partially covered with ash, pour into steeply banked pile against 1 side of grill. Set cooking grate in place, cover, and open lid vent completely. Heat grill until hot, about 5 minutes.

1B For a gas grill Turn all burners to high; cover; and heat grill until hot, about 15 minutes. Leave primary burner on high and turn off other burner(s). (Adjust primary burner as needed to maintain grill temperature between 400 and 450 degrees; if using 3-burner grill, adjust primary burner and second burner.)

2 Whisk flour, baking powder, baking soda, and salt together in large bowl. Using your hands, rub softened butter and shortening into flour until mixture resembles coarse meal. Stir buttermilk into flour mixture until just combined.

3 Using greased ½-cup dry measuring cup, scoop out and drop 8 mounds of dough evenly into 12-inch cast-iron skillet. Brush biscuits with melted butter.

4 Place skillet on cooler side of grill and bake, covered, until biscuits are puffed and beginning to brown at edges, 20 to 30 minutes, rotating skillet halfway through baking. Transfer skillet to wire rack and let biscuits cool for at least 15 minutes. Serve.

Variations

Big and Fluffy Biscuits with Lemon and Dill
Whisk ⅓ cup minced fresh dill and 1 tablespoon grated lemon zest into flour mixture.

Big and Fluffy Biscuits with Orange and Tarragon
Whisk ⅓ cup minced fresh tarragon and 1 tablespoon grated orange zest into flour mixture.

Grilled Fresh Corn Cornbread with Charred Jalapeños and Cheddar

SERVES 6 to 8   **TOTAL TIME** 1 hour, plus 30 minutes cooling

4 jalapeño chiles

2 ears corn, husks and silk removed

2¼ cups (11¼ ounces) cornmeal

1 tablespoon sugar

1 teaspoon baking powder

1 teaspoon baking soda

¾ teaspoon table salt

1½ cups sour cream

½ cup whole milk

¼ cup vegetable oil

5 tablespoons unsalted butter, melted, divided

2 large eggs

8 ounces sharp cheddar cheese, shredded (2 cups), divided

Why This Recipe Works Fire does amazing things for corn, taking it from mild and sweet to earthy and nutty. Toasting cornmeal as well as grilling whole ears of corn makes this skillet bread hearty enough to take on the bold flavors of charred jalapeños and sharp cheddar. The batter is easy to mix outdoors, and the finished bread comes out lofty and golden, with a delectably crisp bottom and a cheese-laced top. Cut into hearty wedges, it's the perfect side for ribs, chili, or really anything off the grill. Don't use stone-ground cornmeal. You will need a 10-inch cast-iron skillet.

1A For a charcoal grill Open bottom vent completely. Light large chimney starter mounded with charcoal briquettes (7 quarts). When top coals are partially covered with ash, pour into steeply banked pile against 1 side of grill. Set cooking grate in place, cover, and open lid vent completely. Heat grill until hot, about 5 minutes.

1B For a gas grill Turn all burners to high; cover; and heat grill until hot, about 15 minutes. Leave primary burner on high and turn off other burner(s). (Adjust primary burner as needed to maintain grill temperature between 400 and 450 degrees; if using 3-burner grill, adjust primary burner and second burner.)

2 Clean and oil cooking grate. Grill jalapeños and corn on hotter side of grill (covered if using gas), turning as needed, until jalapeños are blistered and charred in spots, 7 to 10 minutes, and corn is charred on all sides, 10 to 12 minutes. Transfer jalapeños to cutting board and let cool slightly; stem, seed, and chop fine. Transfer corn to cutting board and let cool slightly; cut kernels from corn. (You should have about 1½ cups.)

3 Place 10-inch cast-iron skillet on hotter side of grill. Add cornmeal and toast, stirring frequently, until fragrant, about 5 minutes. Transfer cornmeal to large bowl. Whisk sugar, baking powder, baking soda, and salt into cornmeal. Whisk in sour cream, milk, oil, ¼ cup melted butter, and eggs until combined. Stir in jalapeños, corn, and 1½ cups cheddar.

4 Brush skillet with remaining 1 tablespoon melted butter. Quickly scrape batter into skillet and smooth top. Sprinkle remaining ½ cup cheddar on top of batter. Place skillet on cooler side of grill and bake, covered, until top is golden brown and toothpick inserted into center comes out clean, 20 to 35 minutes, rotating skillet halfway through baking. Transfer skillet to wire rack and let cornbread cool for 30 minutes. Slice into wedges and serve.

No-Knead Dutch Oven Bread

MAKES 1 loaf   **TOTAL TIME** 1½ hours, plus 13 hours rising and cooling

2¾ cups (15⅛ ounces) bread flour

1½ teaspoons table salt

¼ teaspoon instant or rapid-rise yeast

¾ cup plus 2 tablespoons (7 ounces) water, room temperature

½ cup (4 ounces) mild lager, room temperature

1 tablespoon honey

1 tablespoon distilled white vinegar

Why This Recipe Works The thrill of pulling a beautifully bronzed, rustic loaf from the oven is multiplied when you swap the oven for the grill. Grill-baking this slow-risen, no-knead dough in a preheated Dutch oven over the cooler side of the fire for about an hour produces a loaf with a chewy, open crumb, a golden top, and a deliciously dark and crusty bottom. We prefer to use a mild American lager, such as Budweiser, here; strongly flavored beers will make this bread taste bitter. While the lager adds a nice yeasty flavor, you can substitute an equal amount of water, if you like. You will need a 3- to 5-quart cast-iron Dutch oven; this size is important for helping the dough rise up, not out. Use a bowl that is at least 9 inches wide and 4 inches deep for the second proof in step 4.

1 Whisk flour, salt, and yeast together in large bowl. Using rubber spatula, fold water, beer, honey, and vinegar into flour mixture, scraping up dry flour from bottom of bowl and pressing dough until cohesive and shaggy and all flour is incorporated. Cover tightly with plastic wrap and let sit at room temperature for at least 8 hours or up to 18 hours.

2 Lay 18 by 12-inch sheet of parchment paper on counter and spray lightly with vegetable oil spray. Using greased bowl scraper or your wet fingertips, fold dough over itself by lifting and folding edge of dough toward middle and pressing to seal. Turn bowl 90 degrees and fold dough again; repeat turning bowl and folding dough 6 more times (for a total of 8 folds). Flip dough seam side down in bowl, cover with plastic, and let rest for 15 minutes.

3 Turn out dough seam side up onto lightly floured counter and pat into rough 9-inch circle using your lightly floured hands. Using bowl scraper or your floured fingertips, lift and fold edge of dough toward center, pressing to seal. Repeat 6 more times (for a total of 7 folds), evenly spacing folds around circumference of dough. Press down on dough to deflate, then use bench scraper to gently flip dough seam side down.

4 Using both hands, cup side of dough farthest from you and pull dough toward you, keeping your pinky fingers and sides of palms in contact with counter and applying slight pressure to dough as it drags to create tension. (If dough slides across surface of counter without rolling, remove excess flour. If dough sticks to counter or hands, lightly sprinkle counter or your hands with flour.) Rotate dough ball 90 degrees, reposition dough ball at

top of counter, and repeat pulling dough until taut round ball forms, at least 4 more times. Transfer dough seam side down to center of prepared parchment and cover with inverted large bowl. Let rise until dough has doubled in volume and dough springs back minimally when poked gently with your finger, about 2 hours.

5A   For a charcoal grill Open bottom vent completely. Light large chimney starter mounded with charcoal briquettes (7 quarts). When top coals are partially covered with ash, pour into steeply banked pile against 1 side of grill. Set cooking grate in place and place 3- to 5-quart cast-iron Dutch oven and lid next to each other on grill grate at center of grill. Cover and open lid vent completely. Heat grill until hot, about 5 minutes.

5B   For a gas grill Place 3- to 5-quart cast-iron Dutch oven and lid next to each other on grill grate over primary burner. Turn all burners to high; cover; and heat grill until hot, about 15 minutes. Leave primary burner on high and turn off other burner(s). (Adjust primary burner as needed to maintain grill temperature between 450 and 500 degrees; if using 3-burner grill, adjust primary burner and second burner.)

6   Using sharp knife, make one 6-inch-long, ½-inch-deep slash with swift, fluid motion along top of loaf. Using parchment as sling, carefully transfer dough to hot Dutch oven. Working quickly, reinforce scoring in top of loaf if needed. Top Dutch oven with hot lid. Move to cooler side of grill and bake, covered, for 30 minutes.

7   Carefully remove Dutch oven lid and continue to bake until loaf is golden brown and registers at least 205 degrees, 20 to 40 minutes. Using parchment sling, carefully remove loaf from hot pot and transfer to wire rack; discard parchment. Let cool completely, about 3 hours, before slicing.

Rosemary Focaccia

MAKES 1 loaf   **TOTAL TIME** 1½ hours, plus 2½ hours rising

2½ cups (12½ ounces) all-purpose flour

1¾ teaspoons kosher salt

1 teaspoon instant or rapid-rise yeast

1¼ cups (10 ounces) water, room temperature

¼ cup extra-virgin olive oil, divided

2 tablespoons fresh rosemary leaves

1 teaspoon flake sea salt

Why This Recipe Works The aroma of this herb-spiked focaccia will take you right to Liguria. To create the signature bubbly crumb, you'll use a no-knead mixing method with a highly hydrated dough and give it a good rise and a rest after shaping. Coating the skillet with plenty of olive oil protects the bread from scorching and gives the crust a rich flavor and delectable crunch while allowing for a light, airy crumb. It is important to use fresh, not dried, rosemary here. If proofing the dough in the refrigerator in step 1, let it stand at room temperature for 1 hour before proceeding. You will need a 12-inch cast-iron skillet.

1   Whisk flour, kosher salt, and yeast together in large bowl. Using rubber spatula, fold water into flour mixture, scraping up dry flour from bottom of bowl and pressing dough until cohesive and shaggy and all flour is incorporated. Cover tightly with plastic wrap and let rise at room temperature until doubled in size, 2 to 4 hours. (Alternatively, refrigerate dough until doubled in size, 8 to 18 hours.)

2   Coat bottoms and sides of 12-inch cast-iron skillet with 3 tablespoons oil. Using bowl scraper or your floured fingertips, lift and fold edge of dough toward center, pressing to seal. Repeat 6 more times (for a total of 7 folds), evenly spacing folds around circumference of dough. Use bench scraper to gently transfer dough seam side up into oiled skillet, then flip dough over. Cover loosely with greased plastic and let dough rest for 30 minutes.

3A   For a charcoal grill Open bottom vent completely. Light large chimney starter mounded with charcoal briquettes (7 quarts). When top coals are partially covered with ash, pour into steeply banked pile against 1 side of grill. Set cooking grate in place, cover, and open lid vent completely. Heat grill until hot, about 5 minutes.

3B   For a gas grill Turn all burners to high; cover; and heat grill until hot, about 15 minutes. Leave primary burner on high and turn off other burner(s). (Adjust primary burner as needed to maintain grill temperature between 450 and 500 degrees; if using 3-burner grill, adjust primary burner and second burner.)

4 Using your fingertips, gently press dough round into corners of skillet, taking care not to tear dough. (If dough resists stretching, let it relax for 5 to 10 minutes before trying to stretch it again.) Using fork, poke surface of dough 40 to 45 times. Brush surface of dough with remaining 1 tablespoon oil. Sprinkle rosemary and sea salt evenly over top; cover loosely with greased plastic; and let dough rest until slightly bubbly, about 10 minutes.

5 Place skillet on cooler side of grill and bake, covered, until top and sides are golden brown and edges are crispy, 25 to 30 minutes, rotating skillet halfway through baking.

Transfer skillet to wire rack and let cool for 5 minutes. Remove focaccia from skillet and let cool on wire rack for 30 minutes. Serve warm or at room temperature.

Variation

Focaccia with Fresh Figs and Thyme
Substitute fresh thyme leaves for rosemary. Quarter 6 stemmed figs and press gently into dough after brushing top with oil in step 4. Sprinkle dough with ¼ teaspoon pepper in addition to thyme and sea salt.

Pull-Apart Dinner Rolls

MAKES 12 rolls   **TOTAL TIME** 45 minutes, plus 2 hours rising

¾ cup (6 ounces) warm tap water (110 degrees)

5 tablespoons unsalted butter, melted, divided

1 large egg, separated; white beaten with 1 teaspoon water and ⅛ teaspoon table salt

2 cups (10 ounces) all-purpose flour, plus extra as needed

1⅛ teaspoons instant or rapid-rise yeast

1 teaspoon sugar

1 teaspoon table salt

Why This Recipe Works Dainty indoor dinner rolls, meet your wilder outdoor cousins. Buttery and rich yet light, these deceptively simple gems will impress all guests. The dough is easy to work with and can handle the variances of grill-baking. Thanks to the cast-iron skillet, the rolls turn out with a light, almost fried, crunchy crust that's reminiscent of pan pizza crust. That crust is optimized through baking the rolls in a ring formation so that the bottom and side of each one makes contact with the hot metal. Keep these rolls in the skillet after baking and they'll stay nice and warm— meaning your second (or third) will be just as good as your first. You will need a 10-inch cast-iron skillet.

1 Whisk water, 1 tablespoon melted butter, and egg yolk together in small bowl. In bowl of stand mixer, whisk flour, yeast, sugar, and salt together. Fit stand mixer with dough hook. With mixer on low speed, slowly add water mixture and mix until dough comes together, about 2 minutes. Increase speed to medium and continue to mix until dough is smooth and elastic, about 8 minutes longer. (If after 4 minutes dough is still very sticky, add 1 to 2 tablespoons extra flour; dough should clear sides of bowl but stick to bottom.) Transfer dough to lightly floured counter and knead by hand to form smooth ball, about 1 minute.

2 Place dough in lightly greased large bowl, cover tightly with greased plastic wrap, and let rise until doubled in size, about 1 hour.

3 Brush bottom and sides of 10-inch cast iron skillet with 1 tablespoon melted butter. Transfer dough to lightly floured counter and shape into 12-inch log. Divide log into 12 equal pieces and cover with greased plastic. Working with 1 piece of dough at a time (keep other pieces covered), form into rough ball by stretching dough around your thumb and pinching edges together so that top is smooth. Place ball seam side down on clean counter and, using your cupped hand, drag in small circles until dough feels taut and round. Arrange dough balls around perimeter of skillet, leaving center empty. Brush dough balls with 1 tablespoon melted butter. Cover loosely with greased plastic and let rise until nearly doubled in size, about 1 hour.

4A For a charcoal grill Open bottom vent completely. Light large chimney starter filled with charcoal briquettes (6 quarts). When top coals are partially covered with ash, pour into steeply banked pile against 1 side of grill. Set cooking grate in place, cover, and open lid vent completely. Heat grill until hot, about 5 minutes.

4B For a gas grill Turn all burners to high; cover; and heat grill until hot, about 15 minutes. Leave primary burner on high and turn off other burner(s). (Adjust primary burner as needed to maintain grill temperature between 400 and 450 degrees; if using 3-burner grill, adjust primary burner and second burner.)

5   Brush rolls with egg wash. Place skillet on cooler side of grill and bake, covered, until rolls are golden brown, 10 to 15 minutes, rotating halfway through baking.

6   Transfer skillet to wire rack. Brush rolls with remaining 2 tablespoons melted butter. Cool for 10 minutes. Serve.

Variation
Hand-Mixed Pull-Apart Dinner Rolls
Whisk flour, yeast, sugar, and salt together in large bowl. Using rubber spatula, fold water mixture into flour mixture, scraping up dry flour from bottom of bowl and pressing dough until cohesive and shaggy and all flour is incorporated. Transfer dough to lightly floured counter and knead by hand to form smooth ball, 5 to 7 minutes. (Coat your hands with flour if dough begins to stick.) Proceed with step 2.

7 Don't Forget Dessert

Ultimate S'mores

SERVES 12 (makes 24 s'mores) **TOTAL TIME** 1¼ hours, plus 4 hours setting

Fluffy Vanilla Marshmallows

- 1 **cup water, divided**
- 2½ **tablespoons unflavored gelatin**
- 2 **large egg whites**
- 2 **cups (14 ounces) granulated sugar**
- ½ **cup light corn syrup**
- ¼ **teaspoon table salt**
- 1 **tablespoon vanilla extract**
- ⅔ **cup (2⅔ ounces) confectioners' sugar**
- ⅓ **cup (1⅓ ounces) cornstarch**

S'mores

- 24 **whole honey graham crackers, halved crosswise**
- 12 **(2-ounce) milk chocolate bars, halved crosswise**

Flare Trade

Charcoal Grill Prepare hot single-level fire. Proceed with step 8.

Gas Grill Prepare hot single-level fire. Proceed with step 8.

Why This Recipe Works S'mores are the OG outdoor dessert, designed to be built and consumed around the campfire. This icon of American ingenuity first appeared in print in a Girl Scout booklet in the 1920s and has been adapted in countless ways ever since. You hardly need a recipe, but we've elevated our version to "ultimate" status by including homemade vanilla-scented marshmallows. Making these gooey confections is easy with a stand mixer, and they keep well—so you can get toasting whenever the mood strikes. Three ¼-ounce envelopes of gelatin will yield the 2½ tablespoons needed for this recipe. You'll need a candy thermometer or another thermometer, such as an instant-read probe model, that registers high temperatures. You will also need several long marshmallow skewers (or sturdy sticks). Feel free to embellish your s'mores with nut butter or Nutella.

1 **For the marshmallows** Make foil sling for 13 by 9-inch baking pan by folding 2 long sheets of aluminum foil; first sheet should be 13 inches wide and second sheet should be 9 inches wide. Lay sheets of foil in pan perpendicular to each other, with extra foil hanging over edges of pan. Push foil into corners and up sides of pan, smoothing foil flush to pan. Spray pan with vegetable oil spray.

2 Whisk ½ cup water and gelatin together in bowl and let sit until very firm, about 5 minutes. Add egg whites to bowl of stand mixer fitted with whisk attachment.

3 Combine granulated sugar, corn syrup, salt, and remaining ½ cup water in large saucepan. Bring to boil over medium-high heat and cook, gently swirling saucepan occasionally, until sugar has dissolved completely and mixture registers 240 degrees, 6 to 8 minutes. Off heat, immediately whisk in gelatin mixture until gelatin is dissolved.

4 Working quickly, whip whites on high speed until soft peaks form, 1 to 2 minutes. With mixer running, carefully pour hot syrup into whites, avoiding whisk and bowl as much as possible. Whip until mixture is very thick and stiff and bowl is only slightly warm to touch, about 10 minutes. Reduce speed to low and add vanilla. Slowly increase speed to high and mix until incorporated, about 30 seconds, scraping down bowl as needed. Transfer mixture to prepared pan and spread into even layer using greased rubber spatula. Let sit at room temperature until firm, at least 4 hours.

5 Lightly coat chef's knife with oil spray. Whisk confectioners' sugar and cornstarch together in bowl. Lightly dust top of marshmallows with 2 tablespoons confectioners' sugar mixture. Transfer remaining confectioners' sugar mixture to 1-gallon zipper-lock bag. Place cutting board over pan of marshmallows and carefully invert pan and board. Remove pan and peel off foil.

6 Cut marshmallows crosswise into 6 strips, then cut each strip into 4 squares (marshmallows will be approximate 2-inch squares). Separate marshmallows and add half to confectioners' sugar mixture in bag. Seal bag and shake to coat marshmallows. Using your hands, remove marshmallows from bag and transfer to colander. Shake colander to remove excess confectioners' sugar mixture. Repeat with remaining marshmallows. (Marshmallows can be stored in zipper-lock bag or airtight container at room temperature for up to 2 weeks.)

7 For the s'mores Light 3-layer log cabin fire in open-fire grill (see page 13). When most logs have carbonized and broken down into large coals, spread evenly into 1-inch-thick layer over grill. Arrange any logs that have not broken down on perimeter of fire and top with fresh logs. (Moderate flames will remain as larger coals and logs burn. Continue to maintain hot single-level fire by pulling fresh coals created by burning logs onto spent coals and adding fresh logs in their place.)

8 For each s'more, top 1 graham cracker half with 1 chocolate bar half. Thread 1 marshmallow onto skewer through cut sides. Toast marshmallow 2 to 4 inches above flames until it reaches your idea of perfection. Sandwich toasted marshmallow between prepared graham cracker and second graham cracker half, gently pressing on graham crackers while removing skewer. Hold together between your fingers for a few seconds to let heat melt chocolate. Enjoy immediately.

Skillet Chocolate Chip Cookie

SERVES 8 to 12   **TOTAL TIME** 55 minutes, plus 20 minutes cooling

12 tablespoons unsalted butter, divided

¾ cup packed (5¼ ounces) dark brown sugar

½ cup (3½ ounces) granulated sugar

2 teaspoons vanilla extract

1 teaspoon table salt

1 large egg plus 1 large yolk

1¾ cups (8¾ ounces) all-purpose flour

½ teaspoon baking soda

1 cup (6 ounces) semisweet chocolate chips

Why This Recipe Works Cast-iron skillet cookies are beloved for their crunchy crusts and soft interiors, and those qualities are enhanced when you grill-bake this giant shareable dessert. This recipe makes dual use of the grill, both to brown the butter and to bake the cookie. You can mix the batter on your outdoor prep table (see page 24), slide the skillet onto the grill while it's still hot right after cooking the main course, and then enjoy wedges of warm cookie for dessert. The chocolate chips might melt a bit, creating a marbled effect in the cookie. It'll be just as delicious, but if you want to avoid this, you can pop the chocolate chips in the freezer briefly before using them. You will need a 12-inch cast-iron skillet.

1A For a charcoal grill Open bottom vent completely. Light large chimney starter mounded with charcoal briquettes (7 quarts). When top coals are partially covered with ash, pour evenly over half of grill. Set cooking grate in place, cover, and open lid vent completely. Heat grill until hot, about 5 minutes.

1B For a gas grill Turn all burners to high; cover; and heat grill until hot, about 15 minutes. Leave primary burner on high and turn off other burner(s). (Adjust primary burner as needed to maintain grill temperature between 425 and 450 degrees; if using 3-burner grill, adjust primary burner and second burner.)

2 Place 12-inch cast-iron skillet on hotter side of grill and melt 9 tablespoons butter in skillet. Continue to cook, stirring constantly, until butter is dark golden brown and has nutty aroma and bubbling subsides, 4 to 6 minutes. Transfer browned butter to large bowl; set skillet aside. Whisk remaining 3 tablespoons butter into browned butter until completely melted.

3 Whisk brown sugar, granulated sugar, vanilla, and salt into melted butter until smooth. Whisk in egg and yolk until smooth, about 30 seconds. Let mixture sit for 3 minutes, then whisk for 30 seconds. Repeat process of resting and whisking 2 more times until mixture is thick, smooth, and shiny.

4 Whisk flour and baking soda together in separate bowl, then stir flour mixture into butter mixture until just combined, about 1 minute. Stir in chocolate chips, making sure no flour pockets remain. Transfer dough to now-empty skillet and press into even layer with spatula.

5 Place skillet on cooler side of grill and bake, covered, until cookie is light golden brown and edges are set, 15 to 25 minutes, rotating skillet halfway through baking. Transfer skillet to wire rack and let cool for at least 20 minutes. Slice into wedges and serve.

Skillet Brownie

SERVES 8 to 12   **TOTAL TIME** 1¼ hours, plus 30 minutes cooling

2 ounces marshmallows
(about 8 large marshmallows)

½ cup plus 2 tablespoons warm
tap water

4 tablespoons unsalted butter,
cut into 4 pieces

2 ounces unsweetened
chocolate, chopped fine

⅓ cup (1 ounce) Dutch-processed
cocoa powder

2½ cups (17½ ounces) sugar

½ cup vegetable oil

2 large eggs plus 2 large yolks

2 teaspoons vanilla extract

1¾ cups (8¾ ounces)
all-purpose flour

1 teaspoon table salt

6 ounces bittersweet
chocolate, chopped

Why This Recipe Works Grill-baking this supersize brownie in a cast-iron skillet and slicing it into wedges gives you the best of both worlds—a crispy edge and a fudgy middle—in every serving. To crank up the fudgy texture, this recipe includes an ingredient frequently found in fudge: marshmallows. Bittersweet chocolate chunks stirred into the batter at the end stud the brownie with gooey pockets of lush melted chocolate. Using indirect heat prevents the chocolate from burning and gets this brownie to its sweet spot in about an hour. (In the meantime, enjoy dinner.) In step 2, you can substitute bittersweet or semisweet chocolate chips for the chopped bittersweet chocolate, if desired, but the results will be less gooey. You will need a 12-inch cast-iron skillet.

1   Combine marshmallows, warm water, butter, unsweetened chocolate, and cocoa in large bowl. Microwave at 50 percent power, stirring occasionally, until chocolate is fully melted and mixture is smooth, 2 to 4 minutes. Let cool for 5 minutes.

2   Grease 12-inch cast-iron skillet. Whisk sugar, oil, eggs and yolks, and vanilla into marshmallow mixture until fully combined. Gently whisk in flour and salt until just incorporated. Stir in bittersweet chocolate. Transfer batter to prepared skillet.

3A   For a charcoal grill Open bottom vent completely. Light large chimney starter filled with charcoal briquettes (6 quarts). When top coals are partially covered with ash, pour into steeply banked pile against 1 side of grill. Set cooking grate in place, cover, and open lid vent completely. Heat grill until hot, about 5 minutes.

3B   For a gas grill Turn all burners to high; cover; and heat grill until hot, about 15 minutes. Leave primary burner on high and turn off other burner(s). (Adjust primary burner as needed to maintain grill temperature between 425 and 450 degrees; if using 3-burner grill, adjust primary burner and second burner.)

4   Place skillet on cooler side of grill and bake, covered, until toothpick inserted in center comes out with a few moist crumbs and batter attached (be careful not to overbake; brownie will continue to bake as it cools), 50 minutes to 1 hour 5 minutes, rotating skillet halfway through baking. Transfer skillet to wire rack and let cool for at least 30 minutes. Slice into wedges and serve.

Variations

Spiced Skillet Brownie
Add 1½ teaspoons ground cinnamon, ¼ teaspoon pepper, and ¼ teaspoon cayenne pepper to sugar mixture with flour.

Espresso–Walnut Skillet Brownie
Add 1½ teaspoons instant espresso powder to bowl with cocoa in step 1. Sprinkle batter with ⅓ cup chopped toasted walnuts before baking.

Grilled Stone Fruit

SERVES 4 to 6   **TOTAL TIME** 1 hour

1½ pounds ripe but slightly firm peaches, nectarines, and/or plums, halved and pitted

2 tablespoons unsalted butter, melted

Why This Recipe Works Devouring juicy peak-season peaches, plums, or nectarines raw is classic summertime eating. Modernize these seasonal treats by grilling them: Grilling fruit softens texture, draws out juices, takes aromas to new heights, and intensifies sweetness through caramelization—all made more fabulous by that hint of smoke. It's also a good way to take advantage of the heat of your grill before or after you cook the main course (or during). Simply brush the fruits' cut surfaces with melted butter and grill over high heat to get grill marks; then, place the fruit in a covered pan to finish cooking over indirect heat. For the best results, use high-quality, ripe, in-season fruit. Serve with a drizzle of honey and dollop of whipped cream. You will need a 13 by 9-inch disposable aluminum roasting pan.

1   Brush cut sides of fruit with melted butter.

2A   For a charcoal grill Open bottom vent completely. Light large chimney starter three-quarters filled with charcoal briquettes (4½ quarts). When top coals are partially covered with ash, pour evenly over half of grill. Set cooking grate in place, cover, and open lid vent completely. Heat grill until hot, about 5 minutes.

2B   For a gas grill Turn all burners to high; cover; and heat grill until hot, about 15 minutes. Leave primary burner on high and turn off other burner(s).

3   Clean and oil cooking grate. Arrange fruit cut side down on hotter side of grill and cook (covered if using gas) until grill marks have formed, 5 to 7 minutes, moving fruit as needed to ensure even cooking.

4   Transfer fruit cut side up to disposable pan and cover loosely with aluminum foil. Place pan on cooler side of grill. If using gas, turn primary burner to medium. Cover and cook until fruit is very tender and paring knife slips in and out with little resistance, 10 to 15 minutes. When cool enough to handle, discard skins, if desired. Serve warm or at room temperature.

Flare Trade

Flat-Top Grill Turn all burners to medium-high and heat griddle until hot, about 10 minutes. Turn all burners to medium. Clean griddle. Cook fruit, cut side down, until well browned, 3 to 5 minutes. Flip fruit and continue to cook until fruit is very tender and paring knife slips in and out with little resistance, 5 to 8 minutes; transfer to platter. Discard skins, if desired, and serve.

Open Fire Prepare hot half-grill fire in open-fire grill. Set cooking grate at least 6 inches from coals and flames and heat grill until hot, about 5 minutes. Proceed with step 3.

Glazed Rotisserie Pineapple with Salted Rum Butterscotch Sauce

SERVES 6 to 8   **TOTAL TIME** 1¾ hours

1   cup packed (7 ounces)
    light brown sugar

½   cup heavy cream

8   tablespoons unsalted butter,
    cut into 8 pieces and
    chilled, divided

½   teaspoon table salt

2   tablespoons dark rum

½   teaspoon vanilla extract

1   pineapple

Why This Recipe Works This stunning dessert really shows off what the grill rotisserie is all about. Turning a ripe pineapple over a hot fire caramelizes its surface to a golden brown and brings out an irresistible aroma reminiscent of a tropical cocktail. The heat penetrates to the inside of the fruit, unlocking its juices. The spiral-cut edges pick up glorious color while cradling the fantastic salted rum butterscotch sauce. This recipe can be doubled: Slide the first pineapple about three-quarters of the way down the skewer and then thread the second pineapple onto the skewer. Center the pineapples on the skewer, leaving a 1-inch gap between them. Use caution when threading the rotisserie skewer through the pineapple, as it will require some pressure to push the skewer through the core. We love the appearance and ridges of a spiral-cut pineapple; however, in step 2 you can simply trim the pineapple slightly further to remove the eyes. You will need a motorized rotisserie attachment. If using a charcoal grill, you will need a 13 by 9-inch disposable aluminum roasting pan. Our gas grill instructions are for a three-burner grill. If using a two-burner grill, we recommend cooking with both burners turned to medium.

1   Cook sugar, cream, 4 tablespoons butter, and salt in medium saucepan over medium-high heat, stirring often with rubber spatula, until large bubbles burst on surface of sauce, about 4 minutes. Off heat, carefully stir in remaining 4 tablespoons butter until fully combined, about 1 minute. Stir in rum and vanilla. Transfer sauce to bowl and let cool for 30 minutes (sauce will thicken as it cools). (Sauce can be refrigerated for up to 1 week; reheat in microwave before serving.)

2   Using sharp knife, slice off crown and bottom of pineapple. Holding pineapple upright, pare off rind from top to bottom as thin as possible. Lay fruit on 1 side. Working around pineapple, cut shallow, diagonal V-shaped grooves just deep enough to remove eyes, following their natural spiral pattern.

3   Set pineapple upright on cutting board. Center beveled tip of rotisserie skewer on top of pineapple and carefully push skewer down through core of pineapple. Turn pineapple on its side and continue to thread it onto center of skewer. Attach rotisserie forks to skewer and insert tines into pineapple; secure forks by tightening screws.

4A **For a charcoal grill** Open bottom vent completely and place disposable pan in center of grill. Light large chimney starter mounded with charcoal briquettes (7 quarts). When top coals are partially covered with ash, pour into 2 even piles on either side of disposable pan. Position rotisserie motor attachment on grill so that skewer runs parallel to coals. Cover, open lid vent completely, and heat grill until hot, about 5 minutes.

4B **For a gas grill** Remove cooking grate. Position rotisserie motor attachment on grill and turn all burners to high. Cover and heat grill until hot, about 15 minutes. Turn outside burners to medium-high and turn off center burner. (Adjust outside burners as needed to maintain grill temperature between 450 and 500 degrees.)

5 Brush pineapple with ¼ cup sauce. Attach rotisserie skewer to motor and start motor. Cover and cook for 30 minutes.

6 Brush pineapple with ¼ cup sauce and continue to cook, covered, until tender and lightly charred, 15 to 30 minutes. Transfer pineapple, still on skewer, to cutting board. Using large wad of paper towels in each hand, carefully remove rotisserie forks and skewer from pineapple. Slice pineapple thin and serve with remaining sauce.

Rustic Summer Fruit Tart

SERVES 4 to 6   **TOTAL TIME** 1½ hours, plus 1 hour 40 minutes chilling and cooling

1½ cups (7½ ounces) all-purpose flour

½ teaspoon table salt

10 tablespoons unsalted butter, cut into ½-inch pieces and chilled

4-6 tablespoons ice water

1 pound plums, apricots, peaches, and/or nectarines, halved, pitted, and cut into ½-inch wedges

5 ounces (1 cup) raspberries, blackberries, and/or blueberries

¼ cup (1¾ ounces) sugar, divided, plus extra sugar as needed

Why This Recipe Works One of the best things about ripe summer fruits—their intense juiciness—can spell trouble when they're baked in a tart. Using a cast-iron skillet as a grill-top tart pan is a genius solution: The skillet captures the bubbling fruit juices and transforms them into an irresistible caramel-like glaze. It also acts like a pizza stone, absorbing heat to crisp the bottom crust before the fruit juices can sog it out. A simple mix of stone fruit and berries with a few tablespoons of sugar makes a quick, easy filling. Be sure to taste the fruit before adding sugar; use less sugar if the fruit is very sweet, more if it is tart. Do not add the sugar to the fruit until you're ready to fill and form the tart. You will need a 10-inch cast-iron skillet.

1 Process flour and salt in food processor until combined, about 5 seconds. Scatter butter over top and pulse until mixture resembles coarse sand and butter pieces are size of small peas, about 10 pulses. Continue to pulse, adding water 1 tablespoon at a time, until dough begins to form small curds that hold together when pinched with fingers, about 10 pulses.

2 Turn mixture onto lightly floured counter and gather into rectangular pile. Starting at farthest end, use heel of your hand to smear small amount of dough against counter. Continue to smear dough until all crumbs have been worked. Gather smeared crumbs together in another rectangular pile and repeat process.

3 Press dough into 6-inch disk, wrap tightly in plastic wrap, and refrigerate for 1 hour. (Dough can be refrigerated for up to 2 days.) Before rolling out dough, let it sit on counter to soften slightly, about 10 minutes.

4 Grease 10-inch cast-iron skillet. Roll dough into 12-inch round between 2 large sheets of parchment paper. Remove top piece of parchment, loosely roll dough around rolling pin, and gently unroll it onto prepared skillet. Ease dough into skillet by gently lifting and supporting edge of dough with your hand while pressing into skillet bottom and corners with your other hand. Leave any overhanging dough in place.

5 Gently toss plums, raspberries, and 3 tablespoons sugar together in bowl; toss with additional sugar if needed. Transfer fruit to dough-lined skillet, mounding fruit slightly in middle. Fold in sides of dough over fruit, pleating every 2 to 3 inches as needed; gently pinch pleated dough

to secure, but do not press dough into fruit. Brush dough with water and sprinkle evenly with remaining 1 tablespoon sugar.

6A **For a charcoal grill** Open bottom vent completely. Light large chimney starter mounded with charcoal briquettes (7 quarts). When top coals are partially covered with ash, pour into steeply banked pile against 1 side of grill. Set cooking grate in place, cover, and open lid vent completely. Heat grill until hot, about 5 minutes.

6B **For a gas grill** Turn all burners to high; cover; and heat grill until hot, about 15 minutes. Leave primary burner on high and turn off other burner(s).

(Adjust primary burner as needed to maintain grill temperature between 450 and 475 degrees; if using 3-burner grill, adjust primary burner and second burner.)

7 Place skillet on hotter side of grill and bake, covered, for 10 minutes. Transfer skillet to cooler side of grill and bake, covered, until crust is beginning to brown and juices are bubbling, 30 to 45 minutes, rotating skillet halfway through baking.

8 Transfer skillet to wire rack and let cool for 10 minutes. Gently slide tart onto rack using spatula and let cool until juices have thickened, at least 30 minutes. Serve.

Charred Strawberry Dutch Baby

SERVES 6 to 8   **TOTAL TIME** 1 hour

1 pound strawberries (preferably 1 inch or larger), hulled

3 tablespoons honey, divided

1 cup (5 ounces) all-purpose flour

¼ cup (1 ounce) cornstarch

2 teaspoons grated lemon zest plus 1 teaspoon juice

1 teaspoon table salt

3 large eggs

1¾ cups skim milk

1 tablespoon unsalted butter, melted and cooled

1 teaspoon vanilla extract

2 tablespoons vegetable oil

Confectioners' sugar

Why This Recipe Works Although it's right at home here among the desserts, this gorgeous pancake would work equally well as a weekend breakfast or part of a brunch spread. Charring skewered, honey-brushed strawberries over the fire is a quick route to a fruit topping with sophisticated flavor and silky texture; chop them up and let them sit with lemon juice and more honey while the pancake puffs up crisp and golden in the skillet. For a real treat, serve this Dutch baby with whipped cream, mascarpone, or crème fraîche. Larger strawberries hold up better on the grill; smaller strawberries will also work, but you might need three skewers instead of two and you should monitor the grill and pull them off before they collapse. You can use whole or low-fat milk instead of skim, but the Dutch baby won't be as crisp. You will need two 12-inch metal skewers and a 12-inch cast-iron skillet.

1A   For a charcoal grill Open bottom vent completely. Light large chimney starter filled with charcoal briquettes (6 quarts). When top coals are partially covered with ash, pour evenly over half of grill. Set cooking grate in place, cover, and open lid vent completely. Heat grill until hot, about 5 minutes.

1B   For a gas grill Turn all burners to high; cover; and heat grill until hot, about 15 minutes. Leave primary burner on high and turn other burner(s) to low. (Adjust primary burner as needed to maintain grill temperature between 400 and 425 degrees; if using 3-burner grill, adjust primary burner and second burner.)

2   Thread strawberries onto two 12-inch metal skewers and brush with 1½ tablespoons honey. Whisk flour, cornstarch, lemon zest, and salt together in large bowl. In separate bowl, whisk eggs until frothy, then whisk in milk, melted butter, and vanilla until combined.

3   Grill strawberries on hotter side of grill until tender and charred, 3 to 5 minutes, flipping halfway through grilling. Transfer strawberries to cutting board and let cool slightly, about 5 minutes. Remove strawberries from skewers and cut into quarters. Toss strawberries with remaining 1½ tablespoons honey and lemon juice in separate bowl.

4   Grease 12-inch cast-iron skillet with oil and place on hotter side of grill. Cover and heat skillet until oil is shimmering, about 5 minutes. Transfer skillet to cooler side of grill.

5 Working quickly while skillet preheats, whisk one-third of milk mixture into flour mixture until no lumps remain. Slowly whisk in remaining milk mixture until smooth. Pour batter into skillet and bake, covered, until Dutch baby puffs and turns golden brown along edges, 15 to 20 minutes, rotating skillet halfway through baking.

6 Transfer Dutch baby to cutting board using spatula. Dust with sugar and slice into wedges. Serve immediately, topped with charred strawberry mixture.

Apple Crisp

Topping

- ¾ cup (3¾ ounces) all-purpose flour
- ¾ cup pecans, chopped fine
- ¾ cup old-fashioned rolled oats
- ½ cup packed (3½ ounces) light brown sugar
- ¼ cup (1¾ ounces) granulated sugar
- ½ teaspoon ground cinnamon
- ½ teaspoon table salt
- 8 tablespoons unsalted butter, melted

Filling

- 2½ pounds Golden Delicious apples, peeled, cored, halved, and cut into ½-inch-thick wedges
- ¼ cup (1¾ ounces) granulated sugar
- ¼ teaspoon ground cinnamon
- 2 tablespoons unsalted butter
- ½ cup apple cider
- 2 teaspoons lemon juice

Why This Recipe Works A cast-iron skillet is the key to producing perfectly tender deep-dish apple crisp outdoors. You'll use the skillet to precook the apples, driving off excess juice while adding caramelized flavor. Apple cider, lemon juice, and cinnamon enrich the filling, which you'll cover with a buttery oat-and-pecan blanket before grill-baking the whole thing until golden and fragrant. We like Golden Delicious apples here, but you can use any sweet, crisp apples, including Honeycrisps or Braeburns (don't use Granny Smiths). Rolled oats make the best-textured topping, but quick-cooking oats can be used. You will need a 10-inch cast-iron skillet.

1   For the topping Combine flour, pecans, oats, brown sugar, granulated sugar, cinnamon, and salt in medium bowl. Stir in melted butter until mixture is thoroughly moistened and crumbly.

2   For the filling Toss apples, sugar, and cinnamon together in bowl; set aside.

3A   For a charcoal grill Open bottom vent completely. Light large chimney starter mounded with charcoal briquettes (7 quarts). When top coals are partially covered with ash, pour into steeply banked pile against 1 side of grill. Set cooking grate in place, cover, and open lid vent completely. Heat grill until hot, about 5 minutes.

3B   For a gas grill Turn all burners to high; cover; and heat grill until hot, about 15 minutes. Leave primary burner on high and turn off other burner(s). (Adjust primary burner as needed to maintain grill temperature between 425 and 450 degrees; if using 3-burner grill, adjust primary burner and second burner.)

4   Place 10-inch cast-iron skillet on hotter side of grill and melt butter in skillet. Add apple mixture and cook (covered if using gas), stirring occasionally, until just tender and translucent, 10 to 12 minutes. Transfer skillet to cooler side of grill and gently stir in cider and lemon juice until apples are coated.

5   Sprinkle topping evenly over fruit, breaking up any large chunks. Cover and bake until fruit is tender and topping is golden brown, 20 to 40 minutes, rotating skillet halfway through baking. Transfer skillet to wire rack and let cool for at least 15 minutes. Serve.

Cherry Spoon Cake

SERVES 8 to 10   **TOTAL TIME** 1¼ hours, plus 30 minutes cooling

10 tablespoons unsalted butter, melted and cooled, divided

1½ cups (7½ ounces) plus 2 tablespoons all-purpose flour, divided

1½ cups (10½ ounces) sugar

2½ teaspoons baking powder

¾ teaspoon table salt

1½ cups milk

1 teaspoon grated orange zest

1 teaspoon vanilla extract

1 pound fresh sweet cherries, pitted and halved

Why This Recipe Works This unfussy dessert tops an easy stir-together batter with juicy fresh cherries. As it cooks in a skillet on the grill grate, the bottom and edges of this spoon cake get crusty and nicely browned while the cherries sink into the batter and release their juices, helping to keep the center so moist and soft that you'll want to serve this in bowls, with spoons—and maybe with a scoop of vanilla ice cream on top. Frozen cherries may be substituted for fresh; thaw and drain the cherries before using. You will need a 12-inch cast-iron skillet.

1   Grease 12-inch cast-iron skillet with 2 tablespoons melted butter. Whisk 1½ cups flour, sugar, baking powder, and salt together in large bowl. Whisk milk, orange zest, vanilla, and remaining 8 tablespoons melted butter together in separate bowl. Whisk milk mixture into flour mixture until combined. Pour batter into prepared skillet. Toss cherries with remaining 2 tablespoons flour in separate bowl; set aside.

2A   **For a charcoal grill** Open bottom vent completely. Light large chimney starter three-quarters filled with charcoal briquettes (4½ quarts). When top coals are partially covered with ash, pour into steeply banked pile against 1 side of grill. Set cooking grate in place, cover, and open lid vent completely. Heat grill until hot, about 5 minutes.

2B   **For a gas grill** Turn all burners to high; cover; and heat grill until hot, about 15 minutes. Leave primary burner on high and turn off other burner(s). (Adjust primary burner as needed to maintain grill temperature between 325 and 350 degrees; if using 3-burner grill, adjust primary burner and second burner.)

3   Place skillet on cooler side of grill, spoon cherry mixture evenly over batter, and bake, covered, until top is golden brown and skewer inserted in center comes out clean, 45 to 55 minutes, rotating skillet halfway through baking. Transfer skillet to wire rack and let cool for at least 30 minutes. Serve.

Orange Upside-Down Cake

SERVES 8   **TOTAL TIME** 1½ hours, plus 1 hour 20 minutes cooling

1 pound small navel oranges, blood oranges, and/or Cara Cara oranges

10 tablespoons unsalted butter, melted, divided

1½ cups (10½ ounces) sugar, divided

1 teaspoon cornstarch

⅛ teaspoon plus ½ teaspoon table salt, divided

1 cup (5 ounces) all-purpose flour

1 teaspoon baking powder

½ cup sour cream

2 large eggs

1 teaspoon vanilla extract

2 tablespoons orange marmalade

Why This Recipe Works If you didn't make it yourself, it'd be hard to believe this jewel of a cake came off a grill. It looks stunning but the recipe is simple; if you can peel and slice oranges and stir wet and dry ingredients together, this cake is in your wheelhouse. The sturdy butter cake gets its richness and tang from sour cream. White sugar in the fruit layer contributes a clean sweetness that keeps the orange flavor front and center. A thin layer of orange marmalade brushed over the cooled cake makes for an extra-shiny and extra-citrusy finish. Peeling the oranges by hand (instead of cutting away the peel and pith with a knife) ensures perfectly round slices. You will need a 10-inch cast-iron skillet.

1   Grease 10-inch cast iron skillet, line with parchment paper, then grease parchment. Grate 2 teaspoons zest from 1 orange; set aside. Peel oranges by hand. Using sharp chef's knife or serrated knife, trim ends and slice oranges crosswise into ¼-inch-thick rounds, removing any seeds.

2   Pour 4 tablespoons melted butter over bottom of prepared skillet and swirl to evenly coat. Whisk ½ cup sugar, cornstarch, and ⅛ teaspoon salt together in bowl, then sprinkle mixture evenly over melted butter in skillet. Arrange orange slices in single layer over sugar mixture, nestling slices snugly together and pressing them flat (you may have fruit left over).

3   Whisk flour, baking powder, and remaining ½ teaspoon salt together in large bowl. Whisk sour cream, eggs, vanilla, reserved orange zest, and remaining 1 cup sugar in second large bowl until smooth, about 1 minute. Whisk remaining 6 tablespoons melted butter into sour cream mixture until combined. Whisk flour mixture into sour cream mixture until just combined. Pour batter over oranges in skillet and smooth top.

4A   For a charcoal grill Open bottom vent completely. Light large chimney starter three-quarters filled with charcoal briquettes (4½ quarts). When top coals are partially covered with ash, pour into steeply banked pile against 1 side of grill. Set cooking grate in place, cover, and open lid vent completely. Heat grill until hot, about 5 minutes.

4B   For a gas grill Turn all burners to high; cover; and heat grill until hot, about 15 minutes. Leave primary burner on high and turn off other burner(s). (Adjust primary burner as needed to maintain grill temperature between 325 and 350 degrees; if using 3-burner grill, adjust primary burner and second burner.)

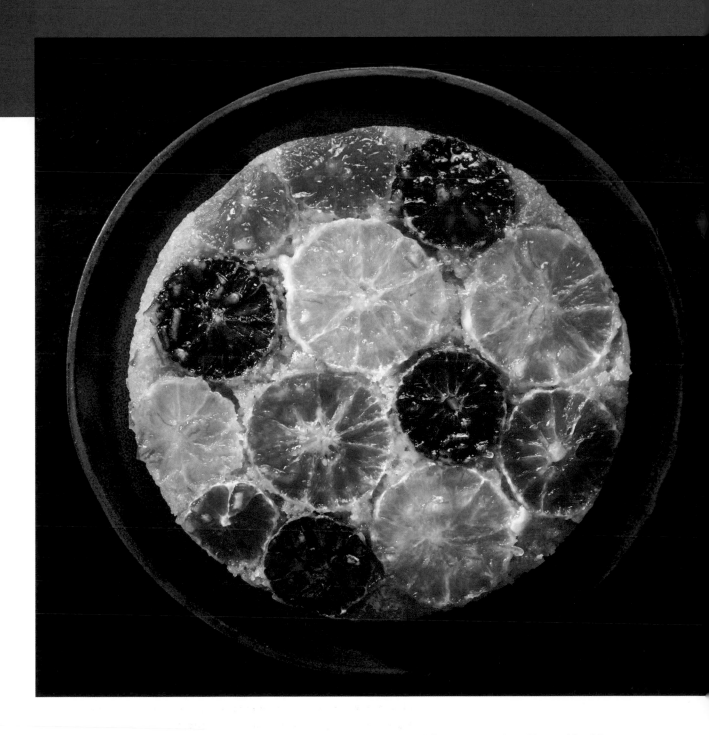

5 Place skillet on cooler side of grill and bake, covered, until golden brown and toothpick inserted in center comes out clean, 35 to 50 minutes, rotating skillet halfway through baking.

6 Transfer skillet to wire rack and let cool for 20 minutes. Run knife around edge of skillet to loosen cake, then invert cake onto serving platter. Discard parchment. Let cake cool for at least 1 hour. Microwave marmalade in bowl until fluid, about 20 seconds. Brush marmalade over top of cake. Serve.

MULLED CIDER

WARM DRINKS AROUND THE FIRE

MULLED WINE & HOT TODDY

Mulled Cider

SERVES 12   **TOTAL TIME** 1 hour

Why This Recipe Works Both savory and sweet aromatic spices complement the sweet-and-tart apple flavor of this make-ahead, serve-a-crowd mulled cider. Perfect for an outdoor fall gathering, its fantastic aroma invites you to stay outdoors just a bit longer when the air turns crisp. For a bit of extra warmth, try the brandied version. To crack the spices, rock the bottom edge of a skillet over them on a cutting board. The amount of brown sugar you add will vary depending on the sweetness of the apple cider; start with the lesser amount and add more as needed. Cinnamon sticks and apple slices also make great garnishes.

1	cinnamon stick, broken into pieces
½	teaspoon black peppercorns, cracked
½	teaspoon coriander seeds, cracked
7	whole cloves
2	quarts apple cider
4	(3-inch) strips orange zest, plus 12 orange slices for garnishing
1–3	tablespoons packed brown sugar

1   Toast cinnamon stick pieces, peppercorns, coriander seeds, and cloves in large saucepan over medium heat, shaking saucepan occasionally, until fragrant, 1 to 3 minutes. Add cider, orange zest, and sugar. Bring to simmer and cook until flavors meld, about 30 minutes, using wide, shallow spoon to skim off any foam that rises to surface.

2   Line fine-mesh strainer with coffee filter and set over large bowl. Strain cider mixture through prepared strainer; discard solids. Serve in warmed mugs, garnishing each portion with orange slice, or return to now-empty saucepan, cover, and keep warm on hot grill grate or flattop until serving. (Mulled cider can be refrigerated for up to 1 week. Reheat on grill or flattop in covered saucepan or Dutch oven.)

Variation
Brandied Mulled Cider
Add 16 ounces brandy to saucepan along with strained cider mixture in step 2. Feel free to substitute bourbon or aged rum for brandy.

Mulled Wine

SERVES 8   **TOTAL TIME** 1½ hours

Why This Recipe Works The best mulled wine is fruity but not too sweet, with deep spice notes. To unlock their full flavor potential, you'll toast the cinnamon sticks, cloves, allspice berries, and peppercorns before simmering them in wine, sugar, and orange zest. After a long, gentle simmer to ensure smooth flavor, stir in a couple of spoonfuls of brandy just before serving for a lightly boozy kick. Any medium- to full-bodied wine, such as Pinot Noir, Côtes du Rhône, or Merlot, works well. To crack the spices, rock the bottom edge of a skillet over them on a cutting board. Offer extra cinnamon sticks as garnishes, if you like.

- 3 cinnamon sticks, broken into pieces
- 10 whole cloves
- 1 teaspoon allspice berries, cracked
- ½ teaspoon black peppercorns, cracked
- 2 (750-ml) bottles red wine
- ½ cup sugar, plus extra for seasoning
- 4 (3-inch) strips orange zest, plus 8 orange slices for garnishing
- 2 ounces brandy

1 Toast cinnamon stick pieces, cloves, allspice berries, and peppercorns in large saucepan over medium heat, shaking saucepan occasionally, until fragrant, 1 to 3 minutes. Add wine, sugar, and orange zest and bring to simmer. Reduce heat to low and partially cover. Simmer gently, stirring occasionally, until flavors meld, about 1 hour.

2 Line fine-mesh strainer with coffee filter and set over large bowl. Strain wine mixture through prepared strainer; discard solids. Stir in brandy and season with extra sugar to taste. Serve in warmed mugs, garnishing each portion with orange slice, or return to now-empty saucepan, cover, and keep warm on hot grill grate or flattop until serving. (Mulled wine can be refrigerated for up to 1 week. Reheat on grill or flattop in covered saucepan or Dutch oven.)

Hot Toddy

SERVES 4   **TOTAL TIME** 10 minutes

Why This Recipe Works Whether made with brandy, whiskey, or even rum, the hot toddy is a delicious cup of comfort that will warm you up whenever there's a chill in the air. Lemon juice and honey in equal amounts make for a rounded flavor. Measure the water after boiling it; even in the short amount of time it takes to boil, you will lose some to evaporation. In addition to the lemon slice, garnish your toddy with a cinnamon stick, if desired. You can use bourbon, Tennessee whiskey, or rum in place of the brandy, if you like.

- 20 ounces boiling water
- 6 ounces brandy
- 2 ounces lemon juice, plus lemon slices for garnishing
- ¼ cup honey

Warm 4 mugs. In each mug, stir 5 ounces boiling water, 1½ ounces brandy, ½ ounce lemon juice, and 1 tablespoon honey until combined and honey has dissolved. Garnish each mug with lemon slice and serve.

Variation

Scotch Hot Toddy
Substitute brewed hot black tea for water and Scotch for brandy.

HOT CHOCOLATE

WARM DRINKS AROUND THE FIRE

SPICED & MOCHA HOT CHOCOLATES

Hot Chocolate

SERVES 12 (makes 3 cups mix)   **TOTAL TIME** 10 minutes

Why This Recipe Works A steaming mug of hot chocolate is bliss on a cozy night by the campfire. Preparing a homemade mix ahead of time means that at a moment's notice you can make a mug (or mugs) of hot chocolate that's deeper and more intensely chocolaty than any store-bought version. The secret is augmenting the cocoa powder with unsweetened chocolate: The cocoa butter in the unsweetened chocolate adds a lush texture. Feel free to spike your hot chocolate by adding 1 ounce of bourbon or peppermint schnapps. To make it extra-fancy, use homemade marshmallows (see page 296) and toast 'em.

Hot Chocolate Mix

- 1 cup sugar
- 6 ounces unsweetened chocolate, chopped fine
- 1 cup unsweetened cocoa powder
- ½ cup nonfat dry milk powder
- 5 teaspoons cornstarch
- 1 teaspoon vanilla extract
- ¾ teaspoon kosher salt

For Serving

- Milk
- Whipped cream (optional)
- Marshmallows (optional)

1 For the hot chocolate mix Process all ingredients in food processor until ground to powder, 30 to 60 seconds. Transfer to airtight container. (Mix can be stored at room temperature for up to 2 months.)

2 For each serving Heat 1 cup milk in small saucepan over medium fire until it starts to steam and bubbles appear around edge of saucepan. Add ¼ cup hot chocolate mix and continue to heat, whisking constantly, until mixture is simmering, 2 to 3 minutes. Pour hot chocolate into mug and serve with whipped cream or marshmallows, if desired.

Variations

Spiced Hot Chocolate

Add 1 teaspoon ground cinnamon, ¾ teaspoon ancho chile powder, and pinch cayenne pepper to processor with other hot chocolate mix ingredients. Continue with step 2. To spike the hot chocolate, add 1 ounce aged rum or chile liqueur to each serving.

Mocha Hot Chocolate

Add ⅓ cup instant espresso powder to processor with other hot chocolate mix ingredients. Continue with step 2. To spike the hot chocolate, add 1 ounce Kahlúa to each serving.

Nutritional Information for Our Recipes

To calculate the nutritional values of our recipes per serving, we used The Food Processor SQL by ESHA research. When using this program, we entered all the ingredients, using weights wherever possible. We also used our preferred brands in these analyses. Any ingredient listed as "optional" was excluded from the analyses. If there is a range in the serving size, we used the highest number of servings to calculate nutritional values. We did not include additional salt or pepper for food that's seasoned to taste.

	CALORIES	TOTAL FAT (G)	SAT FAT (G)	CHOL (MG)	SODIUM (MG)	TOTAL CARB (G)	DIETARY FIBER (G)	TOTAL SUGAR (G)	ADDED SUGAR (G)	PROTEIN (G)
Snacks and Small Plates										
Charred Guacamole	120	11	1.5	0	150	8	5	1	0	2
Baba Ghanoush	180	15	2	0	390	12	5	5	0	3
Grilled Buffalo Chicken Dip with Spicy Monkey Bread	260	13	7	40	1070	27	0	4	0	9
Smoked Nachos	490	28	13	55	650	42	4	2	0	21
Blistered Shishito Peppers	30	2.5	0	0	0	2	1	1	0	0
Smoky Shishito Peppers with Espelette and Lime	30	2.5	0	0	95	3	1	1	0	0
Shishito Peppers with Mint, Poppy Seeds, and Orange	40	2.5	0	0	200	5	2	2	0	1
Grilled Potato Wedges with Lemon-Dill Mayo	500	24	5	10	700	42	0	0	0	6
Watermelon with Grilled Queso de Freir, Serrano, and Pepitas	270	21	10	35	610	9	1	7	1	11
Bruschetta with Marinated Grilled Tomatoes and Fresh Mozzarella	390	19	6	20	550	41	1	8	0	1
Grilled Polenta Wedges with Grilled Scallions and Gorgonzola	190	11	4.5	15	340	19	1	2	2	5
Grilled Polenta Wedges with Grilled Oranges and Ricotta	170	8	2.5	10	160	21	1	4	2	3
Grilled Onion, Pear, and Prosciutto Flatbread	360	18	6	30	990	38	2	10	2	13
Grilled Butternut Squash, Apple, and Goat Cheese Flatbread	320	15	5	10	580	38	2	8	2	9
Malaysian Chicken Satay with Peanut Sauce	380	22	3	140	930	14	1	7	4	32
Grilled Chicken and Vegetable Quesadillas	320	22	7	35	570	21	1	2	0	12
Negimaki	210	8	3	60	790	9	1	7	5	22
Grilled Lamb Kofte	460	38	13	90	480	7	1	3	0	23

	CALORIES	TOTAL FAT (G)	SAT FAT (G)	CHOL (MG)	SODIUM (MG)	TOTAL CARB (G)	DIETARY FIBER (G)	TOTAL SUGAR (G)	ADDED SUGAR (G)	PROTEIN (G)
Snacks and Small Plates (cont.)										
Grilled Clams, Mussels, or Oysters with Soy-Citrus Sauce	70	0.5	0	15	1580	3	0	0	0	11
Grilled Clams, Mussels, or Oysters with Spicy Lemon Butter	120	8	5	35	510	2	0	0	0	9
Grilled Clams, Mussels, or Oysters with Mignonette Sauce	60	0.5	0	15	350	4	0	1	0	9
Gambas a la Plancha	150	6	1	190	320	2	0	0	0	21
Burnt Whiskey Sours	180	0	0	0	0	12	0	11	11	0
Charred Pineapple Margaritas	290	0	0	0	20	33	1	30	24	0
Bloody Marys for a Crowd	120	0	0	0	360	6	1	4	0	1
Smoky Peach Sangria	190	0	0	0	0	17	1	13	6	1
Both Hands Needed										
Smoked Turkey Club Panini	770	59	20	90	1520	28	1	6	0	34
Grilled Red Curry Chicken Sandwiches with Spicy Slaw	680	31	6	135	1180	36	4	13	7	48
Philly-Style Cheesesteaks	920	54	22	195	1560	25	2	6	0	69
Grilled Beer Brats and Onions	740	45	13	85	1700	37	4	8	1	24
Grilled Pork Bánh Mì	570	34	6	90	1280	34	2	14	9	29
Grilled Arayes with Parsley-Cucumber Salad	940	72	25	135	1390	36	5	6	0	39
Grilled Halloumi Wraps	550	29	17	60	1720	43	2	5	0	32
Eggplant and Mozzarella Panini	650	34	11	40	990	52	7	9	0	22
Grilled Turkey Burgers with Spinach and Feta	370	12	8	85	730	23	0	4	0	42
Grilled Turkey Burgers with Miso and Ginger	340	9	6	70	530	26	0	5	0	40
Grilled Turkey Burgers with Herbs and Goat Cheese	390	14	9	80	400	24	0	4	0	44
Smashed Burgers	700	53	14	100	830	25	0	6	0	28
Grilled Smokehouse Barbecue Burgers	720	39	14	155	1400	41	2	16	6	48
Grind-Your-Own Sirloin Burgers	450	22	10	110	800	24	0	4	0	34
Grilled Green Chile and Chorizo Cheeseburgers	1080	81	29	110	2880	31	1	7	0	58
Grilled Harissa Lamb Burgers	680	48	19	130	770	26	1	5	0	34
Salmon Burgers with Asparagus and Lemon-Herb Sauce	560	34	6	70	870	31	3	6	0	32
Grilled Portobello Burgers with Goat Cheese and Arugula	320	18	5	10	440	31	2	8	0	10
Grilled Chicken Tacos with Salsa Verde	630	29	3.5	125	1430	46	3	7	1	44
Tacos al Carbón	380	18	5	75	490	26	1	1	0	27
Tacos al Pastor	300	6	1.5	40	750	45	2	10	0	16
Grilled Swordfish Tacos	600	25	4	100	660	61	4	19	0	35
Smoked Salmon Tacos	700	39	9	90	1440	49	0	17	9	37
Breakfast Burritos with Black Beans and Chorizo	780	46	18	455	2370	55	0	4	0	39

	CALORIES	TOTAL FAT (G)	SAT FAT (G)	CHOL (MG)	SODIUM (MG)	TOTAL CARB (G)	DIETARY FIBER (G)	TOTAL SUGAR (G)	ADDED SUGAR (G)	PROTEIN (G)
Weeknight Dinners										
Grilled Chicken Cobb Salad	780	55	12	335	1720	17	8	6	0	55
Grilled Garam Masala Chicken, Tomatoes, and Naan with Chutney	890	31	4.5	130	1420	108	3	20	0	53
Grilled Pesto Chicken with Cucumber and Cantaloupe Salad	710	59	12	105	880	7	1	4	0	35
Grilled Chicken Thighs with Butternut Squash and Cilantro Vinaigrette	570	35	4	160	1040	30	5	6	0	36
Sweet and Tangy Barbecue Chicken Thighs with Sweet Potatoes and Scallions	530	15	3	160	1360	60	7	33	11	37
Paprika and Lime–Rubbed Chicken with Grilled Vegetable Succotash	550	23	3	160	900	33	7	10	2	57
Stir-Fried Cumin Beef	350	24	5	75	730	7	1	3	2	25
Grilled Steak Fajitas	720	44	11	100	1680	41	2	8	0	39
Grilled Steak Tips, Broccoli, and Red Onion with Anchovy-Garlic Butter	630	44	16	150	1620	12	3	4	0	44
Grilled Cumin-Rubbed Flank Steak with Elote	480	28	8	125	1110	20	3	5	0	42
Japanese Steak House Steak and Vegetables	810	64	22	145	1180	15	3	8	0	44
Grilled Strip Steak and Potatoes with Blue Cheese Butter	640	32	13	155	790	31	0	0	0	57
Bún Chả	400	17	6	55	850	45	1	9	7	18
Grilled Sausages and Polenta with Arugula Salad	400	24	6	35	1030	23	1	2	0	23
Fried Rice with Ham, Gai Lan, and Mushrooms	370	13	1.5	70	540	51	1	5	2	12
Grilled Pork Chops with Plums	270	12	2.5	55	360	18	2	15	7	23
Grilled Pork Tenderloin with Pineapple-Lentil Salad	380	14	2.5	75	520	32	8	14	1	33
Tuscan Pork Ribs with Grilled Radicchio	570	50	13	105	720	7	1	1	0	23
Lamb and Summer Vegetable Kebabs with Grilled Focaccia	460	24	6	95	680	23	2	5	0	37
Grilled Lamb Shoulder Chops with Zucchini and Corn Salad	870	72	26	145	870	16	3	7	0	42
Grilled Shrimp, Corn, and Avocado Salad	540	33	4.5	285	930	29	8	7	0	37
Grilled Shrimp Skewers with Chili Crisp and Napa Cabbage Slaw	420	29	3.5	215	400	11	4	3	0	28
Grilled Tuna Steaks with Cucumber-Mint Farro Salad	610	28	5	45	820	53	6	6	0	38
Grilled Swordfish with Potatoes and Salsa Verde	630	34	6	150	1630	29	4	2	0	49
Grilled Caesar Salad with Salmon	700	48	10	135	850	10	0	4	0	53
Grilled Cod and Summer Squash Packets	450	30	4.5	75	1180	12	3	7	0	34

	CALORIES	TOTAL FAT (G)	SAT FAT (G)	CHOL (MG)	SODIUM (MG)	TOTAL CARB (G)	DIETARY FIBER (G)	TOTAL SUGAR (G)	ADDED SUGAR (G)	PROTEIN (G)
Weeknight Dinners (cont.)										
Grilled Tofu with Charred Broccoli and Peanut Sauce	640	52	5	0	650	20	5	6	0	25
Grilled Tofu and Vegetables with Harissa	240	13	1.5	0	590	19	3	8	0	14
Grilled Peach and Tomato Salad with Burrata and Basil	290	25	9	35	410	12	2	10	0	8
Grilled Vegetable and Halloumi Salad	280	20	8	30	710	18	3	13	0	10
Stir-Fried Sichuan-Style Eggplant	290	22	1.5	0	5	16	4	7	2	7
Weekend Gatherings										
Diner-Style Breakfast	590	33	10	260	700	37	2	6	3	32
Grilled French Toast	580	25	11	150	980	69	0	14	4	18
Shakshuka Breakfast Pizza	450	24	5	195	1240	46	1	9	0	15
Bacon	320	32	12	45	150	1	0	1	1	6
Smoked Chicken Wings	390	28	11	190	1780	7	1	5	4	26
Smoked Citrus Chicken	440	26	7	140	390	5	1	3	0	46
Smoked Bourbon Chicken	900	60	17	300	1250	3	0	1	0	75
Grill-Roasted Butterflied Chicken	660	45	13	225	830	3	0	2	2	56
Grill-Roasted Butterflied Chicken with Barbecue Spice Rub	720	46	13	225	1460	17	2	13	12	57
Grill-Roasted Butterflied Chicken with Ras el Hanout Spice Rub	700	46	13	225	1050	11	4	6	5	57
Pollo a la Brasa	820	63	16	235	1140	4	1	1	0	57
Thai Cornish Game Hens with Chili Dipping Sauce	340	15	4	105	790	33	1	26	26	19
Smoked Turkey	470	18	2.5	230	980	2	0	2	1	70
Grilled Pork Loin with Apple-Cranberry Filling	400	4.5	1.5	115	640	49	1	41	18	39
Grilled Pork Loin with Apple, Cherry, and Caraway Filling	380	4	1.5	115	640	47	1	39	18	39
Memphis-Style Wet Ribs	400	27	9	90	1450	19	1	15	11	19
Kansas City-Style Barbecue Ribs	380	27	9	90	1400	16	1	12	12	18
North Carolina Barbecue Pork	260	9	3	95	1410	11	1	7	0	29
Lexington-Style Barbecue Sauce	45	0	0	0	430	9	0	7	0	0
Eastern North Carolina-Style Barbecue Sauce	40	0	0	0	410	8	0	6	5	0
Cuban-Style Pork with Mojo	390	22	5	110	840	10	1	4	1	36
Smoked Prime Rib	820	68	25	175	1180	2	1	1	0	45
Texas-Style Barbecue Brisket	670	45	17	215	1220	1	1	0	0	62
Texas-Style Smoked Beef Ribs	470	27	12	155	1780	2	1	0	0	51
Rotisserie Leg of Lamb with Cauliflower, Grape, and Arugula Salad	580	33	9	185	1660	14	3	8	0	57

	CALORIES	TOTAL FAT (G)	SAT FAT (G)	CHOL (MG)	SODIUM (MG)	TOTAL CARB (G)	DIETARY FIBER (G)	TOTAL SUGAR (G)	ADDED SUGAR (G)	PROTEIN (G)
Weekend Gatherings (cont.)										
Hot-Smoked Whole Side of Salmon	160	4	1	55	1930	6	0	6	6	23
"Smoked Salmon Platter" Sauce	100	10	1	30	60	0	0	0	0	1
Apple-Mustard Sauce	30	0	0	0	170	5	0	5	1	0
New England Clambake	650	35	14	185	2490	51	5	7	0	38
Grill-Roasted Whole Cauliflower with Tahini-Yogurt Sauce	300	25	4	0	790	18	3	9	7	6
Grilled Vegetable Platter	430	38	10	30	740	20	6	10	0	12
Smoky Tomato and Eggplant Phyllo Pie	420	30	7	20	920	29	3	4	0	12
Over an Open Fire										
Campfire Hot Dogs with Smoky Potato Salad	870	49	15	55	2450	82	2	10	0	25
Chicken Souvlaki	610	17	6	130	1920	61	2	7	1	51
Grilled Jerk Chicken	300	12	3	190	1390	5	1	1	1	41
Kalbi	350	16	6	80	3170	19	1	15	10	30
Thick-Cut Rib Steaks with Ember-Baked Potatoes	920	53	25	225	1120	52	4	2	0	59
Grilled Flank Steak and Vegetables with Chimichurri	470	33	7	105	910	10	3	4	0	35
Fireside Chili	990	58	20	285	1050	35	11	7	1	82
Grilled Harissa-Rubbed Rack of Lamb with Ember-Baked Carrots	460	30	6	105	810	14	5	5	0	36
Grilled Halibut with Spicy Orange and Fennel Salad	430	30	4.5	85	750	9	2	6	0	33
Grilled Whole Trout with Wilted Swiss Chard and Apple-Cherry Relish	710	39	6	165	1530	29	4	20	4	62
Paella for a Crowd	540	15	2.5	135	1050	67	3	3	0	36
Ember-Roasted Beet Salad with Spiced Yogurt and Watercress	230	16	6	10	650	18	5	11	0	7
Grilled Breads										
Grilled Flour Tortillas	170	6	1.5	0	300	25	1	0	0	3
Grilled Flatbreads	440	20	7	65	750	56	2	2	1	10
Hand-Mixed Grilled Flatbreads	440	20	7	65	750	56	2	2	1	10
Grilled Garlic Flatbreads	450	20	7	65	750	58	2	2	1	10
Mana'eesh Za'atar	320	12	2	0	610	45	2	0	0	6
Hand-Mixed Mana'eesh Za'atar	320	12	2	0	610	45	2	0	0	6
Grilled Pizza	720	42	11	40	1390	65	3	5	2	23
Grilled Pizza with Corn, Cherry Tomatoes, Pesto, and Ricotta	680	39	10	35	1290	65	3	3	2	19
Grilled Pizza with Soppressata, Banana Peppers, and Hot Honey	750	44	12	50	1580	65	3	5	2	25
Pizza Dough for the Outdoor Pizza Oven	450	5	1	0	910	85	3	0	0	14

	CALORIES	TOTAL FAT (G)	SAT FAT (G)	CHOL (MG)	SODIUM (MG)	TOTAL CARB (G)	DIETARY FIBER (G)	TOTAL SUGAR (G)	ADDED SUGAR (G)	PROTEIN (G)
Grilled Breads (cont.)										
Whole-Wheat Pizza Dough for the Outdoor Pizza Oven	400	9	1.5	0	910	71	7	0	0	13
Thin-Crust Pizza for the Outdoor Pizza Oven	730	25	11	55	2350	94	4	4	0	30
Big and Fluffy Biscuits	390	21	10	35	590	43	1	2	0	7
Big and Fluffy Biscuits with Lemon and Dill	390	21	10	35	590	43	2	2	0	7
Big and Fluffy Biscuits with Orange and Tarragon	390	21	10	35	590	43	2	2	0	7
Grilled Fresh Corn Cornbread with Charred Jalapeños and Cheddar	470	29	12	100	730	41	4	6	1	14
No-Knead Dutch Oven Bread	210	1	0	0	460	42	1	2	2	7
Rosemary Focaccia	220	7	1	0	520	34	1	0	0	5
Focaccia with Fresh Figs and Thyme	250	8	1	0	510	41	2	6	0	5
Pull-Apart Dinner Rolls	140	5	3	30	230	19	1	0	0	3
Hand-Mixed Pull-Apart Dinner Rolls	140	5	3	30	230	19	1	0	0	3
Don't Forget Dessert										
Ultimate S'mores	270	2.5	1	0	125	62	0	54	50	3
Skillet Chocolate Chip Cookie	340	17	10	60	260	46	1	29	28	4
Skillet Brownie	480	22	8	70	220	73	2	50	44	6
Spiced Skillet Brownie	480	22	8	70	220	73	2	50	44	6
Espresso-Walnut Skillet Brownie	500	24	9	70	220	73	2	51	44	6
Grilled Stone Fruit	80	4	2.5	10	0	10	2	9	0	1
Glazed Rotisserie Pineapple with Salted Rum Butterscotch Sauce	300	17	11	45	160	36	1	33	24	1
Rustic Summer Fruit Tart	380	20	12	50	210	46	3	16	8	5
Charred Strawberry Dutch Baby	420	14	4	150	690	63	3	26	17	1
Apple Crisp	440	23	10	40	160	61	5	40	24	4
Cherry Spoon Cake	340	13	8	35	300	54	1	37	30	4
Orange Upside-Down Cake	420	19	11	95	410	60	1	44	37	4
Mulled Cider	90	0	0	0	5	22	1	19	2	0
Brandied Mulled Cider	180	0	0	0	10	22	1	19	2	0
Mulled Wine	110	0	0	0	15	14	0	14	12	0
Hot Toddy	170	0	0	0	5	19	0	18	17	0
Scotch Hot Toddy	170	0	0	0	5	19	0	18	17	0
Hot Chocolate	190	9	5	5	100	27	5	19	17	5
Spiced Hot Chocolate	190	9	5	5	105	28	5	19	17	5
Mocha Hot Chocolate	190	9	5	5	100	28	5	19	17	5

Conversions and Equivalents

Some say cooking is a science and an art. We would say that geography has a hand in it, too. Flours and sugars manufactured in the United Kingdom and elsewhere will feel and taste different from those manufactured in the United States. So we cannot promise that the loaf of bread you bake in Canada or England will taste the same as a loaf baked in the States, but we can offer guidelines for converting weights and measures. We also recommend that you rely on your instincts when making our recipes. Refer to the visual cues provided. If the dough hasn't "come together in a ball" as described, you may need to add more flour—even if the recipe doesn't tell you to. You be the judge.

The recipes in this book were developed using standard U.S. measures following U.S. government guidelines. The charts below offer equivalents for U.S. and metric measures. All conversions are approximate and have been rounded up or down to the nearest whole number.

Example:

1 teaspoon	=	4.9292 milliliters, rounded up to 5 milliliters
1 ounce	=	28.3495 grams, rounded down to 28 grams

VOLUME CONVERSIONS

U.S.	Metric
1 teaspoon	5 milliliters
2 teaspoons	10 milliliters
1 tablespoon	15 milliliters
2 tablespoons	30 milliliters
¼ cup	59 milliliters
⅓ cup	79 milliliters
½ cup	118 milliliters
¾ cup	177 milliliters
1 cup	237 milliliters
1¼ cups	296 milliliters
1½ cups	355 milliliters
2 cups (1 pint)	473 milliliters
2½ cups	591 milliliters
3 cups	710 milliliters
4 cups (1 quart)	0.946 liter
1.06 quarts	1 liter
4 quarts (1 gallon)	3.8 liters

WEIGHT CONVERSIONS

Ounces	Grams
½	14
¾	21
1	28
1½	43
2	57
2½	71
3	85
3½	99
4	113
4½	128
5	142
6	170
7	198
8	227
9	255
10	283
12	340
16 (1 pound)	454

CONVERSIONS FOR COMMON BAKING INGREDIENTS

Baking is an exacting science. Because measuring by weight is far more accurate than measuring by volume, and thus more likely to produce reliable results, in our recipes we provide ounce measures in addition to cup measures for many ingredients. Refer to the chart below to convert these measures into grams.

Ingredient	Ounces	Grams
Flour		
1 cup all-purpose flour*	5	142
1 cup cake flour	4	113
1 cup whole-wheat flour	5½	156
Sugar		
1 cup granulated (white) sugar	7	198
1 cup packed brown sugar (light or dark)	7	198
1 cup confectioners' sugar	4	113
Cocoa Powder		
1 cup cocoa powder	3	85
Butter†		
4 tablespoons (½ stick or ¼ cup)	2	57
8 tablespoons (1 stick or ½ cup)	4	113
16 tablespoons (2 sticks or 1 cup)	8	227

* U.S. all-purpose flour, the most frequently used flour in this book, does not contain leaveners, as some European flours do. These leavened flours are called self-rising or self-raising. If you are using self-rising flour, take this into consideration before adding leaveners to a recipe.

† In the United States, butter is sold both salted and unsalted. We generally recommend unsalted butter. If you are using salted butter, take this into consideration before adding salt to a recipe.

OVEN TEMPERATURES

Fahrenheit	Celsius	Gas Mark
225	105	¼
250	120	½
275	135	1
300	150	2
325	165	3
350	180	4
375	190	5
400	200	6
425	220	7
450	230	8
475	245	9

CONVERTING TEMPERATURES FROM AN INSTANT-READ THERMOMETER

We include doneness temperatures in many of the recipes in this book. We recommend an instant-read thermometer for the job. Refer to the table above to convert Fahrenheit degrees to Celsius. Or, for temperatures not represented in the chart, use this simple formula:

Subtract 32 degrees from the Fahrenheit reading, then divide the result by 1.8 to find the Celsius reading.

Example:
"Grill chicken until thighs register 175 degrees."

To convert:

175°F − 32   =   143°

143° ÷ 1.8   =   79.44°C, rounded down to 79°C

Index

Note: Page references in *italics* indicate photographs.